THE

PSALMS & CANTICLES

AT

MATTINS & EVENSONG

POINTED TO

THE EIGHT GREGORIAN TONES

FROM THE

Sarum Tonale

BY

THE REV. G. H. PALMER, B. A.

(New Edition, Revised & Enlarged)

WANTAGE
S. Mary's Convent
1963

'Semper in psalmis meditemur, atque
Viribus totis Domino canamus
Dulciter ympnos.'

Gregorius I. Papa.

PRINTED IN GREAT BRITAIN
AT THE UNIVERSITY PRESS, OXFORD
BY VIVIAN RIDLER
PRINTER TO THE UNIVERSITY

INTRODUCTION

THe principal object of this work is to exhibit a method of pointing by means of which any Psalm may be chanted to any one of the eight Tones. In places where Antiphons are in use, as in the Chapels of Religious Communities, some such system is obviously necessary, inasmuch as the melody of the Antiphon determines the Tone and Ending to which its accompanying Psalm is to be sung. Elsewhere, Quire-masters can use their own discretion as to the choice of Tones and Endings.[1]

The method of pointing here adopted consists in the employment of the figures 1 to 8, answering to the Eight Tones. These figures are placed above the syllable on which the Mediation or Ending of the corresponding Tone begins, *i.e.* the syllable on which the reciting note is left. The Tone being once chosen, the singers must confine their attention to its corresponding figure in each half of the verse,[2] *all the other figures being disregarded.*

The principles on which the pointing is regulated are based on the examples found in the Sarum and other English Antiphonals.

The forms of the Tones, with the order of their Endings, are from the Sarum *Tonale*, with additional Endings from other English sources, as shewn in the Table of Tones.

The notation employed is that which is found in English MSS. of the xiijth—xvth centuries, of which the following characters are used in this work :—

1. The Staff of four lines.

2. The two Clefs, C and F which indicate the position of those notes upon the Staff.[3]

---

1 In this edition one or more of the simpler Tones have been prefixed to each Psalm. These are suggested as having been found by experience to work well, but are not intended to preclude the use of others which may happen to be preferred.

2 It will be seen that in a few of the *Endings* of certain Tones, the figure will not serve to indicate the pointing; the reason being that in these Endings the Reciting-note is left sooner, or later, than in those which are more frequently used, and to which the figures apply. See pp. xv—xxj.

3 There is no fixed pitch in Plainsong; the Clef-notes can therefore be transposed at will.

3. The Flat, used only with the note B.

4. The *Punctum*  a single note, the value of which is determined by the syllable to which it is sung.

5. The *Pes* or *Podatus*  an ascending group of two notes.

6. The *Clivis*  a descending group of two notes.

7. The *Torculus*  a triplet.

8. The *Climacus*  a group of three or more descending notes.

9. The *Pes subpunctis* 

10. The *Climacus resupinus* 

Composite groups.

The note-groups in the above list are merely representations of the original 'neums,' and in no case does the form of a note express either its force or duration. Thus the tailed note is not in itself a long, nor the lozenge a short note.

In every group, whether ascending or descending, it is the initial note which receives the *ictus* or impulse of the voice, and from it the second and following notes should flow, in smooth and connected succession. This initial note is not necessarily a strongly accented one: like the single note (No. 4), its force is precisely that of the syllable to which it is allied. In groups of two notes, the second should always be softly sung.

When a group occurs at the close of the Mediation or Ending, if it consist of two notes, both should be slightly retarded; if of three or four, such as Nos. 7 or 8, it will be sufficient to prolong the last note only. But in the case of composite groups, such as Nos. 9 or 10, the *rallentando* affects the two last notes only, as though they were written 

THE TONES OF THE PSALMS

The additional Endings given below are from the English MSS. *Tonalia* of Gisburn (G.), Gloucester (Gl.), Peterborough (P.), Worcester (W.) and York (Y.).

TONE I

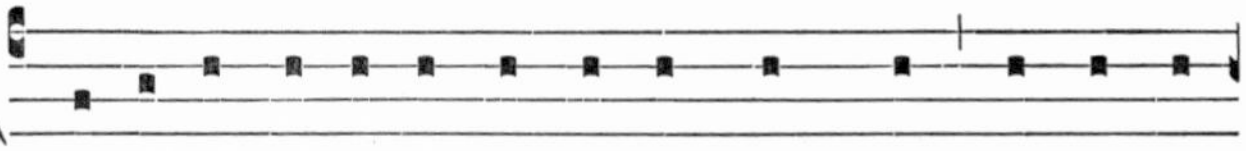

THis is the in-to-na-tion of the First Tone, & this is

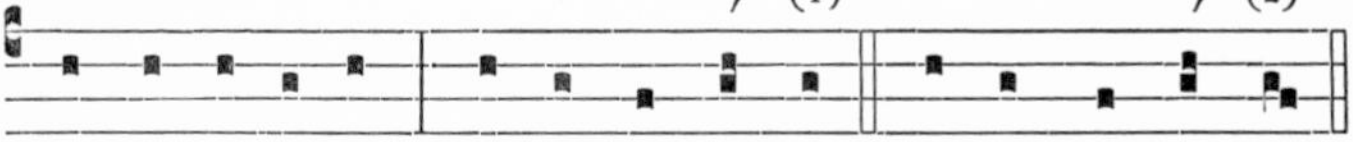

the me-di- a-tion : & this the end-ing. & this the end-ing.

and this the end-ing. and this the end-ing. and this the

end-ing. and this the end- ing. and this the end-ing.

& this the end-ing. & this the ending. & this the ending.

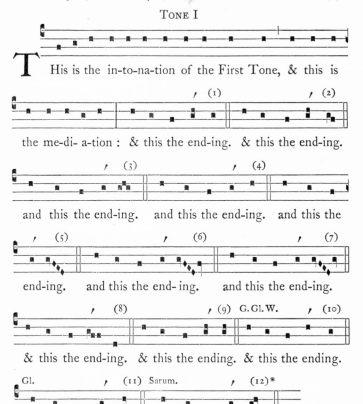

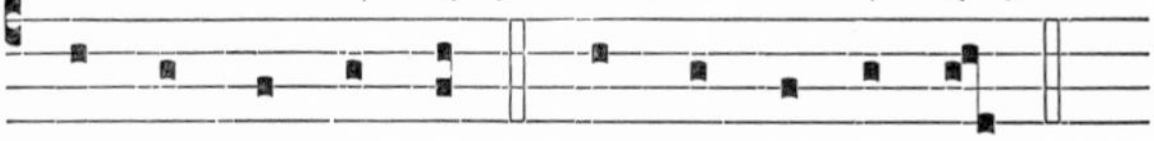

and this the end-ing. and this the end-ing.

¶ *For the Solemn form of Mediation for* Benedictus & Magnificat *see the* Canticles *at the end of the Psalter.*

---

*This Ending does not appear in the *Tonale*, but is given in the *Manuale* to the Psalm *De profundis* in the Order for the Burial of the Dead.

Tone II

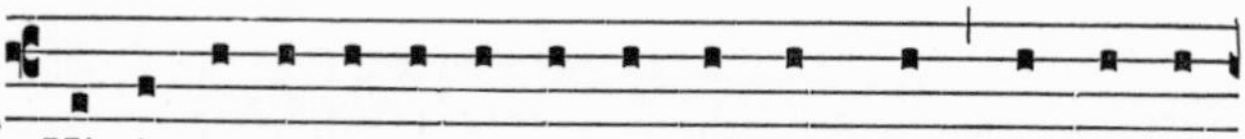

THis is the in-to-nation of the Second Tone, & this is

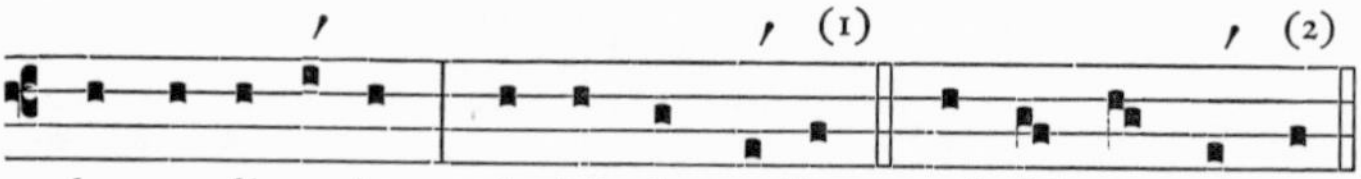

the me-di- a-tion : & this the ending. and this the end-ing.

For the Solemn form of Mediation for Benedictus & Magnificat *see the* Canticles *at the end of the Psalter.*

Tone III

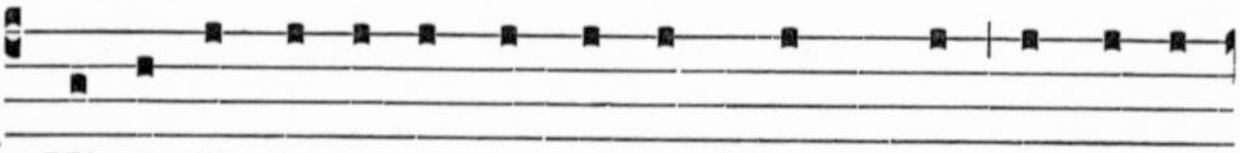

THis is the in-to-na-tion of the Third Tone, & this is

the me-di- a-tion : & this the end-ing. & this the end-ing.

and this the end- ing. and this the end-ing. and this the

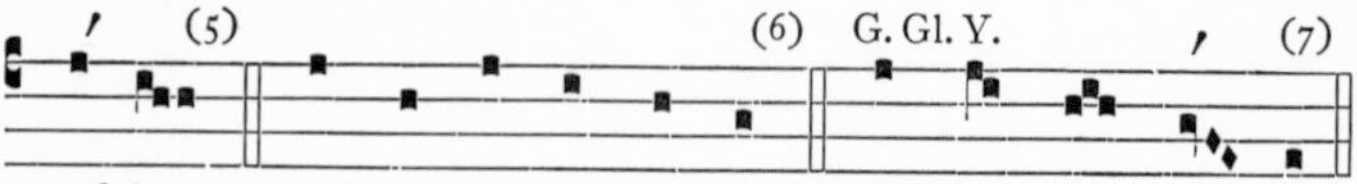

end-ing. and this is the end-ing. and this the end-ing.

and this the end-ing.

Intonation of Benedictus & Magnificat.

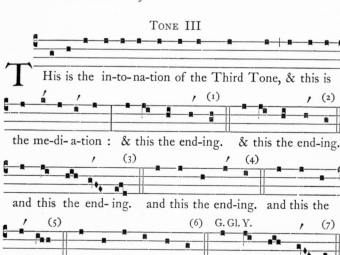

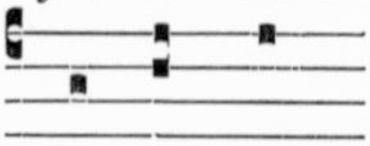

Bles-sed be &c.
My soul doth &c.

Tone IV

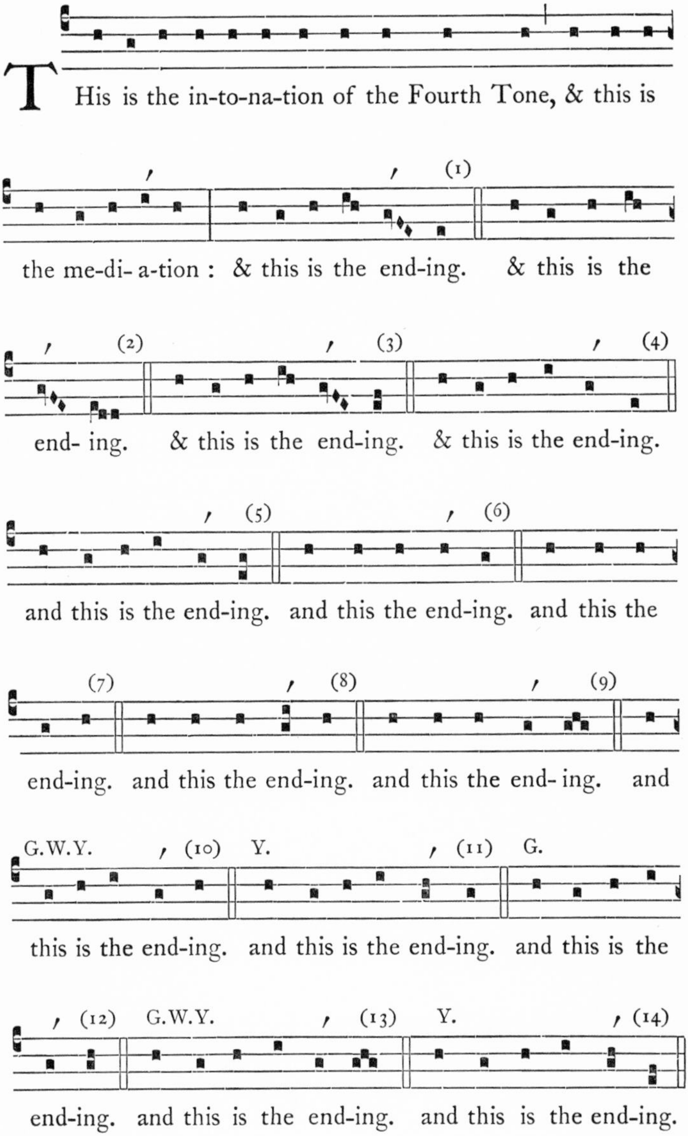
THis is the in-to-na-tion of the Fourth Tone, & this is
(1)
the me-di- a-tion : & this is the end-ing. & this is the
(2) (3) (4)
end- ing. & this is the end-ing. & this is the end-ing.
(5) (6)
and this is the end-ing. and this the end-ing. and this the
(7) (8) (9)
end-ing. and this the end-ing. and this the end- ing. and
G.W.Y. (10) Y. (11) G.
this is the end-ing. and this is the end-ing. and this is the
(12) G.W.Y. (13) Y. (14)
end-ing. and this is the end-ing. and this is the end-ing.

¶ *Some of the above Endings are only used with a type of Antiphon which for certain reasons is transposed a fourth higher than its natural seat. In such cases the entire Tone is thus represented :—*

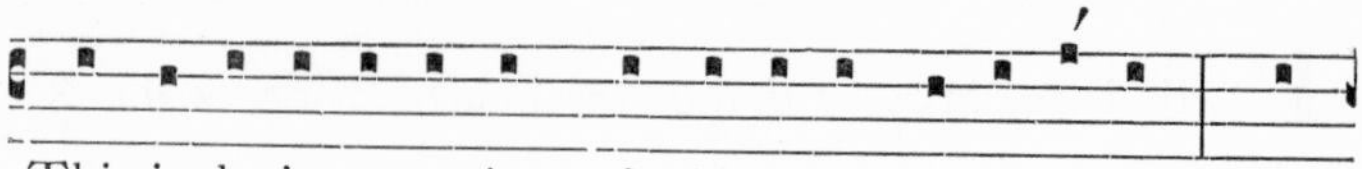

This is the in-to-na-tion ... & this is the me-di- a-tion : and

this is the end-ing.

Endings (5), (11), (12) *&* (13) *are always found similarly transposed, & occasionally* (8), (9) *&* (10) *also.*

¶ *For the Solemn form of Mediation for* Benedictus *&* Magnificat *see the* Canticles *at the end of the Psalter.*

Tone V

THis is the in-to-na-tion of the Fifth Tone, and this is

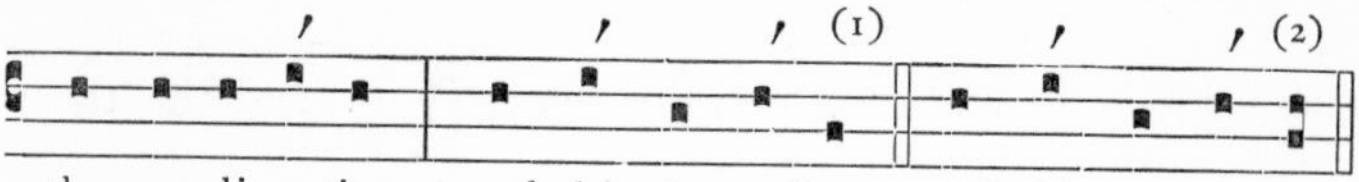

the me-di- a-tion : and this the ending. and this the ending.

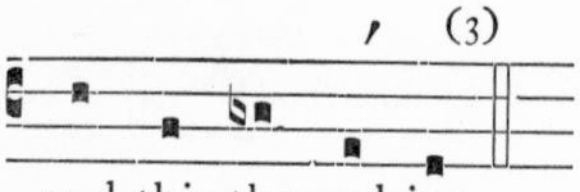

and this the end-ing.

Tone VI

THis is the in-to-nation of the Sixth Tone, and this is

the me- di- a- tion : and this the end-ing.

¶ *For the Solemn form of Mediation for* Benedictus *&* Magnificat *see the* Canticles *at the end of the Psalter.*

Tone VII

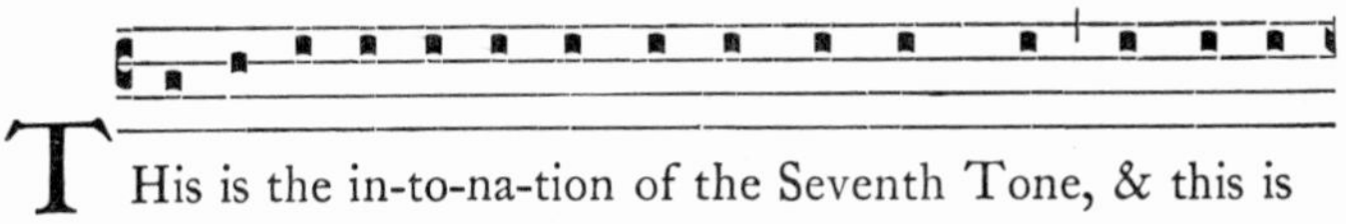
THis is the in-to-na-tion of the Seventh Tone, & this is

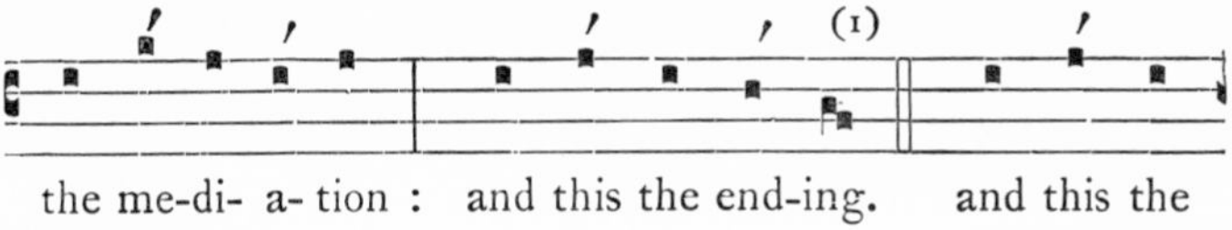
(1)
the me-di- a- tion : and this the end-ing. and this the

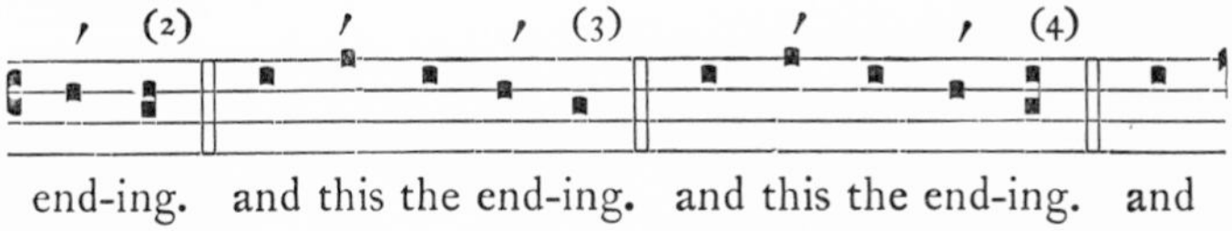
(2) (3) (4)
end-ing. and this the end-ing. and this the end-ing. and

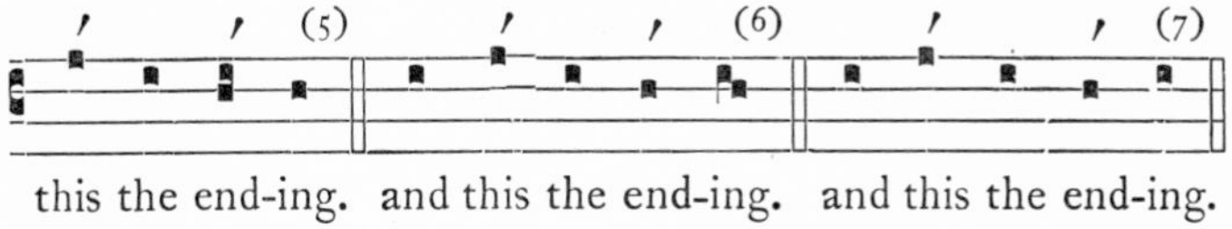
(5) (6) (7)
this the end-ing. and this the end-ing. and this the end-ing.

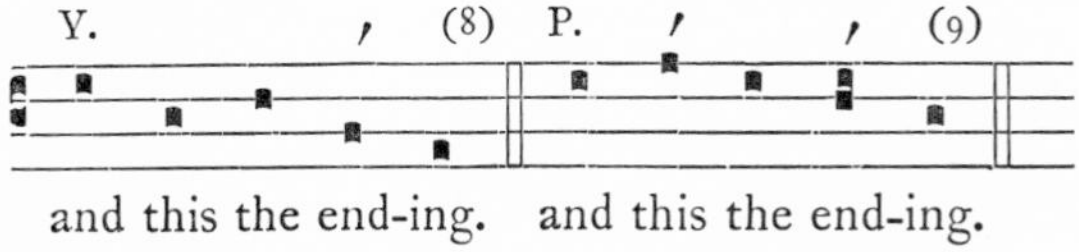
Y. (8) P. (9)
and this the end-ing. and this the end-ing.

Intonation of Benedictus & Magnificat.

Bles- sed be &c.
My soul doth &c.

Tone VIII

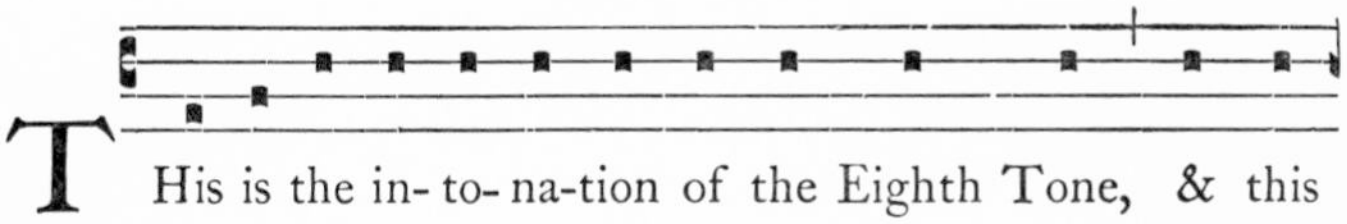
THis is the in- to- na-tion of the Eighth Tone, & this

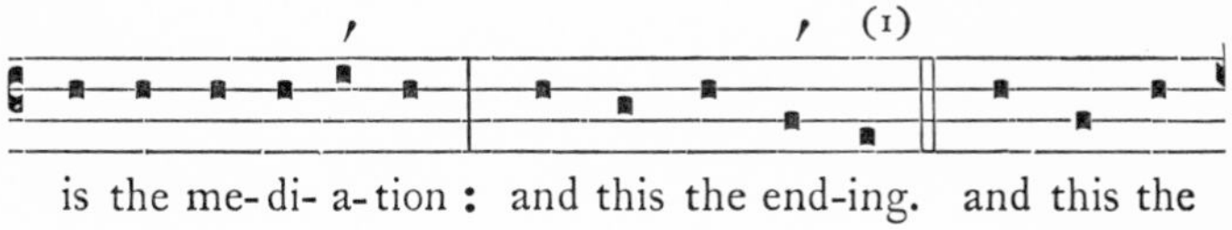
(1)
is the me- di- a- tion : and this the end-ing. and this the

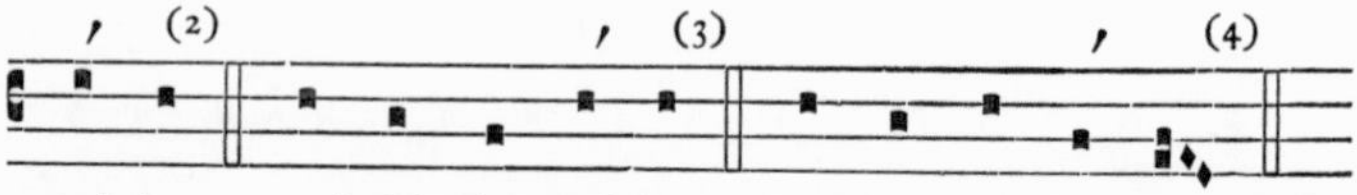

end-ing. and this the end-ing. and this the end-ing.

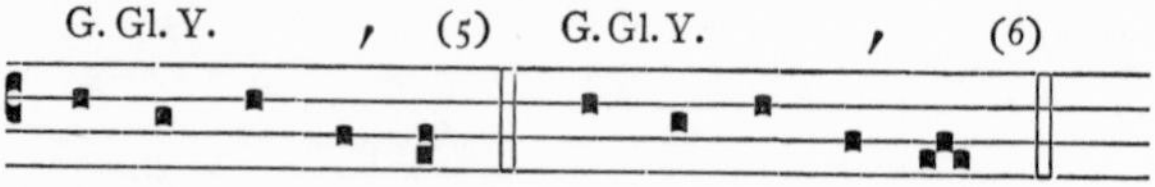

and this the end-ing. and this the end-ing.

¶ *For the Solemn form of Mediation for* Benedictus & Magnificat *see the* Canticles *at the end of the Psalter.*

IRREGULAR OR *Peregrine* TONE

THis is the in- to- na-tion of the Ir-re- gu- lar Tone,

and this is the me-di- a- tion : and this is the full form of

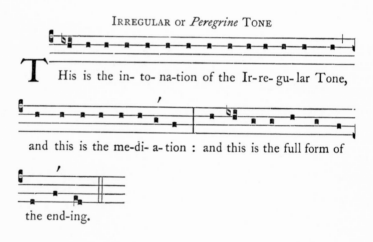

the end-ing.

It will be seen from the foregoing Table that every Tone consists of three melodic inflexions, the Intonation, the Mediation and the Ending. Of these, the first and second are (as regards the Psalms) invariable, whereas the third is found in more or less variety. Each of these must be considered separately.

I. The Intonation. In the Psalms this is used in the *first* verse only; but when two or more Psalms are sung to the same Tone and Ending, the Intonation should not be repeated. In the two principal Gospel Canticles, *Benedictus* and *Magnificat*, the Intonation has a more ornate form,[1] and is used in *every* verse. The Canticles *Benedicite*, *Quicunque* and *Nunc dimittis* are treated as Psalms.[2]

The Intonation of the Psalm-tones being in all cases (except that of the Irregular Tone) strictly syllabic, it follows that when the first half of the opening verse of a psalm contains an insufficient number of syllables for both Intonation and Mediation to be sung in their complete form, one or other of them must be altogether omitted, or one of them (in some cases both) must be abbreviated. The following is a list of these exceptional cases:—

(a) *Entire omission of the* Mediation.

I & VI
III
VII

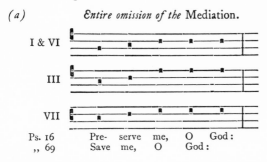

Ps. 16 Pre- serve me, O God:
,, 69 Save me, O God:

---

1 Except in Tone V.

2 The Psalm *Venite exultemus* has from a very early period occupied an important position as the introductory Canticle at Mattins. It was never sung to an ordinary Psalm-tone, (except on the Feast of Epiphany, when it occurred in the course of the Psalms of the third Nocturn), but had its own special Tones, which are probably as ancient as any Plain-chant we possess. Some of these have been adapted to the English text by the Editor of this work. The Easter Anthem *Pascha nostrum* has in this edition been set to one of the

(b) *Abbreviation of the* Intonation.

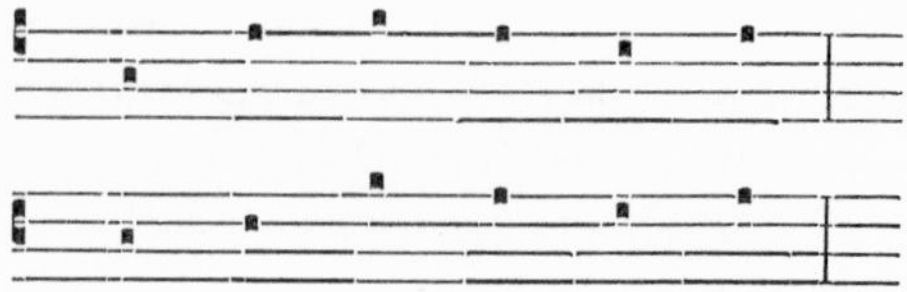

Ps. 61	Hear	my	cry-	ing,	O	God:
,, 113	Praise	the	Lord,	ye	ser-	vants:
,, 132	Lord,	re-	mem-	ber	Da-	vid:

(c) *Abbreviation of both.*

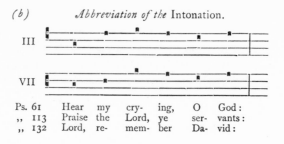

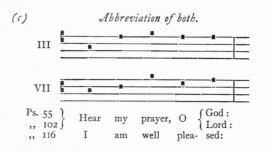

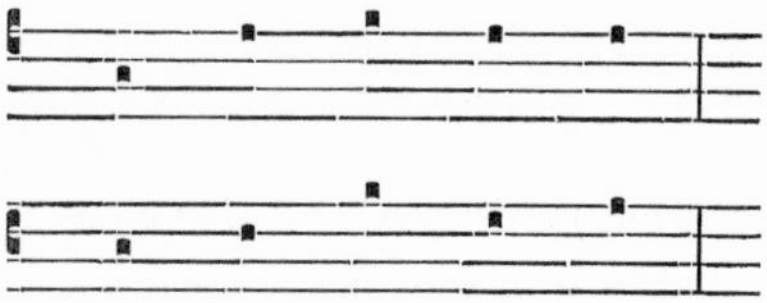

Ps. 55 / ,, 102	Hear	my	prayer,	O	God: / Lord:
,, 116	I	am	well	plea-	sed:

(d) *Entire omission of the* Intonation.

This will be found necessary if Tone IV be used with any Psalm in *(a)*, *(b)* or *(c)*, or with Psalms 23, 46, 63, 76, 119 (*v.* 145), 131, 134 or 148. The Intonation must also be omitted when Tones III & VII are sung to Psalms 23, 63, 76 or 119 (*v.* 145), or when Tone III is used with Psalm 134.

II. The Mediation. This is the inflexion which immediately precedes the colon, or division of the verse. There are eight Mediations, one for each Tone.[1] Two of these, viz. I & VI, have no *fixed*

above-mentioned *Venite*-tones. *Te Deum*, being a Hymn, has its own traditional melody, and was never intended to be treated Psalm-wise. The pointing of the verses by colons, giving it the *appearance* of a Psalm, was an unauthorized introduction of the xvijth century, & the setting of it to Psalm-tones, which was given in previous editions of this book, has now been withdrawn, and its own proper melody has been substituted.

[1] The Irregular Tone is not included.

accent, the first note of the Mediation being always sung to the penultimate syllable, whether accented or not, *e. g.*

I & VI 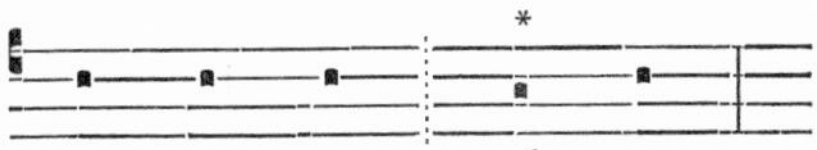

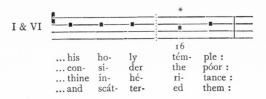

			16	
... his	ho-	ly	tém-	ple :
... con-	si-	der	the	póor :
... thine	in-	hé-	ri-	tance :
... and	scát-	ter-	ed	them :

The other six may be classified as follows :—

Four } Mediations of { *one* accent, viz. II, IV, V & VIII.
Two } Mediations of { *two* accents, viz. III & VII.

Each of these Mediations has, besides its *ordinary* or normal form, an exceptional or *abrupt* method of treatment.

In Mediations of *one* accent this abrupt form is used whenever the syllable immediately before the colon is either an emphatic monosyllable,[1] or the final syllable of an iambic or anapæstic word.

In Mediations of *two* accents the abrupt form is used whenever there is an insufficient number of syllables, or when a strongly accented syllable occurs in the antepenultimate place.

The practical working of these will be seen from the following Tables. The blank note ◘ is used, both here and elsewhere, to indicate the treatment of redundant syllables.

---

1 The *abrupt* form of these Mediations when the final monosyllable is weak, or is in the nature of an enclitic, has now been abandoned. Practical experience has shewn that both rhythm and sense are in many instances seriously affected by its use. A similar course has been followed in the case of Hebrew proper names.

Mediations of *one* accent

Ordinary form

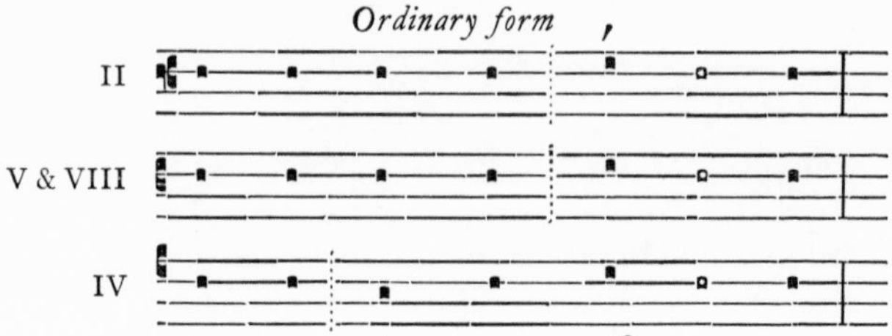

		4		258		
... in	thine	ín-	dig-	na-		tion :
... be-	caúse	of	thine	en-	e-	mies :
... as	the	déw	of	Her-		mon :
... in-	créas-	ed	that	trou-	ble	me :
		Gód	shall	bless		us :

Abrupt form

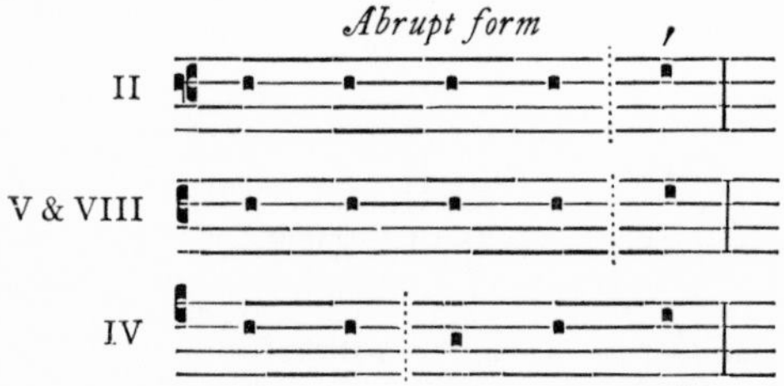

		4		258
... his	tém-	ple	on	high :
... shall	con-	vért	my	soul :
... and	hóuse	of	de-	fence :
... king	for	év-	er-	more :
		This	I	had :

Mediations of *two* accents.

Ordinary form

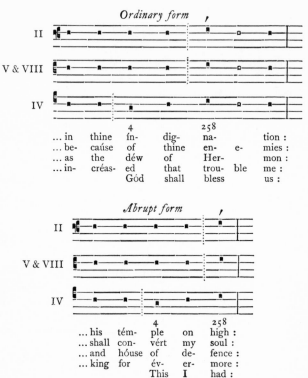

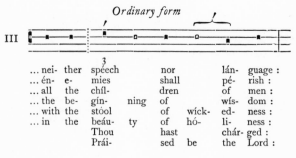

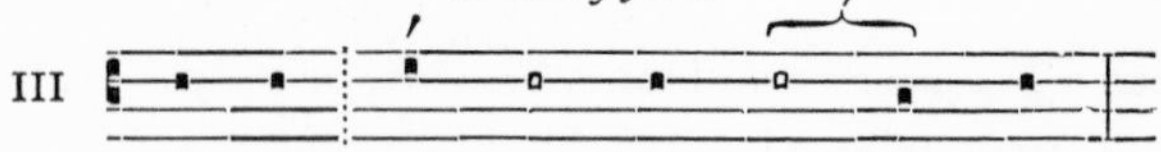

		3					
... nei-	ther	speech		nor		lán-	guage :
... én-	e-	mies		shall		pé-	rish :
... all	the	chíl-		dren		of	men :
... the	be-	gín-	ning	of		wís-	dom :
... with	the	stóol		of	wíck-	ed-	ness :
... in	the	beáu-	ty	of	hó-	li-	ness :
		Thou		hast		chár-	ged :
		Prái-		sed	be	the	Lord :

Abrupt form

III 

3
Who hath máde gréat lights :
For mine éyes have seen :
Thís I had :

Ordinary form

VII 

7
... with an hó- ly wor- ship :
... én- e- mies shall pe- rish :
... in no pé- ril of death :
... the be- gín- ning of wis- dom :
... lo- ving ún- to Is- ra- el :
... in the béau- ty of ho- li- ness :
Gód shall bless us :

Abrupt form

VII 

... and my heárt fáil- eth :
... they be- hóld vá- ni- ty :
For mine éyes have seen :
Thís I had :

III. The Ending, or Difference. This is the inflexion which concludes the Tone. There are 41 Endings in the Sarum *Tonale*,[1] to which 14 have been added from other English sources. Two of these, IV. 7 & 9, have no *fixed* accent, the first note of the Ending always falling on the penultimate syllable, whether accented or not, *e.g.*

IV. 7 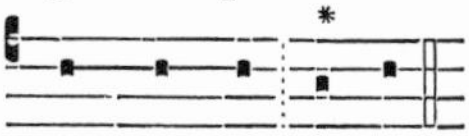

pow- er & gló- ry.
where no wá- ter is.

IV. 9 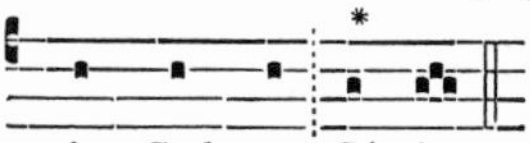

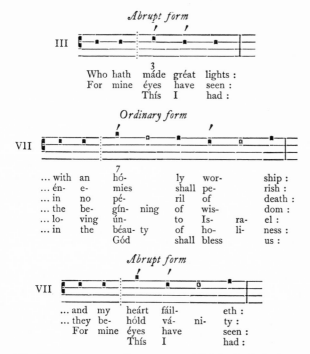

in God my Sá- viour.
to the hó- ly Ghost.

The others may be classified as follows :

Forty three Endings of *one* accent, viz. those of I, II, III, IV (except 7 & 9), VI & VIII, together with V. 3 & VII. 8.

Ten Endings of *two* accents, viz. those of V (except 3) and VII (except 8).

The following Tables will shew the treatment of all the Endings.

[1] The Irregular Tone is not included.

EXAMPLES OF THE ENDINGS

TONE I

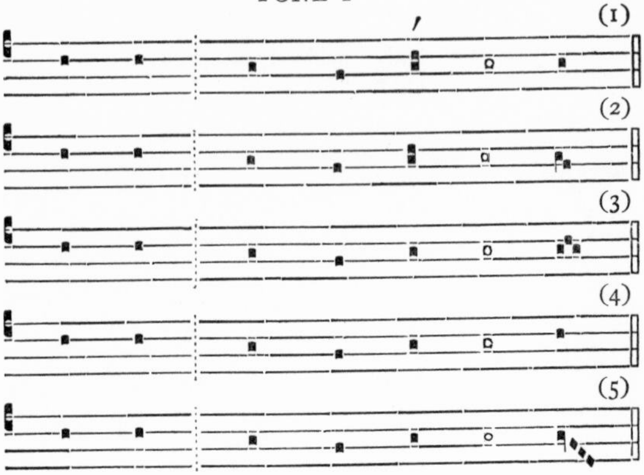

(6) & (7) *are treated as* (5).

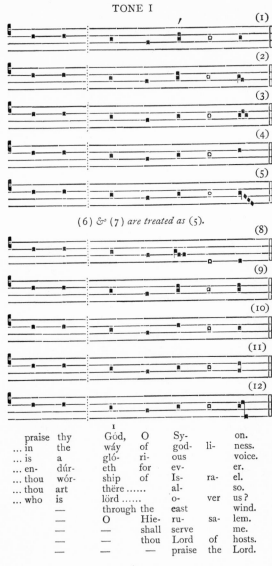

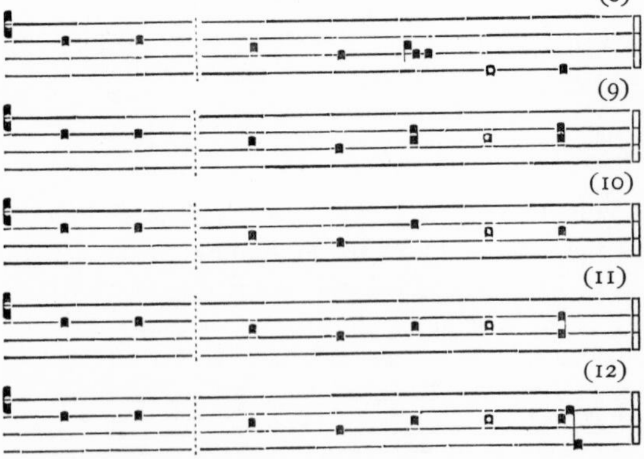

		I				
praise	thy	Gód,	O	Sy-		on.
... in	the	wáy	of	god-	li-	ness.
... is	a	gló-	ri-	ous		voice.
... en-	dúr-	eth	for	ev-		er.
... thou	wór-	ship	of	Is-	ra-	el.
... thou	art	thëre		al-		so.
... who	is	lörd		o-	ver	us?
	—	through	the	east		wind.
	—	O	Hie-	ru-	sa-	lem.
	—	—	shall	serve		me.
	—	—	thou	Lord	of	hosts.
	—	—	—	praise	the	Lord.

TONE II

(1)

(2) *is treated under* Tone VI, *p.* xix.

			2			
praise	thy	Gód,	O	Sy-		on.
... in	the	wáy	of	god-	li-	ness.
... is	a	gló-	ri-	ous		voice.
... en-	dúr-	eth	for	ev-		er.
... thou	wór-	ship	of	Is-	ra-	el.
		—	shall	serve		me.
		—	thou	Lord	of	hosts.
		—	—	praise	the	Lord.

¶ *When an emphatic syllable immediately precedes the syllable which takes the musical accent, the note of the former is re-inforced by the addition of the reciting note, e.g.*

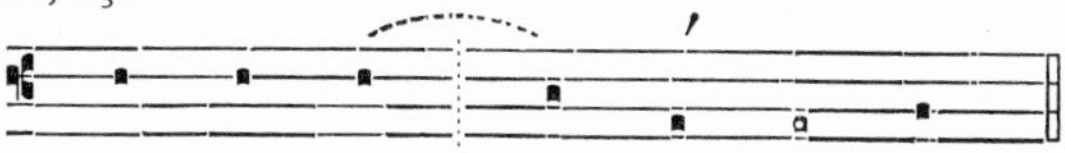

		2			
... thou	art	thëre	al-		so.
... who	is	lörd	o-	ver	us?

The same rule applies to endings (4), (5) *&* (8) *of* Tone III *which are given below.*

TONE III

(1), (2), (3) *&* (7) *are treated under* Tone VI, *p.* xix.

(4)

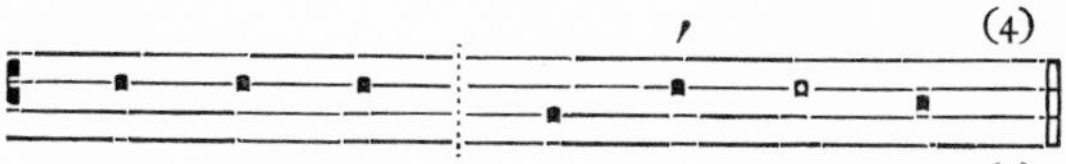

(5)

(6) *is treated under* Tone IV, *pp.* xvj & xvij.

(8)

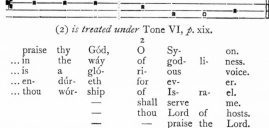

			3			
praise	thy	Gód,	O	Sy-		on.
... in	the	wáy	of	god-	li-	ness.
... is	a	gló-	ri-	ous		voice.
... en-	dúr-	eth	for	ev-		er.
... thou	wór-	ship	of	Is-	ra-	el.
		—	shall	serve		me.
		—	thou	Lord	of	hosts.
		—	—	praise	the	Lord.

TONE IV

(1)

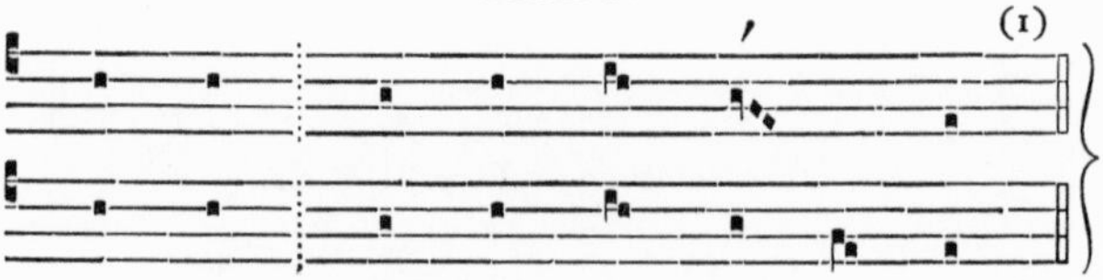

(2) & (3) *are treated as* (1).

(4)

(5)

(6)

(7) & (9) *See p.* xiij.

(8)

(10)

(11)

(12)

(13) *is treated as* (12).

(14)

TONE III

(6)

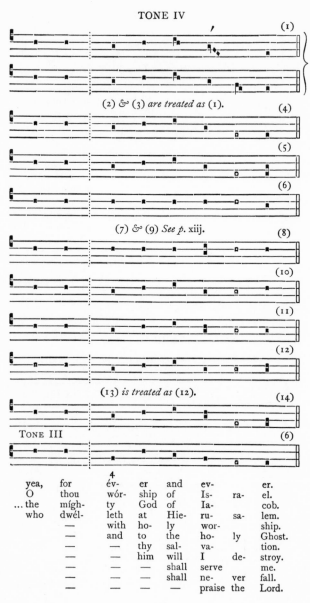

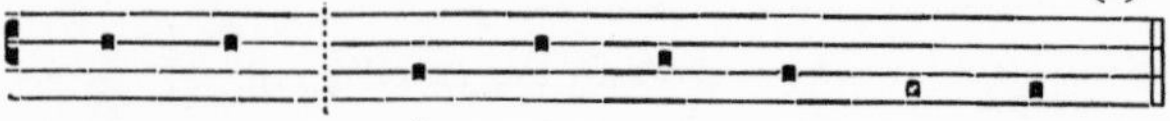

		4					
yea,	for	év-	er	and	ev-		er.
O	thou	wór-	ship	of	Is-	ra-	el.
... the	mígh-	ty	God	of	Ia-		cob.
who	dwél-	leth	at	Hie-	ru-	sa-	lem.
	—	with	ho-	ly	wor-		ship.
	—	and	to	the	ho-	ly	Ghost.
	—	—	thy	sal-	va-		tion.
	—	—	him	will	I	de-	stroy.
	—	—	—	shall	serve		me.
	—	—	—	shall	ne-	ver	fall.
	—	—	—	—	praise	the	Lord.

¶ *In the following and similar examples where the 4th syllable from the end is strongly accented, and is followed by two weaker syllables, the musical accent is transferred to the previous note, to correspond with the verbal accent. The * calls attention to the note of the redundant syllable in these cases.*

(4)

(5)

TONE III (6)

		4					
and	con-	démn	the	ín-	no-	cent	blood.
for	hé	hath	done	már-	vel-	lous	things.
		wórms	and	féa-	ther-	ed	fowls.

¶ *In the following Endings, when an emphatic syllable marked with two dots immediately precedes the syllable which receives the musical accent, the figure* 4 *must be disregarded, and the pointing must follow that of Tone* VI. *e.g.*

(4)

(5)

(10) *& all following Endings are treated in a similar way.*

TONE III (6)

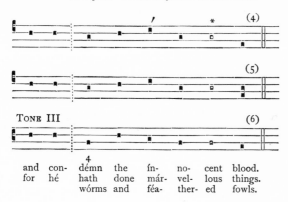

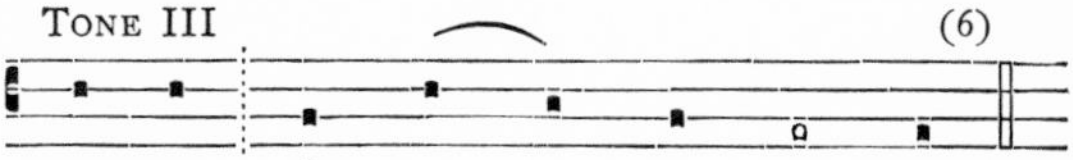

	4	6				
... the	face	of	äll	peo-		ple.
... are	come	to	grëat ...	mi-	se-	ry.
	—	and	slëw ...	migh-	ty	kings.
	—	—	Lörd, ...	hear	my	voice.

praise	thy	God,	O	Sy-		on.
... in	the	way	of	god-	li-	ness.
... is	a	glo-	ri-	ous		voice.
... thou	art	thëre......		al-		so.
... who	is	lörd......		o-	ver	us?
	—	through	the	east		wind.
	—	O	Hie-	ru-	sa-	lem.
	—	—	shall	serve		me.
	—	—	shall	ne-	ver	fall.
	—	—	—	praise	the	Lord.

(3) *is treated under* Tone VIII, *p.* xxj.

¶ *If* two *weak syllables occur between the two musical accents, the former of these is sung to the intermediate note over which the * is placed, e.g.*

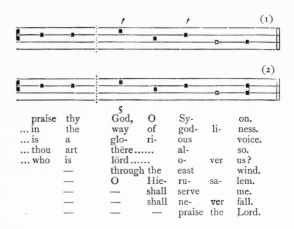

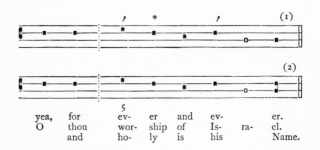

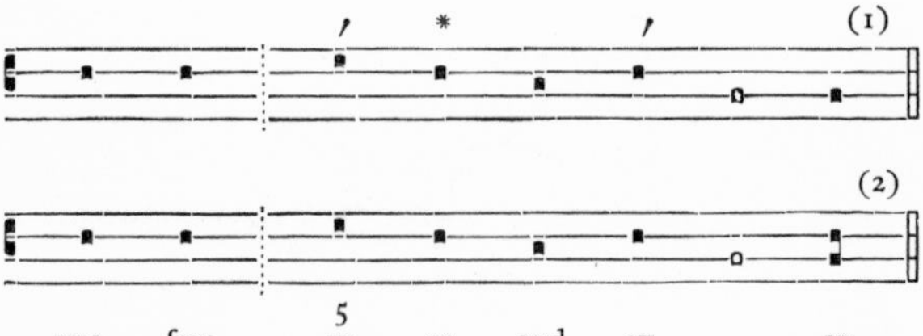

yea,	for	ev-	er	and	ev-		er.
O	thou	wor-	ship	of	Is-	ra-	el.
	and	ho-	ly	is	his		Name.

TONE VI

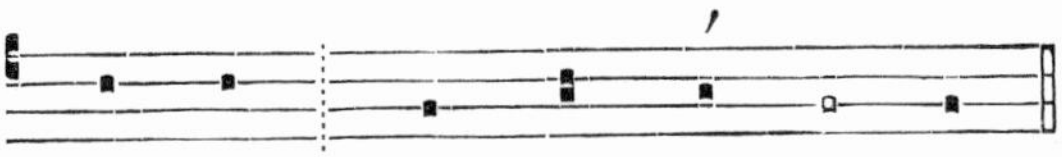

TONE II (2)

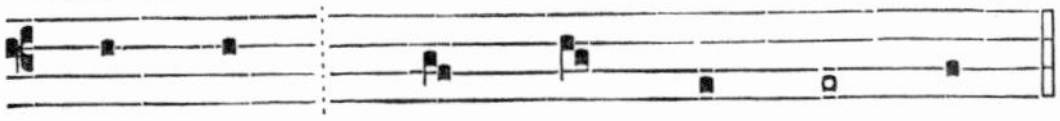

TONE III (1)

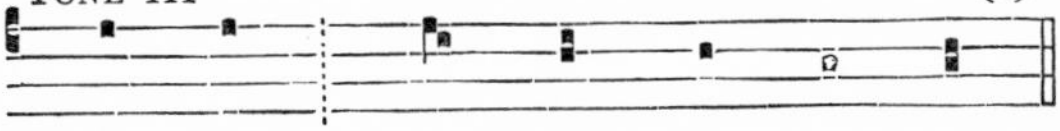

(2) *is treated as* (1).

(3)

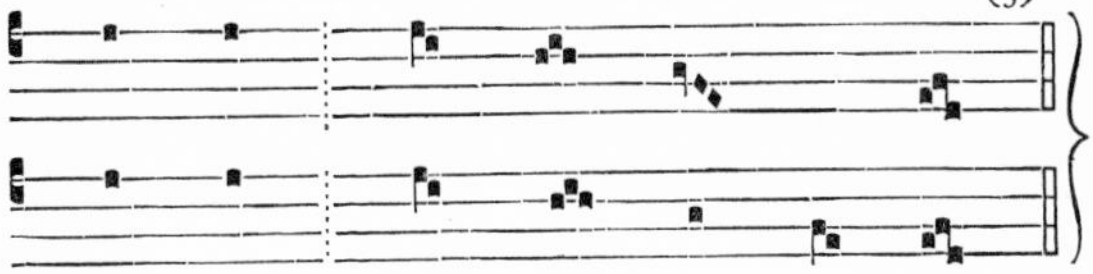

(7) *is treated as* (3).

		6				
praise	thy	Gód,	O	Sy-		on.
in	the	wáy	of	god-	li-	ness.
... en-	dúr-	eth	for	ev-		er.
... thou	wór-	ship	of	Is-	ra-	el.
	—	through	the	east		wind.
	—	O	Hie-	ru-	sa-	lem.
	—	—	but	one		God.
	—	—	shall	ne-	ver	fall.
	—	—	—	praise	the	Lord.

¶ *The * indicates the place of the redundant note in the following Endings, when the accent falls on the* fourth *syllable from the end.* *(See p.* xvij).

TONE VI

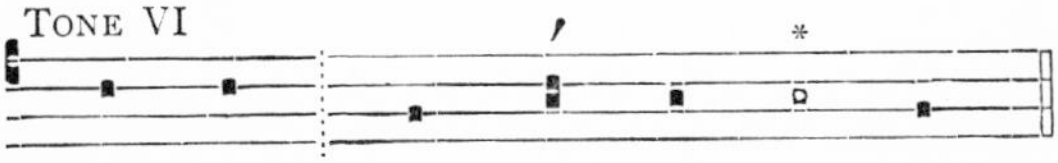

TONE III (1)

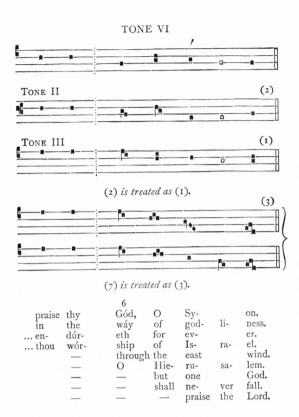

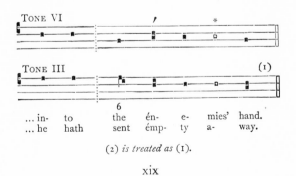

		6				
... in-	to	the	én-	e-	mies'	hand.
... he	hath	sent	émp-	ty	a-	way.

(2) *is treated as* (1).

(1)

(2)

(3)

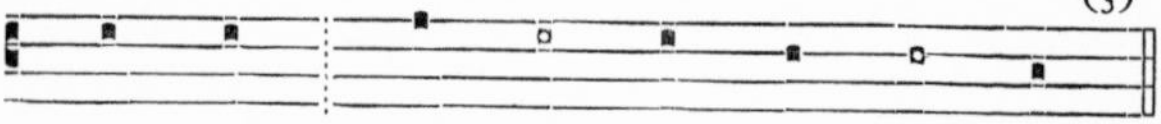

(4)

(5)

(6)

(7)

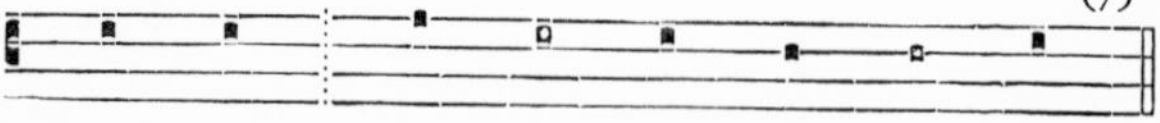

(8) *is treated under* Tone VIII. *p.* xxj.

(9)

		7					
praise	thy	God,		O	Sy-		on.
in	the	way		of	god-	li-	ness.
... is	a	glo-		ri-	ous		voice.
yea,	for	ev-	er	and	ev-		er.
O	thou	wor-	ship	of	Is-	ra-	el.
... thou	art	thëre			al-		so.
... who	is	lörd			o-	ver	us ?
	—	through		the	east		wind.
	—	O		Hie-	ru-	sa-	lem.
	—	—		shall	serve		me.
	—	—		thou	Lord	of	hosts.
	—	—		—	praise	the	Lord.

TONE VIII

(1)

(4), (5) & (6) *are treated as* (1).

(2)

(3). *See page* xxij.

TONE V (3)

TONE VII (8)

		8				
praise	thy	Gód,	O	Sy-		on.
in	the	wáy	of	god-	li-	ness.
... en-	dúr-	eth	for	ev-		er.
... thou	wór-	ship	of	Is-	ra-	el.
... thou	art	thëre		al-		so.
... who	is	lörd		o-	ver	us?
	—	through the		east		wind.
	—	O	Hie-	ru-	sa-	lem.
	—	—	but	one		God.
	—	—	shall	ne-	ver	fall.
	—	—	—	praise	the	Lord.

¶ *The * shews the place of the redundant note in the following Endings, when the accent falls on the* fourth *syllable from the end.* (*See p.* xvij).

(1)

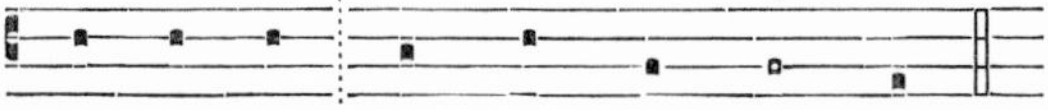

(4), (5) & (6) *are treated as* (1).

(2)

TONE V (3)

TONE VII (8)

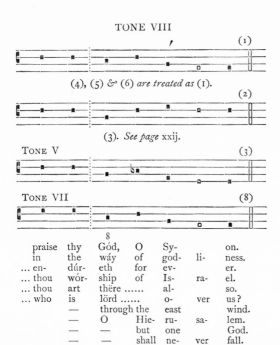

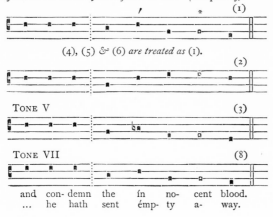

and	con-	demn	the	ín	no-	cent	blood.
...	he	hath	sent	émp-	ty	a-	way.

VIII. 3 is not, strictly speaking, an Ending, but an inflexion which was commonly used as a *metrum* or Mediation in the chanting of the Lessons, Benedictions and Short Chapters in the Quire-Services. As the Ending of a Psalm-tone it is found in the Sarum *Tonale*, but is assigned to three Psalms only, viz. 130, 145 & 147 (vv. 1—11), when sung at Vespers on Ferias. It has not been suggested for use in this edition, as its pointing greatly depends on the accentuation of the last four syllables. But if used, it must be remembered that when the final syllable is emphatic, and is preceded by two syllables of less importance, the reciting-note is left on the former of these, and the final note of the Ending is necessarily omitted. In such cases the figure 8 will not indicate the pointing, as the following examples will shew:—

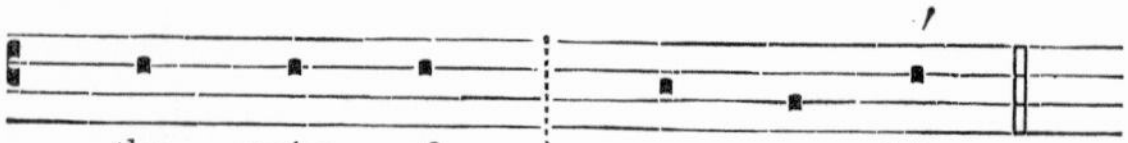

the	voíce	of	my	com-	plaínt.
might	be	knówn	un-	to	mén.
		from	all	his	síns

Where the final syllable is weak, the ordinary pointing of Tone VIII must be followed.

The Irregular or *Peregrine* Tone is probably of Byzantine origin, and was introduced into France in the ixth century. Even in the xth century it was styled *tonus novissimus*, and it was not till the beginning of the xjth that it came into general use. Since that time it has been included in the various *Tonalia* under the head of Tone VIII. Owing to the complex nature of its Ending (as given in English MSS.) it requires to be noted throughout to any Psalm or Canticle with which it is used. (*Cf.* pp. 252, 266 & 274).

N.B. A full point to the left of the figure 4 (and, more rarely, of figures 6 & 8) in the second half of a verse, will occasionally be met with in the course of the Psalter, (*e.g.* in Pss. xxxv. 5 & 6, lxiij. 10, & cxiij. 6). Where this occurs, it will be found desirable to prefix the Reciting-note to the first note of the Ending.

On the choice of Tones and Endings

It has been already stated that where Antiphons are in use, the Antiphon determines both the Tone and its Ending. But where they are not in question, the simpler Tones for the Psalms are much to be preferred. At the same time, it must be admitted that there are some Psalms in which, if Tones II, IV, V or VIII were chosen, the constant recurrence of the abrupt Mediation would have an unpleasing, not to say tiresome, effect. In such cases, those Tones are best avoided.

As regards the Endings, the more ornate ones should, as a rule, be restricted to the Gospel Canticles. Moreover, amongst these ornate Endings there are a few which have such a lack of 'finality' that they cannot be recommended for general use. Such are I. 7, III. 3, IV. 2 & 3, and VIII. 4. These are examples of what is called *epíthesis* or augmentation. They are, in fact, extensions of simpler forms, and were intended to meet or 'dovetail into' the opening phrase of some particular Antiphon. Thus I. 7 is merely an augmented form of I. 5, III. 3 of III. 7, IV. 2 & 3 of IV. 1, & VIII. 4 of VIII. 6. These Endings are undoubtedly relics of a time when the Antiphon was sung alternately with every verse of the Psalm. There are, however, other instances of *epithetic* Endings, such as I. 6 (from I. 5), IV. 5 (from IV. 4), V. 2 (from V. 1) & VII. 4 (from VII. 3), which may be quite legitimately used.

Hints for Chanting

(1) Remember that the *words* are of the first importance.

(2) Do not mistake *accent* for *length*. *Accent* is merely the momentary stress or impulse of the voice given to a particular syllable, and never involves a *lengthening* of that syllable.

(3) In the recitation, remember that no syllable, however strong, should be *prolonged*, and that no syllable, however weak, should be *clipped*. Some syllables have more weight than others, and consequently take a little more time to articulate; but, this being duly allowed for, the recitation should be as *even*, and the syllables as nearly *equal* in length as is consistent with good reading. Any tendency to measured rhythm, (such as that of a dotted crotchet followed by a quaver,) must be sedulously avoided.

(4) In both Mediation and Ending, the syllable which takes the *final* musical accent should be slightly retarded, (where it will bear it).

(5) There should be a *marked* pause, or rather *silence*, at the colon in every verse. To ensure this, it is suggested that the singers should mentally repeat the two previous syllables, (*e.g.* 'féar him', 'Gén-tiles'); or, in the case of the second syllable being strongly accented, (*e.g.* 'his árm', 'have séen',) should consider that syllable as of double length.

(6) All Hebrew words should be pronounced *more Romano.*

The two clauses of the 'Gloria Patri' should be sung *alternately*, like the rest of the Psalm, and *not* by the full Quire. (See the rubrick following the Ps. *Venite* at Mattins.)

The pointing is here given once for all :—

Glory be to the [37]Fa-ther, and [4]to [16]the [258]Son : [4]and [15678]to [23]the holy Ghost.

As it was in the beginning, is now, and [347]ev-er [12568]shall be : world [4]with-[15678]out [23]end. A-men.

The 'Annexed Copy of the Sealed Book' has been followed in this work, both for the text, and for the division of the verses.

PROPER PSALMS ON CERTAIN DAYS

	Mattins	*Evensong*		*Mattins*	*Evensong*
Christmas-day	19, 45, 85	89, 110, 132	*Easter-day*	2, 57, 111	113, 114, 118
Ash-Wednesday	6, 32, 38	102, 130, 143	*Ascension-day*	8, 15, 21	24, 47, 108
Good Friday	22, 40, 54	69, 88	*Whitsun-day*	48, 68	104, 145

THE

PSALMS OF DAVID

At Mattins

DAY I Ps. I *Beatus vir, qui non abiit* i. I *or* 4

BLessed is the man that hath not walked in the counsel
347 12568
of the ungodly, | nor stood in the way of sin-ners :
457 168 23
and hath not sat in the seat of the scornful.
37 4 16 258
2 But his delight is in the law of the Lord : and in his law
4 6 123578
will he exer-cise him-sëlf day and night.
37 4 16 258
3 And he shall be like a tree planted by the wa-ter side :
4 6 123578
that will bring forth his fruit in düe season.
347 12568
4 His leaf also shall not wi- ther : and look, whatsoever he
4 15678 23
do-eth, it shall prosper.
37 4 16 258
5 As for the ungodly, it is not so with them : but they are
4 6 123578
like the chaff, | which the wind scattereth away from the fäce
of the earth.

37 4
6 Therefore the ungodly shall not be able to stand in the
12568 4 15678 23
judge-ment : neither the sinners in the congrega-tion of the
righteous.

37 4 12568
7 But the Lord knoweth the way of the righ-teous : and
457 168 23
the way of the un-god- ly shall perish.

Ps. 2 *Quare fremuerunt* iij. 4 *or* viij. 1

347 12568
WHy do the heathen so furiously rage to- ge- ther : and
457 168 23
why do the people i-ma- gine a vain thing ?

37
2 The kings of the earth stand up, & the rulers take coun-
4 12568 .4 15678 23
sel to- ge- ther : against the Lord, and a-gainst his An-ointed.
347 12568 4 15678 23
3 Let us break their bonds a-sun-der : & cast a- way their
cords from us.

37 4 16 258
4 He that dwelleth in heaven shall laugh them to scorn :
4 15678 23
the Lord shall have them in de-rision.

37 4 16 258
5 Then shall he speak unto them in his wrath : and vex
4 15678 23
them in his sore dis-pleasure.
3 47 16 258 4 15678 23
6 Yet have I set my King : upon my ho-ly hill of Syon.
37 4 16
7 I will preach the law, whereof the Lord hath said un-to
258 4 15678 23
me : Thou art my Son, this day have I be-gotten thee.

8 Desire of me, and I shall give thee the heathen for
347 258 16 4
thine in-he- ri-tance : and the utmost parts of the earth for
15678 23
thy pos-session.

347 12568
9 Thou shalt bruise them with a rod of i- ron : and break
4 15678 23
them in pieces like a pot- ter's vessel.

37 4 16 258
10 Be wise now there-fore, O ye kings : be learned, ye that
4 15678 23
are judg-es of the earth.

3 47 16 258 4 15678 23
11 Serve the Lord in fear : and rejoice un-to him with
reverence.

37 4
12 Kiss the Son, lest he be angry, and so ye perish from the
16 258
right way : if his wrath be kindled, yea but a little, | blessed
4 15678 23
are all they that put their trust in him.

Ps. 3 *Domine, quid multiplicati* vj *or* vij. I

37 4 258 16
LOrd, how are they in-creas-ed that trou-ble me : many are
4 15678 23
they that rise a-gainst me.

37 4 16 258
2 Many one there be that say of my soul : There is no help
4 15678 23
for him in his God.

347 12568
3 But thou, O Lord, art my de- fen-der : thou art my wor-
4 15678 23
ship, and the lift-er up of my head.

37 4 16 258
4 I did call upon the Lord with my voice : and he heard
457 168 23
me out of his holy hill.

37 4 16 258 4
5 I laid me down and slept, and rose up a-gain : for the
15678 23
Lord sus-tained me.

347 12568
6 I will not be afraid for ten thousands of the peo-ple : that
4 15678 23
have set themselves a-gainst me round about.

37 4 16 258
7 Up, Lord, and help me, O my God : for thou smitest all
mine enemies upon the cheek-bone ; thou hast broken the
457 168 23
teeth of the un-godly.

37 4 16 258
8 Salvation belongeth un-to the Lord : and thy blessing is
4 15678 23
up- on thy people.

Ps. 4 *Cum invocarem* viij. 1

37 4 258 16
HEar me when I call, O God of my righ-teous-ness : thou
hast set me at liberty when I was in trouble ; have
4 15678 23
mercy upon me, and heark-en un- to my prayer.

347 12568
2 O ye sons of men, how long will ye blas-pheme mine ho-
.4 15678 23
nour : & have such pleasure in vanity, & seek af- ter leasing ?

3 Know this also, that the Lord hath chosen to himself the
37 4 12568 .4 15678 23
man that is god-ly : when I call upon the Lord, he will hear me.

347 12568
4 Stand in awe, & sin not : commune with your own heart,
4 15678 23
and in your cham-ber, and be still.

347 258 16 4 6 123578
5 Offer the sacri-fice of righ-teous-ness : and put your trüst
in the Lord.

37 4 16 258 4 15678 23
6 There be ma-ny that say : Who will shew us any good ?

347 16 258 4 15678 23
7 Lord, lift thou up : the light of thy coun-te-nance up-on us.

37 4 16 258
8 Thou hast put glad-ness in my heart : since the time that
4 15678 23
their corn and wine and oil in-creased.

37 4 16 258
9 I will lay me down in peace, and take my rest : for it is
4 15678 23
thou Lord only, that makest me dwell in safety.

Ps. 5 *Verba mea* ij. 1 *or* viij. 2

347 16 258 4 15678 23
POnder my words, O Lord : consider my me- di-tation.

37
2 O hearken thou unto the voice of my calling, my King
4 16 258 4 15678 23
and my God : for unto thee will I make my prayer.

3 47 16 258
3 My voice shalt thou hear be-times, O Lord : early in the
4 15678 23
morning will I direct my prayer unto thee, and will look up.

37 4 258 16
4 For thou art the God that hast no plea-sure in wick-ed-
4 15678 23
ness : neither shall a-ny e- vil dwell with thee.

37 4 16 258
5 Such as be foolish shall not stand in thy sight : for thou
4 15678 23
hatest all them that work vanity.

347 12568
6 Thou shalt destroy them that speak leas-ing : the Lord
4 15678 23
will abhor both the blood-thirs-ty and de-ceitful man.

7 But as for me, I will come into thine house, | even upon
347 12568
the multitude of thy mer-cy : and in thy fear will I worship
4 15678 23
toward thy ho- ly temple.

37 4
8 Lead me, O Lord, in thy righteousness, be-cause of mine
258 16 4 15678 23
en- e-mies : make thy way plain be-fore my face.

37 4 16 258
9 For there is no faith-fulness in his mouth : their inward
4 15678 23
parts are ve- ry wickedness.

347 258 16 4 15678 23
10 Their throat is an o-pen se-pul-chre : they flat-ter with
their tongue.

11 Destroy thou them, O God ; let them perish through
347 12568
their own i-ma-gi- na- tions : cast them out in the multitude

457 168 23
of their ungodliness, | for they have re- bel- led a- gainst thee.
37 4 16 258
12 And let all them that put their trust in thee re-joice :
they shall ever be giving of thanks, because thou defendest
4 15678 23
them ; they that love thy Name shall be joy- ful in thee ;
347 12568
13 For thou, Lord, wilt give thy blessing un-to the righ-
457 168
teous : and with thy favourable kindness wilt thou de-fend him
23
as with a shield.

At Evensong

DAY I Ps. 6 *Domine, ne in furore* ij. I

347 12568
O Lord, rebuke me not in thine in-dig- na- tion : neither
4 15678 23
chasten me in thy dis-pleasure.
37 4 16 258
2 Have mercy upon me, O Lord, for I am weak : O Lord,
4 15678 23
heal me, for my bones are vexed.
347 12568 4 15678
3 My soul also is sore trou-bled : but Lord, how long wilt
23
thou punish me ?
37 4 16 258 4
4 Turn thee, O Lord, and de-li-ver my soul : O save me
15678 23
for thy mercies' sake.
37 4 16 258
5 For in death no man re-mem-ber-eth thee : and who
4 6 123578
will give thee thänks in the pit ?
37 4 16
6 I am weary of my groaning ; every night wash I my
258 4 15678 23
bed : and water my couch with my tears.

347 12568
7 My beauty is gone for ve-ry trou-ble : and worn away
4 15678 23
because of all mine enemies.
37 4 258 16
8 Away from me, all ye that work va- ni-ty : for the Lord
457 168 23
hath heard the voice of my weeping.
347 12568 4 15678 23
9 The Lord hath heard my pe- ti- tion : the Lord will re-
ceive my prayer.
347 12568
10 All mine enemies shall be confounded, and sore vex-ed :
4 6 123578
they shall be turned back, and put to shäme suddenly.

Ps. 7 *Domine Deus meus* i. I *or* 3

3 47 16 258
O Lord my God, in thee have I put my trust : save me
4 15678 23
from all them that persecute me, and de-liver me;
37 4 12568
2 Lest he devour my soul, like a lion, and tear it in pie-
4 15678 23
ces : while there is none to help.
37 4 16 258
3 O Lord my God, if I have done a-ny such thing : or if
457 168 23
there be any wick-ed-ness in my hands;
347 12568
4 If I have rewarded evil unto him that dealt friend-ly with
·4 15678
me : yea, I have delivered him that without any cause is
23
mine enemy;
347 12568
5 Then let mine enemy persecute my soul, & take me :
yea, let him tread my life down upon the earth, | and lay
4 15678 23
mine ho- nour in the dust.

6 Stand up, O Lord, in thy wrath, | and lift up thyself,

347 258 16
because of the indignation of mine en- e-mies : arise up for me
4 15678 23
in the judgement that thou hast com-manded.

347 12568
7 And so shall the congregation of the people come a-bout
4 15678 23
thee : for their sakes therefore lift up thy-self again.

37 4
8 The Lord shall judge the people; give sentence with me,
16 258
O Lord : according to my righteousness, | and according to
4 15678 23
the innocen-cy that is in me.

37 4 16 258
9 O let the wickedness of the ungodly come to an end :
4 6 123578
— but güide thou the just.

347 16 258 4 15678 23
10 For the righ-teous God : trieth the ve- ry hearts & reins.
37 4 16 258 457 168 23
11 My help com-eth of God : who preserveth them that are
true of heart.

347 12568
12 God is a righteous Judge, strong and pa-tient : & God
4 15678 23
is pro-vok- ed every day.

37 4 16 258
13 If a man will not turn, he will whet his sword : he hath
4 15678 23
bent his bow, and made it ready.

37 4 16 258
14 He hath prepared for him the in-stru-ments of death :
4 15678 23
he ordaineth his arrows against the per- se-cutors.

347 12568
15 Behold, he travail-eth with mis-chief : he hath concei-
4 15678 23
ved sorrow, and brought forth un-godliness.

37 4 16 258
16 He hath graven and dig-ged up a pit : and is fallen him-
4 15678 23
self into the destruction that he made for other.

37 4 16 258
17 For his travail shall come up-on his own head : and his
4 15678 23
wickedness shall fall on his own pate.

347 258
18 I will give thanks unto the Lord, according to his righ-
16 457 168 23
teous-ness : & I will praise the Name of the Lord most High.

Ps. 8 *Domine, Dominus noster* viij. 2

37 4 16
O Lord our Governour, how excellent is thy Name in all the
258 4 15678 23
world : thou that hast set thy glory a-bove the heavens!

2 Out of the mouth of very babes and sucklings hast thou
37 4 258 16
ordained strength, be-cause of thine en- e-mies : that thou
457 168 23
mightest still the enemy, and the a-venger.

37 4
3 For I will consider thy heavens, even the works of thy
12568 4 15678 23
fin-gers : the moon and the stars, which thou hast or-dained.

37 4 16 258
4 What is man that thou art mind-ful of him : and the son
4 15678 23
of man, that thou vi- si-test him?

347 12568
5 Thou madest him lower than the an-gels : to crown
457 168 23
him with glo- ry and worship.

37 4 16
6 Thou makest him to have dominion of the works of thy
258 4 15678 23
hands : & thou hast put all things in subjec-tion un-der his feet;

347 12568 4 6 123578
7 All sheep and ox-en : yea, and the beästs of the field;

37 4 16 258
8 The fowls of the air, and the fish-es of the sea : & what-
4 6 123578
soever walketh through the päths of the seas.

347 258 16 4 15678 23
9 O Lord our Go-ver-nour : how excellent is thy Name in
all the world!

At Mattins

DAY 2 Ps. 9 *Confitebor tibi* i. 4 *or* vij. 7

37 4 16 258
I Will give thanks unto thee, O Lord, with my whole heart :
4 68 157 23
I will speak of all thy mar-vel-lous works.

3 47 16 258
2 I will be glad and re-joice in thee : yea, my songs will
4 15678 23
I make of thy Name, O thou most Highest.

37 4 16 258
3 While mine ene-mies are dri-ven back : they shall fall
4 15678 23
and pe-rish at thy presence.

37 4 16 258
4 For thou hast maintained my right and my cause : thou
4 15678 23
art set in the throne that judgest right.

37 4 12568
5 Thou hast rebuked the heathen, & de-stroy'd the un-god-
457 168 23
ly : thou hast put out their name for ev- er and ever.

37 4 16
6 O thou enemy, destructions are come to a per-pe-tu-al
258
end : even as the cities which thou hast destroyed : their me-
457 168 23
morial is pe-rish-ed with them.

347 12568
7 But the Lord shall en-dure for ev- er : he hath also pre-
4 15678 23
pared his seat for judgement.

347 258 16
8 For he shall judge the world in righ-teous-ness : and
457 168 23
minister true judgement un- to the people.

37 4 12568
9 The Lord also will be a defence for the op-press-ed :
.4 15678 23
even a refuge in due time of trouble.

37 4 16
10 And they that know thy Name will put their trust in

258 4 15678 23
thee : for thou, Lord, hast never fail-ed them that seek thee.

37 4 12568
11 O praise the Lord which dwell-eth in Sy-on : shew the
4 15678 23
peo-ple of his doings.

37
12 For when he maketh inquisition for blood, he re-mem-
4 16 258 4 6 123578
ber-eth them : and forgetteth not the com-pläint of the poor.

13 Have mercy upon me, O Lord; consider the trouble
347 12568 4
which I suffer of them that hate me : thou that liftest me up
15678 23
from the gates of death.

14 That I may shew all thy praises within the ports of the
37 4 12568 4 15678 23
daugh-ter of Sy-on : I will rejoice in thy sal-vation.

37 4 16 258
15 The heathen are sunk down in the pit that they made :
4 6 123578
in the same net which they hid privily, is their föot taken.

37 4 12568
16 The Lord is known to ex-e-cute judge-ment : the un-
457 168 23
godly is trapped in the work of his own hands.

37 4 16 258
17 The wicked shall be turn-ed in-to hell : and all the peo-
4 15678 23
ple that for-get God.

347 12568
18 For the poor shall not alway be for-got-ten : the patient
457 168 23
abiding of the meek shall not pe-rish for ever.

37 4 16 258
19 Up, Lord, and let not man have the up-per hand : let
457 168 23
the heathen be judg- ed in thy sight.

3 47 16 258
20 Put them in fear, O Lord : that the heathen may know
4 15678 23
them-selves to be but men.

Ps. 10 *Ut quid, Domine* i. 4

347 16 258
WHy standest thou so far off, O Lord : and hidest thy
4 15678 23
face in the need-ful time of trouble?

37 4 16 258
2 The ungodly for his own lust doth per-se-cute the poor :
4 15678 23
let them be taken in the crafty wiliness that they have i-magined.

347 16 258
3 For the ungodly hath made boast of his own heart's de-sire :
4 15678 23
and speaketh good of the covetous, whom God ab-horreth.

37 4 16 258
4 The ungodly is so proud that he car-eth not for God :
4 15678 23
neither is God in all his thoughts.

347 12568
5 His ways are al-way grie-vous : thy judgements are far
4 15678 23
above out of his sight, | and therefore defieth he all his enemies.

37 4 16
6 For he hath said in his heart, | Tush, I shall ne-ver be cast
258 457 168 23
down : there shall no harm hap-pen un-to me.

3 47 16 258
7 His mouth is full of cur-sing, de- ceit, & fraud : under his
4 15678 23
tongue is ungod-li- ness and vanity.

37 4 16 258
8 He sitteth lurking in the thievish cor-ners of the streets :
and privily in his lurking dens doth he murder the innocent;
4 15678 23
his eyes are set a-gainst the poor.

37 4
9 For he lieth waiting secretly, | even as a lion lurketh he in
16 258 4 68 157 23
his den : that he may ra-vish the poor.

37 4 16 258 4 15678 23
10 He doth ra-vish the poor : when he getteth him in- to
his net.

37 4 16 258
11 He falleth down, and hum-bleth him-self : that the con-

457 168 23
gregation of the poor may fall into the hands of his captains.
347 12568
12 He hath said in his heart, | Tush, God hath for-got-ten :
4 15678 23
he hideth away his face, and he will ne- ver see it.
37 4 16 258 4 6
13 Arise, O Lord God, and lift up thine hand : — for-
123578
gët not the poor.

37 4 16 258
14 Wherefore should the wick-ed blas-pheme God : while
457 168 23
he doth say in his heart, | Tush, thou God car-est not for it.
347 12568 457 168
15 Surely thou hast seen it : for thou beholdest un-god- li-
23
ness and wrong.

37 4 16 258
16 That thou mayest take the matter in-to thine hand :
the poor committeth himself unto thee; for thou art the
4 15678 23
help-er of the friendless.

347 12568
17 Break thou the power of the ungodly and ma-li-cious :
4 15678 23
take away his ungodliness, and thou shalt find none.
37 4 12568
18 The Lord is King for ev-er and ev-er : and the heathen
4 6 123578
are pe-rish-ed oüt of the land.
37 4 16 258
19 Lord, thou hast heard the de-sire of the poor : thou pre-
457 168 23
parest their heart, and thine ear heark-en-eth thereto;
37 4 16 258
20 To help the fatherless and poor un-to their right : that
457 168 23
the man of the earth be no more ex-alt- ed a-gainst them.

Ps. 11 *In Domino confido* ij. 1 *or* iij. 1

37 4 16 258
IN the Lord put I my trust : how say ye then to my soul,
4 15678 23
that she should flee as a bird un-to the hill?

2 For lo, the ungodly bend their bow, | and make ready their
347 12568
arrows with-in the qui-ver : that they may privily shoot at
457 168 23
them which are true of heart.

37 4 16 258 457 168
3 For the foundations will be cast down : and what hath
23
the righteous done?

347 12568 4
4 The Lord is in his ho-ly tem-ple : the Lord's seat
15678 23
is in heaven.

37 4 16 258 4
5 His eyes con-si-der the poor : and his eyelids try the
15678 23
chil-dren of men.

37 4 12568
6 The Lord al-low-eth the righ-teous : but the ungodly,
4 15678 23
and him that delighteth in wicked-ness doth his soul abhor.

7 Upon the ungodly he shall rain snares, | fire and brimstone,
347 12568 4 15678 23
storm and tem-pest : this shall be their por-tion to drink.

347 258 16
8 For the righteous Lord lov-eth righ-teous-ness : his coun-
4 15678 23
tenance will behold the thing that is just.

At Evensong

DAY 2 Ps. 12 *Salvum me fac* i. 2 *or* vij. 1

37 4 16 258
HElp me, Lord, for there is not one god-ly man left : for the
4 15678 23
faithful are minished from among the chil-dren of men.

347 12568
2 They talk of vanity every one with his neigh-bour :
4 15678 23
they do but flatter with their lips, and dissem-ble in their
double heart.

3 47 16 258
3 The Lord shall root out all de-ceit-ful lips : and the
4 15678 23
tongue that speak-eth proud things.

37 4 16 258
4 Which have said, With our tongue will we pre-vail : we
4 6 123578
are they that ought to speak ; who is Lörd over us ?

347 12568
5 Now for the comfortless troubles' sake of the nee-dy :
.4 15678 23
and because of the deep sigh- ing of the poor.

37 4 16 258
6 I will up, saith the Lord : and will help every one from
4 15678 23
him that swelleth against him, and will set him at rest.

37 4 16 258
7 The words of the Lord are pure words : even as the silver
457 168 23
which from the earth is tried, | and purified se- ven times in
the fire.

37 4 16 258
8 Thou shalt keep them, O Lord : thou shalt preserve him
457 168 23
from this gene- ra- tion for ever.

37 4 16 258
9 The ungodly walk on ev- e- ry side : when they are exal-
4 6 123578
ted, the children of men are püt to rebuke.

Ps. 13 *Usquequo, Domine* ij. 1 *or* iij. 5

347 12568
HOw long wilt thou forget me, O Lord, for ev-er : how
4 15678 23
long wilt thou hide thy face from me ?

37
2 How long shall I seek counsel in my soul, and be so vex-
4 16 258 4 15678 23
ed in my heart : how long shall mine ene-mies tri-umph
over me ?

3 47 16 258
3 Consider, and hear me, O Lord my God : lighten mine
4 15678 23
eyes, that I sleep not in death.

37 4 12568
4 Lest mine enemy say, I have pre-vail-ed a-gainst him :
4 15678 23
for if I be cast down, | they that trouble me will re-joice at it.
347 12568 4
5 But my trust is in thy mer-cy : and my heart is joyful in
15678 23
thy sal-vation.

37 4
6 I will sing of the Lord, because he hath dealt so lov-ing-ly
12568 4 15678 23
with me : yea, I will praise the Name of the Lord most Highest.

Ps. 14 *Dixit insipiens* iv. 6

37 4 16 258 4 15678 23
THe fool hath said in his heart : — There is no God.

347
2 They are corrupt, and become abominable in their
12568 4 6 123578
do- ings : there is none that do-eth gööd, no not one.

37 4
3 The Lord looked down from heaven upon the chil-dren
16 258 4 6
of men : to see if there were any that would under-stand, and
123578
sëek after God.

4 But they are all gone out of the way, | they are altogether
347 12568 4 6 123578
become a-bo-mi-na-ble : there is none that do-eth gööd, no
not one.

5 Their throat is an open sepulchre, | with their tongues
347 12568 4 15678 23
have they de-ceiv-ed : the poison of asps is un- der their lips.

37 4 258 16
6 Their mouth is full of curs-ing and bit-ter-ness : their feet
4 15678 23
are swift to shed blood.

7 Destruction and unhappiness is in their ways, and the way
37 4 16 258 4 15678 23
of peace have they not known : there is no fear of God be-
fore their eyes.

37 4
8 Have they no knowledge, that they are all such work-ers
12568 +
of mis-chief : eating up my people as it were bread, | and call
15678 23
not up-on the Lord ?

347 16
9 There were they brought in great fear, even where no fear
258 4 15678 23
was : for God is in the genera-tion of the righteous.

37 4 16
10 As for you, ye have made a mock at the coun-sel of the
258 4 6 123578
poor : because he put-teth his trüst in the Lord.

11 Who shall give salvation unto Israel out of Syon ?
347 12568
When the Lord turneth the captivity of his peo-ple : then
457 168 23
shall Iacob rejoice, and Is- ra- el shall be glad.

At Mattins

DAY 3 Ps. 15 *Domine, quis habitabit* v. 2 *or* viij. 5

347 12568
LOrd, who shall dwell in thy ta-ber-na-cle : or who shall
4 15678 23
rest up- on thy holy hill ?

37 4 16 258
2 Even he that leadeth an un-cor-rupt life : and doeth the
4 15678 23
thing which is right, | and speaketh the truth from his heart.

3 He that hath used no deceit in his tongue, | nor done evil
347 12568 4 15678 23
to his neigh-bour : and hath not slan-der- ed his neighbour.

37 4 16
4 He that setteth not by himself, but is lowly in his own
258 4 15678 23
eyes : and maketh much of them that fear the Lord.

37 4
5 He that sweareth unto his neighbour, and disap-point-eth
16 258 4 6 123578
him not : though it were to his öwn hindrance.

347 258 16
6 He that hath not given his money up-on u-su-ry : nor
4 15678 23
taken reward a-gainst the innocent.
37 4 16 258 4 15678 23
7 Whoso do-eth these things : — — shall never fall.

Ps. 16 *Conserva me, Domine* i. 1

37 4 16 258 4 15678 23
PRe-serve me, O God : for in thee have I put my trust.
37 4 16 258
2 O my soul, thou hast said un-to the Lord : Thou art
4 15678 23
my God, | my goods are no- thing unto thee.
37 4 16 258
3 All my delight is upon the saints that are in the earth :
4 15678 23
and upon such as ex- cel in virtue.
37 4 16 258 4 15678 23
4 But they that run af-ter an-o-ther god : shall have great
trouble.
347 12568
5 Their drink-offerings of blood will I not of-fer : neither
4 15678 23
make mention of their names with-in my lips.
37
6 The Lord himself is the portion of mine inheritance, and
4 16 258 4 15678 23
of my cup : thou shalt main-tain my lot.
37 4 16 258
7 The lot is fallen unto me in a fair ground : yea, I have
4 15678 23
a good-ly heritage.
37 4 12568
8 I will thank the Lord for giv-ing me warn-ing : my reins
4 6 123578
also chasten me in the nïght-season.
347 12568
9 I have set God al-ways be-fore me : for he is on my right
457 168 23
hand, there-fore I shall not fall.

37 4 12568
10 Wherefore my heart was glad, and my glo-ry re-joi-ced :
4 15678 23
my flesh al- so shall rest in hope.

3 47 16 258
11 For-why thou shalt not leave my soul in hell : neither
4 15678 23
shalt thou suffer thy Holy One to see cor-ruption.

12 Thou shalt shew me the path of life ; in thy presence is
37 4 16 258 457 168
the ful-ness of joy : and at thy right hand there is plea-sure
23
for evermore.

Ps. 17 *Exaudi, Domine* iij. 5 *or* vij. 7

7 4 16 258
HEar the right, O Lord, con-si-der my com-plaint : and
4 15678 23
hearken unto my prayer, that goeth not out of feigned lips.

347 12568
2 Let my sentence come forth from thy pre-sence : and let
457 168 23
thine eyes look upon the thing that is equal.

3 Thou hast proved and visited mine heart in the night-
37 4 12568
season ; thou hast tried me, and shalt find no wick-ed-ness in
4 15678 23
me : for I am utterly purposed that my mouth shall not offend.

37
4 Because of men's works, that are done against the words
4 16 258 457 168 23
of thy lips : I have kept me from the ways of the de-stroyer.

37 4 16 258 4 15678
5 O hold thou up my go-ings in thy paths : that my foot-
23
steps slip not.

347 12568
6 I have called upon thee, O God, for thou shalt hear me :
4 15678 23
incline thine ear to me, and heark-en un- to my words.

7 Shew thy marvellous loving-kindness, | thou that art the

37 4 16 258
Saviour of them which put their trust in thee : from such as
4 15678 23
re- sist thy right hand.

37 4 16 258 457
8 Keep me as the ap-ple of an eye : hide me under the sha-
168 23
dow of thy wings,

37 4 258 16
9 From the un-god-ly that trou-ble me : mine enemies
4 15678 23
compass me round about to take a-way my soul.

37 4 16 258 .4
10 They are inclosed in their own fat : and their mouth
15678 23
speak-eth proud things.

37 4 16 258
11 They lie waiting in our way on ev-e-ry side : turning
4 .6 123578
their eyes döwn to the ground;

37 4 16 258
12 Like as a lion that is gree-dy of his prey : and as it were
4 15678 23
a lion's whelp, | lurking in se- cret places.

347 16 258
13 Up, Lord, disappoint him, and cast him down : deliver
4 15678 23
my soul from the ungodly, which is a sword of thine.

14 From the men of thy hand, O Lord, | from the men, I
3 47 16 258
say, and from the e-vil world : which have their portion in
4 15678 23
this life, | whose bellies thou fillest with thy hid treasure.

37 4 16 258
15 They have chil-dren at their de-sire : and leave the rest
4 15678 23
of their sub-stance for their babes.

37 4 258 16
16 But as for me, I will behold thy pre-sence in righ-teous-
4
ness : & when I awake up after thy likeness, | I shall be sa-tis-
15678 23
fi- ed with it.

At Evensong

DAY 3 Ps. 18 *Diligam te, Domine* i. 2 *or* v. 2

I Will love thee, O Lord, my strength; the Lord is my
37 4 16 258
stony rock, and my de-fence : my Saviour, my God, and
my might, in whom I will trust, | my buckler, the horn also
4 15678 23
of my salva-tion, and my refuge.

347 12568
2 I will call upon the Lord, which is worthy to be prai-sed :
4 15678 23
so shall I be safe from mine enemies.

37 4 16 258
3 The sorrows of death com-pas-sed me : and the overflow-
4 6 123578
ings of ungod-li-ness mäde me afraid.

347 12568
4 The pains of hell came a-bout me : and the snares of
.4 15678 23
death o- ver-took me.

37 4 16 258 4
5 In my trouble I will call up-on the Lord : and com-plain
15678 23
un- to my God.

347 12568
6 So shall he hear my voice out of his ho-ly tem-ple : and
4 15678
my complaint shall come before him, | it shall enter e-ven in-
23
to his ears.

37 4 12568
7 The earth trem-bled & qua-ked : the very foundations al-
4 6 123578
so of the hills shook, & were remov-ed, be-caüse he was wroth.

347 12568
8 There went a smoke out in his pre-sence : and a consu-
4 15678 23
ming fire out of his mouth, so that coals were kin-dled at it.

37 4 16 258
9 He bowed the heavens al-so, and came down : and it was
.4 15678 23
dark un- der his feet.

3 47 16 258
10 He rode upon the Che-rubyn, and did fly : he came fly-
4 6 123578
ing up-on the wïngs of the wind.
3 47 16 258
11 He made dark-ness his se-cret place : his pavilion round
4 15678 23
about him, | with dark water, and thick clouds to cover him.
347 12568
12 At the brightness of his presence his clouds re-mov-ed :
4 15678 23
hail-stones, and coals of fire.

13 The Lord also thundered out of heaven, and the Highest
347 12568 4 15678 23
gave his thun-der : hail-stones, and coals of fire.
37 4 16 258
14 He sent out his arrows, and scat-ter-ed them : he cast
4 15678 23
forth light-nings, and de-stroyed them.

15 The springs of waters were seen, | and the foundations of
37 4 16 258
the round world were discovered, at thy chi-ding, O Lord : at
4 15678 23
the blasting of the breath of thy dis-pleasure.
347 12568
16 He shall send down from on high to fetch me : and shall
4 15678 23
take me out of ma-ny waters.

17 He shall deliver me from my strongest enemy, and from
347 12568 4 15678 23
them which hate me : for they are too migh-ty for me.
37 4 12568
18 They prevented me in the day of my trou-ble : but the
4 15678 23
Lord was my up-holder.
347 258 16
19 He brought me forth also into a place of li-ber-ty : he
4 15678 23
brought me forth, | even because he had a fa- vour unto me.
347 12568
20 The Lord shall reward me after my righ-teous deal-ing :

4 15678 23
according to the cleanness of my hands shall he re- com-
pense me.

37 4 16 258
21 Because I have kept the ways of the Lord : and have
.4 15678 23
not forsaken my God, as the wicked doth.

3 47 16 258
22 For I have an eye un-to all his laws : and will not cast
4 15678 23
out his com-mand-ments from me.

347 12568 6
23 I was also uncor-rupt be-fore him : and eschew-ed mine
123578
öwn wickedness.

347
24 Therefore shall the Lord reward me after my righ-teous
12568 .4 15678
deal-ing : and according unto the cleanness of my hands in
23
his eye-sight.

347 12568
25 With the holy thou shalt be ho- ly : and with a perfect
4 15678 23
man thou shalt be perfect.

37 4 16 258
26 With the clean thou shalt be clean : and with the fro-
4 15678 23
ward thou shalt learn frowardness.

37 4 258 16
27 For thou shalt save the people that are in ad-ver-si-ty :
4 15678 23
and shalt bring down the high looks of the proud.

347 12568
28 Thou also shalt light my can-dle : the Lord my God
4 15678 23
shall make my dark-ness to be light.

37 4 16 258
29 For in thee I shall dis-com-fit an host of men : and with
4 .68 157 23
the help of my God I shall leap o- ver the wall.

37 4 16 258
30 The way of God is an un-de-fi-led way : the word of

the Lord also is tried in the fire; he is the defender of all them
4 15678 23
that put their trust in him.

37 4 16 258 4
31 For who is God, but the Lord : or who hath a-ny
15678 23
strength ex-cept our God?

3 47 16 258
32 It is God, that girdeth me with strength of war : and
4 6 123578
ma-keth my wäy perfect.

37 4 16 258 457 168 23
33 He maketh my feet like harts' feet : and set-teth me up
on high.

3 47 16 258
34 He teach-eth mine hands to fight : and mine arms shall
457 168 23
break e- ven a bow of steel.

347 12568
35 Thou hast given me the defence of thy sal-va-tion : thy
457 168
right hand also shall hold me up, | and thy loving cor-rec-tion
23
shall make me great.

37 4 16 258
36 Thou shalt make room enough un-der me for to go :
4 15678 23
that my foot-steps shall not slide.

347 12568
37 I will follow upon mine enemies, and o-ver-take them :
4 15678 23
neither will I turn again till I have de-stroyed them.

37 4 16 258
38 I will smite them, that they shall not be a-ble to stand :
·4 15678 23
but fall un- der my feet.

347 12568
39 Thou hast girded me with strength un-to the bat-tle :
457 168 23
thou shalt throw down mine e- ne-mies under me.

347
40 Thou hast made mine enemies also to turn their backs
12568 ·4 15678 23
up-on me : and I shall de-stroy them that hate me.

347 12568
41 They shall cry, but there shall be none to help them : yea,
4 15678 23
even unto the Lord shall they cry, but he shall not hear them.
37 4 16 258
42 I will beat them as small as the dust be-fore the wind :
4 6 123578
I will cast them out as the cläy in the streets.
347 12568
43 Thou shalt deliver me from the strivings of the peo-ple :
457 168 23
and thou shalt make me the head of the heathen.
3 47 16 258 4 15678 23
44 A people whom I have not known : — — shall serve me.
347 12568
45 As soon as they hear of me, they shall o-bey me : but
4 15678 23
the strange children shall dis- sem- ble with me.
37 4 16 258 457 168
46 The strange chil-dren shall fail : and be afraid out of
23
their prisons.
347 12568
47 The Lord liveth, and blessed be my strong help-er : and
4 15678 23
praised be the God of my sal-vation.
347 12568
48 Even the God that seeth that I be a-ven-ged : and sub-
4 15678 23
dueth the peo-ple unto me.

49 It is he that delivereth me from my cruel enemies, | and
347 12568 4
setteth me up above mine ad-ver-sa-ries : thou shalt rid me
15678 23
from the wicked man.

50 For this cause will I give thanks unto thee, O Lord, a-
347 12568 4 15678 23
mong the Gen-tiles : and sing prai-ses un- to thy Name.
37 4 16 258
51 Great prosperity giveth he un-to his King : and shew-
4
eth loving-kindness unto David his Anointed, | and unto his
15678 23
seed for evermore.

At Mattins

DAY 4 Ps. 19 *Cæli enarrant* iij. 5

THe heavens declare the [37]glo-[4]ry [16]of [258]God : and the firmament [457]shew-[168]eth [23]his handiwork.

2 One day [37]tel-[4]leth an-[12568]o-ther : and one night certi-[457]fi-[168]eth
[23]an-other.

3 There is neither [347]speech nor [12568]lan-guage : but their voices
[4]are [15678]heard [23]a-mong them.

4 Their sound is gone out [37]in-[4]to [16]all [258]lands : and their words
in-[4]to [6]the [123578]ënds of the world.

5 In them hath he set a taber-[37]na-cle [4]for [16]the [258]sun : which
cometh forth as a bridegroom out of his chamber, | and rejoi-
ceth as a [457]gi-[168]ant [23]to run his course.

6 It goeth forth from the uttermost part of the heaven, |
and runneth about unto the [37]end of [4]it [16]a-[258]gain : and there is
nothing [4]hid [15678]from [23]the heat thereof.

7 The law of the Lord is an undefiled law, con-[37]vert-[4]ing [16]the
[258]soul : the testimony of the Lord is sure, | and giveth wisdom
[4]un-[15678]to [23]the simple.

8 The statutes of the Lord are right, [3]and re-[47]joice [16]the [258]heart :
the commandment of the Lord is pure, and giv-[4]eth [15678]light [23]un-to
the eyes.

9 The fear of the Lord is clean, and en-[37]dur-[4]eth for [12568]e- ver :

4 15678 23
the judgements of the Lord are true, & righ-teous al- to-gether.
37 4
10 More to be desired are they than gold, | yea, than much
16 258 4 15678 23
fine gold : sweeter also than ho-ney, and the honey-comb.
3 47 16 258
11 Moreover by them is thy ser-vant taught : and in keep-
4 15678 23
ing of them there is great reward.
37 4 12568
12 Who can tell how oft he of-fen-deth : O cleanse thou
4 15678 23
me from my secret faults.

13 Keep thy servant also from presumptuous sins, | lest they
347 258 16
get the do-min-ion o-ver me : so shall I be undefiled, | and in-
4 15678 23
no-cent from the great offence.
37 4 16
14 Let the words of my mouth, and the medi-ta-tion of my
258 57 4 168 23
heart : be alway ac-cep-ta- ble in thy sight.
258* 4 15678 23
15 O Lord : my strength, and my re-deemer.

Ps. 20 *Exaudiat te Dominus* iv. 5 *or* vij. 1

347 12568
THe Lord hear thee in the day of trou-ble : the Name
4 15678 23
of the God of Ia- cob de-fend thee.
347 12568
2 Send thee help from the sanc-tu- a- ry : and strengthen
4 15678 23
thee out of Syon.
347 258 16 4 6 123578
3 Remember all thy of- fer-ings : and ac-cept thy bürnt-
sacrifice.
3 47 16 258 4 15678 23
4 Grant thee thy heart's de-sire : and ful- fil all thy mind.
3
5 We will rejoice in thy salvation, | & triumph in the Name

*In the other Tones the Mediation is wholly omitted.

of the [47]Lord [16]our [258]God : the Lord perform [.4]all [15678]thy [23]pe-titions.

6 Now know I that the Lord helpeth his Anointed, | and
will hear him from his [347]ho-ly [12568]hea-ven : even with the wholesome [457]strength [168]of [23]his right hand.

7 Some put their trust in chariots, and [347]some in [12568]hor-ses : but
we will remember the [457]Name [168]of [23]the Lord our God.

8 They are brought [347]down, and [12568]fal-len : but we are [457]ri-[168]sen,
[23]and stand upright.

9 Save, Lord, | and hear us, O [347]King of [12568]hea-ven : when [4]we
[15678]call [23]up-on thee.

Ps. 21 *Domine, in virtute tua* i. 2

THe King shall rejoice [3]in thy [47]strength, [16]O [258]Lord : exceed-
ing glad shall he be [4]of [15678]thy [23]sal-vation.

2 Thou hast given [3]him his [47]heart's [16]de-[258]sire : and hast not
denied him the [4]re-[15678]quest [23]of his lips.

3 For thou shalt prevent him with the [37]bles-[4]sings of [12568]good-
ness : and shalt set a crown of [.4]pure [15678]gold [23]up-on his head.

4 He asked life of thee, and thou gavest [37]him [4]a [16]long [258]life :
even for [457]ev-[168]er [23]and ever.

5 His honour is great in [347]thy sal-[12568]va-tion : glory and great
worship shalt [4]thou [15678]lay [23]up-on him.

6 For thou shalt give him ever-[37]last-[4]ing fe-[258]li-[16]ci-ty : and
make him glad with the [457]joy [168]of [23]thy countenance.

37 4 16 258
7 And-why because the King putteth his trust in the Lord :
4 15678 23
and in the mercy of the most Highest he shall not mis-carry.

3 47 16 258
8 All thine ene-mies shall feel thy hand : thy right hand
4 15678 23
shall find out them that hate thee.

37 4 16
9 Thou shalt make them like a fiery oven in time of thy
258
wrath : the Lord shall destroy them in his displeasure, | and
.4 15678 23
the fire shall con-sume them.

37 4 16 258
10 Their fruit shalt thou root out of the earth : and their
4 15678 23
seed from among the chil-dren of men.

37 4 12568
11 For they intended mis-chief a-gainst thee : and imagined
4 15678 23
such a device as they are not a- ble to perform.

37 4 16 258
12 Therefore shalt thou put them to flight : and the strings
4 15678 23
of thy bow shalt thou make ready a-gainst the face of them.

37 4 16 258
13 Be thou exalted, Lord, in thine own strength : so will
4 15678 23
we sing, and praise thy power.

At Evensong

DAY 4 Ps. 22 *Deus, Deus meus* i. 8 *or* ij. 1

347 258
MY God, my God, look upon me ; why hast thou for-sa-
16 4
ken me : and art so far from my health, and from the
15678 23
words of my complaint ?

37 4 16 258
2 O my God, I cry in the day-time, but thou hear-est not :
457 168 23
and in the night-season al- so I take no rest.

37 4 12568 457 168 23
3 And thou con-tin-u-est ho-ly : O thou wor-ship of Israel.
37 4 16 258
4 Our fathers ho-ped in thee : they trusted in thee, and
4 15678 23
thou didst de-liver them.

347 12568
5 They called upon thee, and were hol-pen : they put their
4 15678 23
trust in thee, and were not con-founded.

37 4 16 258
6 But as for me, I am a worm and no man : a very scorn of
4 15678 23
men, and the out-cast of the people.

37 4 16 258
7 All they that see me laugh me to scorn : they shoot out
4 6 123578
their lips, and shake their heads, saying :

347 258 16
8 He trusted in God that he would de-liv-er him : let him
4 15678 23
deliver him, if he will have him.

37 4 16 258
9 But thou art he that took me out of my mo-ther's womb :
4 15678 23
thou wast my hope, when I hanged yet up- on my mother's
breasts.

37 4 16 258
10 I have been left unto thee ever since I was born : thou
4 15678 23
art my God, e-ven from my mother's womb.

3 47 16 258
11 O go not from me, for trou-ble is hard at hand : and
4 15678 23
there is none to help me.

347 12568
12 Many oxen are come a-bout me : fat bulls of Basan
4 15678 23
close me in on every side.

37 4 16 258
13 They gape up-on me with their mouths : as it were a
4 15678 23
ramping and a roar-ing lion.

37 4 16
14 I am poured out like water, | and all my bones are out of

258 457 168 23
joint : my heart also in the midst of my body is e- ven like
melting wax.

15 My strength is dried up like a potsherd, | & my tongue
37 4 16 258 457 168 23
clea-veth to my gums : and thou shalt bring me in- to the dust
of death.

347 12568
16 For many dogs are come a-bout me : and the council of
4 15678 23
the wicked lay-eth siege a-gainst me.

347
17 They pierced my hands and my feet; I may tell all
16 258 457 168 23
my bones : they stand staring and look-ing up-on me.

37 4 12568
18 They part my gar-ments a-mong them : and cast lots
4 15678 23
up- on my vesture.

37 4 16 258
19 But be not thou far from me, O Lord : thou art my
457 168 23
succour, haste thee to help me.

37 4 16 258
20 Deliver my soul from the sword : my darling from the
15678 23
pow- er of the dog.

37 4 16 258
21 Save me from the li-on's mouth : thou hast heard me
457 168 23
also from among the horns of the unicorns.

347 12568
22 I will declare thy Name un-to my bre-thren : in the
4 15678 23
midst of the congrega-tion will I praise thee.

347 12568
23 O praise the Lord, ye that fear him : magnify him, all
4 15678 23
ye of the seed of Iacob, | and fear him, all ye seed of Israel.

37 4
24 For he hath not despised nor abhorred the low es-tate of
16 258
the poor : he hath not hid his face from him, | but when he
4 15678 23
called un-to him he heard him.

347 12568
25 My praise is of thee in the great con-gre-ga-tion : my
4 15678 23
vows will I perform in the sight of them that fear him.

347 12568
26 The poor shall eat, and be sa-tis- fi- ed : they that seek
4 15678 23
after the Lord shall praise him ; your heart shall live for ever.

27 All the ends of the world shall remember themselves,
37 4 16 258
and be turned un-to the Lord : and all the kindreds of the
457 168 23
nations shall wor-ship be-fore him.

37 4 16 258
28 For the king-dom is the Lord's : & he is the Governour
4 15678 23
a-mong the people.

37 4 16 258 457 168 23
29 All such as be fat up-on earth : have eat-en, and
worshipped.

347 12568
30 All they that go down into the dust shall kneel be-fore
4 15678 23
him : and no man hath quick-en- ed his own soul.

347 12568
31 My seed shall serve him : they shall be counted unto
4 15678 23
the Lord for a ge- ne-ration.

347
32 They shall come, and the heavens shall de-clare his
258 16 4 15678 23
righ-teous-ness : unto a people that shall be born, whom the
Lord hath made.

Ps. 23 *Dominus regit me* iv. 4 *or* viij. 1

347 12568 4 15678 23
THe Lord is my shep-herd : therefore can I lack nothing.
4 37 12568
2 He shall feed me in a green pas-ture : and lead me
457 168 23
forth beside the wa-ters of comfort.

347 16 258
3 He shall con-vert my soul : and bring me forth in the
4 15678 23
paths of righteous-ness, for his Name's sake.

4 Yea, though I walk through the valley of the shadow of
347 12568
death, I will fear no e- vil : for thou art with me ; thy rod
4 6 123578
and thy stäff comfort me.

347
5 Thou shalt prepare a table before me against them that
258 16 4
trou-ble me : thou hast anointed my head with oil, | and my
15678 23
cup shall be full.

6 But thy loving-kindness and mercy shall follow me all
37 4 16 258 4 15678
the days of my life : and I will dwell in the house of the Lord
23
for ever.

At Mattins

DAY 5 Ps. 24 *Domini est terra* vj.

37 4 16 258
THe earth is the Lord's, and all that there-in is : the com-
4 15678 23
pass of the world, and they that dwell therein.

37 4 16 258 4
2 For he hath founded it up-on the seas : and prepar-ed
15678 23
it up-on the floods.

37 4 16 258
3 Who shall ascend into the hill of the Lord : or who
4 15678 23
shall rise up in his holy place?

37 4 16 258
4 Even he that hath clean hands, and a pure heart : and
that hath not lift up his mind unto vanity, | nor sworn to
4 15678 23
de-ceive his neighbour.

37 4 16 258
5 He shall receive the bles-sing from the Lord : and righ-
4 15678 23
teousness from the God of his sal-vation.

347 12568
6 This is the generation of them that seek him : even of
4 15678 23
them that seek thy face, O Iacob.

3
7 Lift up your heads, O ye gates, | and be ye lift up, ye ev-
47 16 258 457 168 23
er-last-ing doors : and the King of glo- ry shall come in.

347 12568
8 Who is the King of glo-ry : it is the Lord strong and
457 168 23
mighty, | even the Lord migh-ty in battle.

3
9 Lift up your heads, O ye gates, | and be ye lift up, ye ev-
47 16 258 457 168 23
er-last-ing doors : and the King of glo- ry shall come in.

347 12568
10 Who is the King of glo- ry : even the Lord of hosts, | he
4 15678 23
is the King of glory.

Ps. 25 *Ad te, Domine, levavi* ij. 1

UNto thee, O Lord, will I lift up my soul; my God, I
37 4 16 258
have put my trust in thee : O let me not be confound-
4 15678 23
ed, | neither let mine ene-mies tri- umph over me.

347 12568
2 For all they that hope in thee shall not be a-sham-ed : but
457 168 23
such as transgress without a cause shall be put to con-fusion.

3 47 16 258 4 15678 23
3 Shew me thy ways, O Lord : and teach me thy paths.

347 12568
4 Lead me forth in thy truth, and learn me : for thou art
4 15678
the God of my salvation; in thee hath been my hope all
23
the day long.

347 12568
5 Call to remembrance, O Lord, thy ten-der mer-cies : and
4 68 157 23
thy loving-kindnesses, which have been ev- er of old.

37 4 16 258
6 O remember not the sins and of-fen-ces of my youth :
.4 15678
but according to thy mercy think thou upon me, O Lord, for
23
thy goodness.

37 4 16 258
7 Gracious and righ-teous is the Lord : therefore will he
.4 15678 23
teach sin-ners in the way.

347 12568
8 Them that are meek shall he guide in judge-ment : and
4 15678 23
such as are gentle, them shall he learn his way.

37 4 16 258
9 All the paths of the Lord are mer-cy and truth : unto
4 15678 23
such as keep his covenant, and his tes- ti-monies.

37 4 16 258 4
10 For thy Name's sake, O Lord : be merciful unto my
15678 23
sin, for it is great.

37 4 16 258
11 What man is he, that fear-eth the Lord : him shall he
4 15678 23
teach in the way that he shall choose.

37 4 16 258 4 68 157 23
12 His soul shall dwell at ease : and his seed shall in-he-rit
the land.

347 12568
13 The secret of the Lord is among them that fear him :
457 168 23
and he will shew them his covenant.

37 4 16 258
14 Mine eyes are ever looking un-to the Lord : for he shall
4 .6 123578
pluck my feet oüt of the net.

37 4 12568
15 Turn thee unto me, and have mer-cy up- on me : for I
4 15678 23
am deso-late, and in misery.

347 12568
16 The sorrows of my heart are en-lar-ged : O bring thou
457 168 23
me out of my troubles.

347 258 16 4 15678
17 Look upon my adversi-ty and mi-se-ry : and for-give
23
me all my sin.

37 4 16 258
18 Consider mine enemies, how ma-ny they are : and they
4 15678 23
bear a tyran-nous hate a-gainst me.

347 258 16
19 O keep my soul, and de-liv-er me : let me not be con-
4 15678 23
founded, | for I have put my trust in thee.

347 12568
20 Let perfectness and righteous dealing wait up-on me :
4 15678 23
for my hope hath been in thee.

37 4 16 258 4 15678 23
21 Deliver Is-ra-el, O God : out of all his troubles.

Ps. 26 *Judica me, Domine* i. 4

347 12568
BE thou my Judge, O Lord, | for I have walked in-no-cent-
4
ly : my trust hath been also in the Lord, | there-fore
15678 23
shall I not fall.

347 12568 4 15678
2 Examine me, O Lord, and prove me : try out my reins
23
and my heart.

3 47 16 358
3 For thy loving-kindness is ev-er be-fore mine eyes : and
4 15678 23
I will walk in thy truth.

34 7 12568
4 I have not dwelt with vain per-sons : neither will I have
457 168 23
fellowship with the de-ceitful.

347 12568
5 I have hated the congregation of the wick-ed : and will
457 168 23
not sit a-mong the un-godly.

37 4 16 258
6 I will wash my hands in inno-cen-cy, O Lord : and so
457 168 23
will I go to thine altar.

347 12568
7 That I may shew the voice of thanks- giv- ing : and tell
4 15678 23
of all thy wondrous works.

37 4 16 258
8 Lord, I have loved the habi-ta-tion of thy house : and the
4 15678 23
place where thine ho- nour dwelleth.

347 12568
9 O shut not up my soul with the sin- ners : nor my life
4 6 123578
with the blöod-thirsty.

347 258 16 4 15678
10 In whose hands is wick-ed-ness : and their right hand
23
is full of gifts.

347 12568
11 But as for me, I will walk in-no-cent-ly : O deliver me,
457 168 23
and be mer-ci- ful unto me.

3 47 16 258 4
12 My foot stand-eth right : I will praise the Lord in the
15678 23
con-gre-gations.

At Evensong

DAY 5 PS. 27 *Dominus illuminatio* i. II *or* vj.

37 4
THe Lord is my light and my salvation; whom then shall
16 258
I fear : the Lord is the strength of my life ; of whom
4 15678 23
then shall I be afraid ?

2 When the wicked, even mine enemies & my foes, | came

37 4 16 258 4 15678 23
upon me to eat up my flesh : they stum-bled and fell.

3 Though an host of men were laid against me, | yet shall
37 4 16 258
not my heart be a-fraid : and though there rose up war against
4 15678 23
me, | yet will I put my trust in him.
37 4 16
4 One thing have I desired of the Lord, which I will re-
258
quire : even that I may dwell in the house of the Lord all the
days of my life, | to behold the fair beauty of the Lord, and to
457 168 23
vi- sit his temple.
347
5 For in the time of trouble he shall hide me in his ta-ber-
12568
na-cle : yea, in the secret place of his dwelling shall he hide
4 15678 23
me, | and set me up up- on a rock of stone.
37 4 16 258 4
6 And now shall he lift up mine head : above mine ene-mies
15678 23
round a-bout me.
34 7
7 Therefore will I offer in his dwelling an oblation with great
12568 457 168 23
glad-ness : I will sing, and speak prai-ses un-to the Lord.
37 4 16 258
8 Hearken unto my voice, O Lord, when I cry un-to thee :
457 168 23
have mercy up-on me, and hear me.
37 4 16 258 4
9 My heart hath talked of thee, Seek ye my face : Thy face,
15678 23
Lord, will I seek.
37 4 16 258
10 O hide not thou thy face from me : nor cast thy ser-
4 15678 23
vant a-way in dis-pleasure.
347 12568
11 Thou hast been my suc-cour : leave me not, neither for-
4 15678 23
sake me, | O God of my sal-vation.

37 4 12568 ·4
12 When my father & my mo-ther for-sake me : the Lord
15678 23
ta- keth me up.

3 47 16 258
13 Teach me thy way, O Lord : and lead me in the right
457 168 23
way, be-cause of mine enemies.

347 12568
14 Deliver me not over into the will of mine ad-ver-sa-ries :
4 15678 23
for there are false witnesses risen up against me, and such as
speak wrong.

347 12568
15 I should utter-ly have faint-ed : but that I believe verily
457 168 23
to see the goodness of the Lord in the land of the living.

4 37 12568
16 O tarry thou the Lord's lei-sure : be strong, and he shall
4 6 123578
comfort thine heart, | and put thou thy trüst in the Lord.

Ps. 28 *Ad te, Domine* iij. I

3 47 16 258
UNto thee will I cry, O Lord, my strength : think no
scorn of me, | lest if thou make as though thou hearest
4 15678 23
not, I become like them that go down in-to the pit.

37 4 16
2 Hear the voice of my humble petitions, when I cry un-to
258 4
thee : when I hold up my hands towards the mercy-seat of thy
15678 23
ho- ly temple.

3 O pluck me not away, | neither destroy me with the un-
347 12568
godly and wick-ed do-ers : which speak friendly to their
4 15678 23
neighbours, | but ima-gine mis- chief in their hearts.

37 4 16 258
4 Reward them ac-cor-ding to their deeds : and according
4 15678 23
to the wickedness of their own in-ventions.

37 4 16 258
5 Recompense them after the work of their hands : pay
4 15678 23
them that they have de-served.

6 For they regard not in their minds the works of the
37 4 16 258
Lord, | nor the ope-ra-tion of his hands : therefore shall he
·4 15678 23
break them down, and not build them up.

37 4 16 258
7 Prai-sed be the Lord : for he hath heard the voice of my
457 168 23
hum-ble pe-titions.

8 The Lord is my strength and my shield ; my heart hath
347 12568
trusted in him, and I am help-ed : therefore my heart danceth
4 15678 23
for joy, | and in my song will I praise him.

37 4 16 258
9 The Lord is my strength : and he is the wholesome de-
4 15678 23
fence of his An-ointed.

347
10 O save thy people, and give thy blessing unto thine in-
258 16 4 15678 23
he-ri-tance : feed them, and set them up for ever.

Ps. 29 *Afferte Domino* v. 2

37
BRing unto the Lord, O ye mighty, | bring young rams
4 16 258 ·4 15678 23
un-to the Lord : ascribe unto the Lord wor-ship and
strength.

37 4 16 258
2 Give the Lord the honour due un-to his Name : worship
4 15678 23
the Lord with ho- ly worship.

37 4 12568
3 It is the Lord that com-mand-eth the wa-ters : it is the
457 168 23
glorious God that ma-keth the thunder.

4 It is the Lord that ruleth the sea; the voice of the Lord
347 12568 4 68 157
is mighty in o-pe-ra-tion : the voice of the Lord is a glo-
23
ri-ous voice.

37 4 258 16
5 The voice of the Lord break-eth the ce-dar-trees : yea,
457 168 23
the Lord breaketh the ce-dars of Libanus.

37 4 16 258
6 He maketh them also to skip like a calf : Libanus also,
4 6 123578
and Sirion, like a yoüng unicorn.

7 The voice of the Lord divideth the flames of fire; the voice
37 4 258 16
of the Lord sha-keth the wil-der-ness : yea, the Lord shaketh
4 15678 23
the wil-der-ness of Cades.

8 The voice of the Lord maketh the hinds to bring forth
4 37 12568
young, | and discovereth the thick bush-es : in his temple doth
457 168 23
every man speak of his honour.

347 258 16
9 The Lord sitteth a-bove the wa-ter-flood : and the Lord
4 15678 23
remaineth a King for ever.

347 12568
10 The Lord shall give strength un-to his peo-ple : the
4 15678 23
Lord shall give his people the bles-sing of peace.

At Mattins

DAY 6 Ps. 30 *Exaltabo te, Domine* i. 1

3 47 16 258
I Will magnify thee, O Lord, for thou hast set me up : and
4 15678 23
not made my foes to tri-umph over me.

37 4 16 258 4 15678 23
2 O Lord my God, I cri-ed un-to thee : and thou hast
healed me.

37 4 16 258
3 Thou, Lord, hast brought my soul out of hell : thou hast
4 6 123578
kept my life from them that go döwn to the pit.
37 4 16 258
4 Sing praises unto the Lord, O ye saints of his : and give
4 15678 23
thanks unto him for a remem-brance of his holiness.

5 For his wrath endureth but the twinkling of an eye, |
37 4 16 258
and in his plea-sure is life : heaviness may endure for a night, |
4 15678 23
but joy com-eth in the morning.
347 12568
6 And in my prosperity I said, | I shall never be re-mov-ed :
4 15678 23
thou, Lord, of thy goodness hast made my hill so strong.
37 4 16 258 4 15678 23
7 Thou didst turn thy face from me : and I was troubled.
37 4 16 258 4
8 Then cried I un-to thee, O Lord : and gat me to my
15678 23
Lord right humbly.
37 4 16 258 4 6 123578
9 What profit is there in my blood : when I go döwn to
the pit?
37 4 16 258 457 168
10 Shall the dust give thanks un-to thee : or shall it de-
clare thy truth?
37 4 12568 4
11 Hear, O Lord, and have mer-cy up-on me : Lord, be
15678 23
thou my helper.
37 4 16 258
12 Thou hast turned my hea-viness in-to joy : thou hast put
4 15678 23
off my sackcloth, | and gird-ed me with gladness.
37 4
13 Therefore shall every good man sing of thy praise with-
12568 4 15678 23
out cea-sing : O my God, I will give thanks un-to thee for
ever.

Ps. 31 *In te, Domine, speravi* ij. 1

37
IN thee, O Lord, have I put my trust, | let me never be put
4 12568 4 15678 23
to con- fu- sion : deliver me in thy righteousness.
37 4 16 258 ·4 15678 23
2 Bow down thine ear to me : make haste to de-liver me.
37 4 16 268
3 And be thou my strong rock, and house of de-fence :
4 15678 23
that thou may-est save me.
347 12568
4 For thou art my strong rock, and my cas-tle : be thou
4 15678 23
also my guide, | and lead me for thy Name's sake.
37 4 12568
5 Draw me out of the net that they have laid pri-vi-ly for
4 15678 23
me : for thou art my strength.
347 12568
6 Into thy hands I com-mend my spi-rit : for thou hast re-
4 15678 23
deemed me, O Lord, thou God of truth.
347 258 16
7 I have hated them that hold of super-sti-tious va- ni-ties :
4 6 123578
and my trust hath bëen in the Lord.
347 12568
8 I will be glad, & rejoice in thy mer-cy : for thou hast con-
457 168 23
sidered my trouble, | & hast known my soul in ad-versities.
37 4 258 16
9 Thou hast not shut me up into the hand of the en- e-my :
457 168 23
but hast set my feet in a large room.
347 12568
10 Have mercy upon me, O Lord, for I am in trou-ble :
·4 15678
& mine eye is consumed for very heaviness, | yea, my soul and
23
my body.
347 258 16 4 15678
11 For my life is waxen old with hea-vi-ness : & my years
23
with mourning.

347 258 16
12 My strength faileth me, because of mine in-i-qui-ty :
·4 15678 23
and my bones are con-sumed.

13 I became a reproof among all mine enemies, | but es-
347 12568
pecially a-mong my neigh-bours : & they of mine acquaintance
4
were afraid of me; & they that did see me without | con-vey'd
6 123578
them-sëlves from me.

3 47 16 258
14 I am clean forgotten, as a dead man out of mind : I am
4 15678 23
become like a bro-ken vessel.

347 258 16
15 For I have heard the blasphemy of the mul-ti-tude : and
fear is on every side, | while they conspire together against me,
4 15678 23
and take their counsel to take a-way my life.
3 47 16 258 ·4
16 But my hope hath been in thee, O Lord : I have said,
15678 23
Thou art my God.

37 4
17 My time is in thy hand; deliver me from the hand of
258 16 4 15678 23
mine en- e-mies : and from them that per- se-cute me.
37 4 258 16
18 Shew thy servant the light of thy coun-te-nance : and
4 15678 23
save me for thy mercies' sake.

37 4
19 Let me not be confounded, O Lord, | for I have call-ed
12568
up-on thee : let the ungodly be put to confusion, | and be put
4 15678 23
to si- lence in the grave.
347 12568
20 Let the lying lips be put to si- lence : which cruelly,
4 15678 23
disdainfully, and despitefully, speak a-gainst the righteous.

21 O how plentiful is thy goodness, | which thou hast laid up

347 12568
for them that fear thee : and that thou hast prepared for them
4 15678 23
that put their trust in thee, | even be- fore the sons of men !

22 Thou shalt hide them privily by thine own presence
37 4 12568
from the pro-vo-king of all men : thou shalt keep them se-
4 15678 23
cretly in thy taberna-cle from the strife of tongues.

37 4 16 258
23 Thanks be to the Lord : for he hath shewed me mar-
4 6 123578
vellous great kindness in a ströng city.

347 16 258 4
24 And when I made haste, I said : I am cast out of the
15678 23
sight of thine eyes.

37 4 16 258
25 Nevertheless, thou heardest the voice of my prayer :
4 15678 23
when I cri- ed unto thee.

37 4 16 258
26 O love the Lord, all ye his saints : for the Lord pre-
4 6
serveth them that are faithful, | and plenteously reward-eth the
123578
pröud doer.

37 4 16 258
27 Be strong, and he shall es-tab-lish your heart : all ye
4 6 123578
that put your trüst in the Lord.

At Evensong

DAY 6 Ps. 32 *Beati quorum* iv. 4 *or* vj.

347 12568
BLessed is he whose unrighteousness is for-giv-en : and
4 15678 23
whose sin is covered.

37 4 16
2 Blessed is the man unto whom the Lord im-pu-teth no
258 4 15678 23
sin : and in whose spi-rit there is no guile.

37 4 16 258
3 For while I held my tongue : my bones consumed away
457 168 23
through my dai- ly com-plaining.

3 47 16 258
4 For thy hand is heavy up-on me day and night : and my
4 15678 23
moisture is like the drought in summer.

37 4 16 258
5 I will acknowledge my sin un-to thee : and mine unrigh-
4 15678 23
teous-ness have I not hid.

37 4 16 258
6 I said, I will confess my sins un-to the Lord : & so thou
457 168 23
forgavest the wick-ed-ness of my sin.

7 For this shall everyone that is godly make his prayer unto
37 4 16 258
thee, | in a time when thou may-est be found : but in the
4 15678 23
great water-floods they shall not come nigh him.

37 4
8 Thou art a place to hide me in, | thou shalt pre-serve me
12568 457 168 23
from trou-ble : thou shalt compass me about with songs of de-
liverance.

37
9 I will inform thee, and teach thee in the way where-in
4 16 258 4 15678 23
thou shalt go : and I will guide thee with mine eye.

347
10 Be ye not like to horse and mule, which have no un-der-
12568
stand-ing : whose mouths must be held with bit and bridle,
4 15678 23
lest they fall up-on thee.

37 4 12568
11 Great plagues remain for the un-god-ly : but whoso put-
4 15678 23
teth his trust in the Lord, | mercy embra-ceth him on every side.

37 4 16 258
12 Be glad, O ye righteous, and re-joice in the Lord : and
457 168 23
be joyful, all ye that are true of heart.

Ps. 33 *Exultate iusti* iij. 5

347 12568
REjoice in the Lord, O ye righ-teous : for it becometh well
4 15678 23
the just to be thankful.

3 47 16 258
2 Praise the Lord with harp : sing praises unto him with
4 15678 23
the lute, | and in-stru-ment of ten strings.

37 4 16 258
3 Sing unto the Lord a new song : sing praises lustily unto
4 6 123578
him with a göod courage.

3 47 16 258 4 15678 23
4 For the word of the Lord is true : and all his works are
faithful.

347 12568
5 He loveth righteous-ness and judge-ment : the earth is
4 15678 23
full of the good-ness of the Lord.

3 47 16 258
6 By the word of the Lord were the hea-vens made : and
4 15678 23
all the hosts of them by the breath of his mouth.

37
7 He gathereth the waters of the sea together, as it were up-
4 16 258 4 15678 23
on an heap : and layeth up the deep, as in a treasure-house.

347 16 258
8 Let all the earth fear the Lord : stand in awe of him, all
4 6 123578
ye that dwëll in the world.

37 4 16 258 4 15678 23
9 For he spake, and it was done : he command-ed, and it
stood fast.

37 4 16
10 The Lord bringeth the counsel of the hea-then to
258
naught : and maketh the devices of the people to be of none
457 168 23
effect, | and casteth out the coun-sels of princes.

347 12568
11 The counsel of the Lord shall en-dure for ev- er : and
4 15678 23
the thoughts of his heart from generation to ge- ne-ration.
347 12568
12 Blessed are the people whose God is the Lord Ie- ho- va :
4
and blessed are the folk, | that he hath chosen to him to be
15678 23
his in-heritance.

13 The Lord looked down from heaven, | and beheld all
37 4 16 258
the chil-dren of men : from the habitation of his dwelling |
4 6 123578
he considereth all them that dwëll on the earth.
37 4 16 258 4 15678
14 He fashioneth all the hearts of them : and un-der-stand-
23
eth all their works.
37 4
15 There is no king that can be saved by the mul-titude of
16 258 4 15678 23
an host : neither is any mighty man deli-ver- ed by much
strength.
3 47 16 258
16 A horse is counted but a vain thing to save a man :
4 15678 23
neither shall he deliver any man by his great strength.
347 12568
17 Behold, the eye of the Lord is upon them that fear him :
4 15678 23
and upon them that put their trust in his mercy.
3 47 16 258 4
18 To de-li-ver their soul from death : and to feed them
15678 23
in the time of dearth.
37 4 16 258
19 Our soul hath patiently tar-ried for the Lord : for he is
4 15678 23
our help and our shield.
3 47 16 258
20 For our heart shall re-joice in him : because we have
4 15678 23
ho-ped in his holy Name.

347 12568
21 Let thy merciful kindness, O Lord, be up-on us : like
4 15678 23
as we do put our trust in thee.

Ps. 34 *Benedicam Domino* v. 2 *or* viij. 1

37 4 16 258
I Will alway give thanks un-to the Lord : his praise shall
4 15678 23
ev-er be in my mouth.

37 4 16 258
2 My soul shall make her boast in the Lord : the humble
4 15678 23
shall hear there- of, and be glad.

37 4 16 258 4 15678
3 O praise the Lord with me : & let us magnify his Name
23
to-gether.

347 12568
4 I sought the Lord, and he heard me : yea, he delivered
4 15678 23
me out of all my fear.

347 258 16
5 They had an eye unto him, and were ligh-ten-ed : and
4 15678 23
their faces were not a-shamed.

4 23578 16
6 Lo, the poor crieth, and the Lord hear-eth him : yea, and
4 15678 23
saveth him out of all his troubles.

347 12568
7 The angel of the Lord tarrieth round about them that fear
4 15678 23
him : and de- li- ver-eth them.

37 4 12568
8 O taste and see, how gra-cious the Lord is : blessed is
4 15678 23
the man that trust-eth in him.

37 4 16 258
9 O fear the Lord, ye that are his saints : for they that
4 15678 23
fear him lack nothing.

347 12568
10 The lions do lack, and suf-fer hun-ger : but they who

4 6 123578
seek the Lord shall want no man-ner of thïng that is good.
37 4 16 258
11 Come, ye children, and heark-en un-to me : I will teach
4 6 123578
you the fëar of the Lord.
37 4 16 258 4 15678
12 What man is he that lust-eth to live : and would fain
23
see good days?
347 12568 4 15678 23
13 Keep thy tongue from e- vil : and thy lips, that they
speak no guile.
37 4 16 258 4 15678 23
14 Eschew e-vil, and do good : seek peace, and en-sue it.
37 4 12568
15 The eyes of the Lord are o-ver the righ-teous : and his
4 15678 23
ears are o-pen un- to their prayers.
37 4
16 The countenance of the Lord is against them that do
12568 4 15678 23
e- vil : to root out the remem-brance of them from the earth.
4 23578 16
17 The righteous cry, and the Lord hear-eth them : and
4 15678 23
delivereth them out of all their troubles.
3 47 16 258
18 The Lord is nigh unto them that are of a con-trite heart :
4 15678 23
and will save such as be of an hum-ble spirit.
347 12568
19 Great are the troubles of the righ-teous : but the Lord
4 6 123578
deli-ver-eth hïm out of all.
3 47 16 258 4 15678 23
20 He keep-eth all his bones : so that not one of them is
broken.
37 4 12568
21 But misfortune shall slay the un-god-ly : and they that
4 15678 23
hate the righ-teous shall be desolate.

37 4 12568
22 The Lord delivereth the souls of his ser-vants : and all
4 15678 23
they that put their trust in him shall not be destitute.

At Mattins

DAY 7 Ps. 35 *Judica, Domine* iv. 1 *or* 5

37 4 16
PLead thou my cause, O Lord, with them that strive with
258 4 15678 23
me : and fight thou against them that fight a-gainst me.
347 12568 ·4 15678 23
2 Lay hand upon the shield and buck-ler : and stand up to
help me.

3 Bring forth the spear, | and stop the way against them
347 12568 4 15678 23
that per-se-cute me : say unto my soul, | I am thy sal-vation.

37
4 Let them be confounded, and put to shame, that seek af-
4 16 258
ter my soul : let them be turned back, and brought to confu-
4 15678 23
sion, | that ima-gine mis-chief for me.

37 4 16 258
5 Let them be as the dust be-fore the wind : and the angel
·4 15678 23
of the Lord scat-ter-ing them.

347 258 16
6 Let their way be dark and slip-pe-ry : and let the angel of
·4 15678 23
the Lord per- se-cute them.

3
7 For they have privily laid their net to de-stroy me with-
47 16 258 4 15678
out a cause : yea, even without a cause have they made a pit
23
for my soul.

8 Let a sudden destruction come upon him unawares, | and
37 4 16 258
his net, that he hath laid pri-vily, catch him-self : that he may
4 6 123578
fall in-to his öwn mischief.

37 4 16 258 4
9 And, my soul, be joy-ful in the Lord : it shall rejoice in
15678 23
his sal-vation.

10 All my bones shall say, Lord, who is like unto thee, |
37 4 16 258
who deliverest the poor from him that is too strong for him :
4 15678 23
yea, the poor, and him that is in misery, | from him that
spoileth him?

37 4 16 258
11 False witnes-ses did rise up : they laid to my charge
4 15678 23
things that I knew not.

37 4 16 258 4 15678
12 They rewarded me e-vil for good : to the great dis-com-
23
fort of my soul.

13 Nevertheless, when they were sick, I put on sack-cloth, |
347 12568
and humbled my soul with fast-ing : and my prayer shall turn
4 6 123578
in-to mine öwn bosom.

347
14 I behaved myself as though it had been my friend, or my
12568 4 15678 23
bro-ther : I went heavily, as one that mourn-eth for his mother.

15 But in mine adversity they rejoiced, | & gathered them-
347 12568
selves to-ge-ther : yea, the very abjects came together against
4 15678 23
me unawares, | making mouths at me, and ceased not.

347 12568
16 With the flatterers were bu-sy mock-ers : who gnashed
4 15678 23
up-on me with their teeth.

37 4 16 258
17 Lord, how long wilt thou look up-on this : O deliver my
soul from the calamities which they bring on me, | and my
4 15678 23
dar-ling from the lions.

347 12568
18 So will I give thee thanks in the great con-gre- ga- tion :
4 15678 23
I will praise thee a-mong much people.

347
19 O let not them that are mine enemies triumph over me
12568 457
un- god- ly : neither let them wink with their eyes that hate
168 23
me with-out a cause.

3 47 16 258
20 And-why their com-mu-ning is not for peace : but they
4 15678 23
imagine deceitful words against them that are qui- et in the
land.

3 47 16 258
21 They gaped upon me with their mouths, and said : Fie
4 15678 23
on thee, fie on thee, we saw it with our eyes.

3 47 16 258
22 This thou hast seen, O Lord : hold not thy tongue
4 15678 23
then, | go not far from me, O Lord.

347 12568
23 Awake, and stand up to judge my quar-rel : avenge thou
4 15678 23
my cause, my God, and my Lord.

347 258 16
24 Judge me, O Lord my God, according to thy righ-teous-
4 15678 23
ness : and let them not tri-umph over me.

25 Let them not say in their hearts, | There, there, so
347 12568 4 15678 23
would we have it : neither let them say, We have de-voured.

26 Let them be put to confusion and shame together that
37 4 12568
re-joice at my trou-ble : let them be clothed with rebuke and
4 15678 23
dishonour, that boast them-selves a-gainst me.

347
27 Let them be glad and rejoice, that favour my righ-teous
12568
deal-ing : yea, let them say alway, | Blessed be the Lord, who

4 15678 23
hath pleasure in the prosperi-ty of his servant.

347 258
28 And as for my tongue, it shall be talking of thy righ-
16 .4 15678 23
teous-ness : and of thy praise all the day long.

Ps. 36 *Dixit iniustus* i. 2 *or* ij. 1

37 4 12568
MY heart sheweth me the wickedness of the un-god-ly :
4 15678 23
that there is no fear of God be-fore his eyes.

37 4 16 258
2 For he flattereth himself in his own sight : until his
4 15678 23
abomina-ble sin be found out.

37 4 16 258
3 The words of his mouth are unrighteous, & full of de-ceit :
4 15678 23
he hath left off to behave himself wise-ly, and to do good.

3
4 He imagineth mischief upon his bed, | & hath set him-self
47 16 258 4 15678 23
in no good way : neither doth he abhor any thing that is evil.

37 4 12568
5 Thy mercy, O Lord, reacheth un-to the hea-vens : and
4 68 157 23
thy faith-ful-ness un-to the clouds.

3 4 7 12568
6 Thy righteousness standeth like the strong moun-tains :
4 15678 23
thy judgements are like the great deep.

7 Thou, Lord, shalt save both man and beast; how excellent
37 4 16 258
is thy mer-cy, O God : & the children of men shall put their
457 168 23
trust under the sha-dow of thy wings.

3 7 4 16
8 They shall be satisfied with the plen-teous-ness of thy
258 457
house : and thou shalt give them drink of thy pleasures, as out
168 23
of the river.

3 47 16 258 4 15678
9 For with thee is the well of life : and in thy light shall
23
we see light.

347
10 O continue forth thy loving-kindness unto them that
12568 457 168 23
know thee : and thy righteousness unto them that are true
of heart.

347 12568
11 O let not the foot of pride come a-gainst me : and let
4 15678 23
not the hand of the un-god- ly cast me down.

347 258 16
12 There are they fallen, all that work wick-ed-ness : they
4 15678 23
are cast down, | and shall not be a- ble to stand.

At Evensong

DAY 7 PS. 37 *Noli æmulari* i. 1 *or* 4

37 4 12568
FRet not thyself because of the un-god-ly : neither be thou
4 15678 23
envious against the e- vil doers.

37 4 16 258
2 For they shall soon be cut down like the grass : and be
4 15678 23
withered e-ven as the green herb.

3 47 16 258
3 Put thou thy trust in the Lord, and be do-ing good :
4 15678 23
dwell in the land, and ve-ri- ly thou shalt be fed.

37 4 16 258 4 15678 23
4 De-light thou in the Lord : and he shall give thee thy
heart's desire.

37 4 16
5 Commit thy way unto the Lord, and put thy trust in
258 4 68 157 23
him : and he shall bring it to pass.

37 4 16 258
6 He shall make thy righteousness as clear as the light : and
4 15678 23
thy just deal-ing as the noon-day.

347 12568
7 Hold thee still in the Lord, | and abide patient-ly up-on
him : but grieve not thyself at him whose way doth prosper, |
4 15678 23
against the man that doeth af-ter e- vil counsels.

347 12568
8 Leave off from wrath, and let go dis-plea-sure : fret not
4 6 123578
thyself, | else shalt thou be mov-ed to dö evil.

37 4 16 258
9 Wicked doers shall be root-ed out : & they that patiently
4 68 157 23
abide the Lord, | those shall in-he-rit the land.

37 4 16 258
10 Yet a little while, and the ungodly shall be clean gone :
4 15678 23
thou shalt look after his place, and he shall be away.

37 4 16 258
11 But the meek-spirited shall pos-sess the earth : and shall
4 15678 23
be refreshed in the mul-ti-tude of peace.

37 4 16 258
12 The ungodly seeketh coun-sel a-gainst the just : and
4 15678 23
gnasheth up- on him with his teeth.

37 4 16 258
13 The Lord shall laugh him to scorn : for he hath seen
4 15678 23
that his day is coming.

3 47
14 The ungodly have drawn out the sword, and have bent
16 258
their bow : to cast down the poor & needy, | and to slay such
.4 15678 23
as are of a right con-ver-sation.

37 4 16 258
15 Their sword shall go through their own heart : & their
.4 15678 23
bow shall be broken.

3 47 16 258
16 A small thing that the righ-teous hath : is better than
457 168 23
great riches of the un-godly.

347 12568
17 For the arms of the ungodly shall be bro-ken : and the
457 168 23
Lord up-hold-eth the righteous.

37 4 12568
18 The Lord knoweth the days of the god-ly : and their
4 15678 23
inheritance shall en-dure for ever.

37 4 16 258
19 They shall not be confounded in the pe-ri-lous time :
.4 15678 23
and in the days of dearth they shall have enough.

20 As for the ungodly they shall perish, | and the enemies
37 4 16 258
of the Lord shall consume as the fat of lambs : yea, even as
4 15678 23
the smoke shall they con-sume away.

37 4 16 258
21 The ungodly borroweth, and pay-eth not a-gain : but
4 15678 23
the righteous is mer-ci- ful and liberal.

3 47 16 258
22 Such as are blessed of God shall pos-sess the land : and
4 15678 23
they that are cursed of him shall be rooted out.

347 12568
23 The Lord ordereth a good man's go-ing : and maketh
457 168 23
his way ac-cep- ta-ble to himself.

37 4 16 258
24 Though he fall, he shall not be cast a-way : for the
457 168 23
Lord up-hold-eth him with his hand.

37 4 16 258
25 I have been young, and now am old : and yet saw I
.4 15678 23
never the righteous forsaken, | nor his seed beg-ging their bread.

347 12568 4
26 The righteous is ever merci-ful, and lend-eth : and his
15678 23
seed is blessed.

37 4 16 258 4 15678
27 Flee from evil, and do the thing that is good : and dwell
23
for evermore.

37 4 16 258
28 For the Lord loveth the thing that is right : he forsaketh
457 168 23
not his that be godly, | but they are pre-ser-ved for ever.

347 258 16
29 The unrighteous shall be pun-ish-ed : as for the seed of
4 15678 23
the ungodly, it shall be rooted out.

37 4 16 258 4
30 The righteous shall in-he-rit the land : and dwell there-
15678 23
in for ever.

37 4 12568
31 The mouth of the righteous is exer-ci-sed in wis-dom :
457 168 23
and his tongue will be talk-ing of judgement.

37 4 16 258 4 15678 23
32 The law of his God is in his heart : and his go-ings
shall not slide.

37 4 12568 457
33 The ungodly se-eth the righ-teous : and seeketh oc-ca-
168 23
sion to slay him.

37 4 16 258
34 The Lord will not leave him in his hand : nor condemn
4 15678 23
him when he is judged.

35 Hope thou in the Lord, and keep his way, | and he shall
3 47 16 258
promote thee, that thou shalt pos-sess the land : when the un-
4 15678 23
godly shall pe-rish, thou shalt see it.

34 7 12568
36 I myself have seen the ungodly in great pow-er : and
4 6 123578
flourishing like a grëen bay-tree.

37 4 16 258
37 I went by, and lo, he was gone : I sought him, but his
4 15678 23
place could no-where be found.

37 4 16
38 Keep innocency, | and take heed unto the thing that is
258 4 6 123578
right : for that shall bring a man peäce at the last.

37 4 12568
39 As for the transgressors, they shall pe-rish to-ge-ther :
4 6 123578
and the end of the ungodly is, they shall be root-ed oüt at the
last.

37 4 16 258
40 But the salvation of the righteous com-eth of the Lord :
4 15678 23
who is also their strength in the time of trouble.

37 4 12568
41 And the Lord shall stand by them, and save them : he
shall deliver them from the ungodly, and shall save them, |
4 15678 23
because they put their trust in him.

At Mattins

DAY 8 Ps. 38 *Domine, ne in furore* i. 8

347 12568
PUt me not to rebuke, O Lord, in thine an-ger : neither
457 168 23
chasten me in thy hea-vy dis-pleasure.

347 16 258 ·4 15678
2 For thine arrows stick fast in me : and thy hand pres-
23
seth me sore.

347 12568
3 There is no health in my flesh, because of thy dis-plea-
457 168 23
sure : neither is there any rest in my bones, by rea-son of
my sin.

37 4 16 258
4 For my wickednesses are gone o-ver my head : and are
457 168 23
like a sore burden, too hea-vy for me to bear.

37 4 16 258 4 15678 23
5 My wounds stink, and are cor-rupt : — through my
foolishness.

37 4 258 16
6 I am brought into so great trou-ble and mi- se-ry : that I
4 15678 23
go mourn-ing all the day long.

347 16 258
7 For my loins are filled with a sore dis-ease : and there is
4 15678 23
no whole part in my body.

4 37 12568
8 I am feeble, and sore smit-ten : I have roared for the very
457 168 23
dis-qui- et-ness of my heart.

37 4 16 258 4
9 Lord, thou knowest all my de-sire : and my groan-ing
15678 23
is not hid from thee.

347 258 16
10 My heart panteth, | my strength hath fail-ed me : and
4 15678 23
the light of mine eyes is gone from me.

347
11 My lovers and my neighbours did stand looking up-on my
12568 4 15678 23
trou-ble : and my kins-men stood a-far off.

347 16 258
12 They also that sought after my life laid snares for me :
and they that went about to do me evil talked of wickedness, |
.4 15678 23
and imagined de-ceit all the day long.

347 12568
13 As for me, I was like a deaf man, and heard not : and
4 15678 23
as one that is dumb, who doth not o- pen his mouth.

37 4 16 258 4
14 I became even as a man that hear-eth not : and in whose
15678 23
mouth are no reproofs.

3 47 16 258
15 For in thee, O Lord, have I put my trust : thou shalt
4 15678 23
answer for me, O Lord my God.

16 I have required that they, even mine enemies, | should not

347 258 16
tri-umph o-ver me : for when my foot slipt, | they rejoiced
457 168 23
great-ly a-gainst me.

37 4 16 258
17 And I, truly, am set in the plague : and my heaviness
457 168 23
is ev- er in my sight.

347 258 16 457 168
18 For I will con-fess my wick-ed-ness : and be sor-ry
23
for my sin.

347 12568
19 But mine enemies live, and are migh-ty : and they that
457 168 23
hate me wrongfully are ma-ny in number.

347 12568
20 They also that reward evil for good are a-gainst me :
4 15678 23
because I follow the thing that good is.

3 47 16 258 4 15678 23
21 Forsake me not, O Lord my God : be not thou far
from me.

347 12568 4 15678 23
22 Haste thee to help me : O Lord God of my sal-vation.

Ps. 39 *Dixi, custodiam* ij. i

37 4 16 258 4 15678 23
I Said, I will take heed to my ways : that I of-fend not in
my tongue.

347 12568
2 I will keep my mouth, as it were with a bri-dle : while
457 168 23
the un-god-ly is in my sight.

34 7 12568
3 I held my tongue, and spake no-thing : I kept silence,
4 15678 23
yea, even from good words, | but it was pain and grief to me.

4 My heart was hot within me, | and while I was thus mu-
4 37 12568 4 15678 23
sing, the fire kind-led : & at the last I spake with my tongue.

37 4 16
5 Lord, let me know mine end, | and the num-ber of my
258 4 15678 23
days : that I may be certified how long I have to live.
37 4 16 258
6 Behold, thou hast made my days as it were a span long :
and mine age is even as nothing in respect of thee ; and verily
4 15678 23
every man living is al-to- ge- ther vanity.
3
7 For man walketh in a vain shadow, | and disquiet-eth
47 16 258 4 15678
him-self in vain : he heapeth up riches, | and cannot tell who
23
shall gather them.
37 4 16 258 4
8 And now, Lord, what is my hope : truly my hope is
15678 23
e- ven in thee.
347 12568
9 Deliver me from all mine of-fen-ces : and make me not
4 15678 23
a rebuke un- to the foolish.
3 47 16 258 4 6
10 I became dumb, and o-pened not my mouth : for it was
123578
thy doing.
37 4 16 258
11 Take thy plague a-way from me : I am even consumed
457 168 23
by the means of thy heavy hand.

12 When thou with rebukes dost chasten man for sin, | thou
makest his beauty to consume away, | like as it were a moth
37 4 12568 4 15678 23
fret-ting a gar-ment : every man there-fore is but vanity.
37
13 Hear my prayer, O Lord, | and with thine ears con-si-
4 12568 4 15678 23
der my call-ing : hold not thy peace at my tears.
347 258 16 4
14 For I am a stranger with thee, and a so-jour-ner : as
15678 23
all my fathers were.

37 4 16 258
15 O spare me a little, that I may re-co-ver my strength :
4 15678 23
before I go hence, and be no more seen.

Ps. 40 *Expectans expectavi* vj.

3 47 16 258
I Waited pa-tiently for the Lord : and he inclined unto me,
4 15678 23
and heard my calling.

347
2 He brought me also out of the horrible pit, | out of the mire
16 258 4 15678 23
& clay : & set my feet upon the rock, | & or-der- ed my goings.
37 4 16 258
3 And he hath put a new song in my mouth : even a
4 15678 23
thanksgiv-ing un- to our God.
37 4 16 258 4 6 123578
4 Many shall see it, and fear : and shall put their trüst in
the Lord.

37 4 16 258
5 Blessed is the man that hath set his hope in the Lord : &
4 15678 23
turned not unto the proud, | & to such as go a-bout with lies.

6 O Lord my God, | great are the wondrous works which
347 12568
thou hast done, | like as be also thy thoughts which are to us-
4 6 123578
ward : & yet there is no man that or-der-eth thëm unto thee.
37 4 16 258
7 If I should de-clare them, and speak of them : they should
4 15678 23
be more than I am a- ble to express.
3 47 16 258
8 Sacrifice and meat-offer-ing thou would-est not : but mine
.4 15678 23
ears hast thou opened.
347 12568
9 Burnt-offerings, and sacrifice for sin, hast thou not re-quir-
4 15678 23
ed : then said I, Lo, I come.

10 In the volume of the book it is written of me, | that I
37 4 16 258
should fulfil thy will, O my God : I am content to do it; yea,
4 15678 23
thy law is with-in my heart.

347
11 I have declared thy righteousness in the great con-gre-
12568 4 15678 23
ga- tion : lo, I will not refrain my lips, O Lord, & that thou
knowest.

3 47 16 258
12 I have not hid thy righteous-ness with-in my heart : my
4 15678 23
talk hath been of thy truth, | and of thy sal-vation.

37 4 16 258
13 I have not kept back thy loving mer-cy and truth : from
.4 15678 23
the great con-gre-gation.

37 4 16 258
14 Withdraw not thou thy mercy from me, O Lord : let
4 15678 23
thy loving-kindness and thy truth al- way pre-serve me.

15 For innumerable troubles are come about me ; | my sins
37 4 16 258
have taken such hold upon me that I am not a-ble to look up :
yea, they are more in number than the hairs of my head, | and
4 15678 23
my heart hath failed me.

347 258 16
16 O Lord, let it be thy pleasure to de-li- ver me : make
4 15678 23
haste, O Lord, to help me.

17 Let them be ashamed, and confounded together, | that
347 12568
seek after my soul to de-stroy it : let them be driven back-
4 15678 23
ward, and put to rebuke, that wish me evil.

37 4 16 258
18 Let them be desolate, and re-ward-ed with shame : that
4 15678 23
say unto me, Fie upon thee, fie up-on thee.

3 47 16 258
19 Let all those that seek thee be joy-ful and glad in thee :
4 15678 23
and let such as love thy salvation say alway, | The Lord be
praised.

347 12568 ·4 15678 23
20 As for me, I am poor and nee-dy : but the Lord car- eth
for me.

347 12568
21 Thou art my helper and my re-deem-er : make no long
457 168 23
tar- ry-ing, O my God.

At Evensong

DAY 8 Ps. 41 *Beatus qui intelligit* iij. 4 *or* iv. 4

347 12568
BLessed is he that considereth the poor and nee-dy : the
4 15678 23
Lord shall deliver him in the time of trouble.

2 The Lord preserve him and keep him alive, | that he may
37 4 16 258
be bles-sed up-on earth : and deliver not thou him into the
457 168 23
will of his enemies.

37 4 16 258
3 The Lord comfort him, when he lieth sick up-on his bed :
4 15678 23
make thou all his bed in his sickness.

37 4 16 258
4 I said, Lord, be mer-ciful un-to me : heal my soul, for I
457 168 23
have sin-ned a-gainst thee.

347 12568 4
5 Mine enemies speak e-vil of me : When shall he die, and
6 123578
his näme perish ?

347 258 16
6 And if he come to see me, he speak-eth va- ni-ty : and his
heart conceiveth falsehood within himself, | and when he com-
4 15678 23
eth forth he telleth it.

37 4 12568
7 All mine enemies whisper to-ge-ther a-gainst me : even
457 168 23
against me do they i-ma-gine this evil.
347 12568
8 Let the sentence of guiltiness pro-ceed a-gainst him : and
4 15678 23
now that he lieth, let him rise up no more.
347 12568
9 Yea, even mine own familiar friend, whom I trust-ed :
4 15678 23
who did also eat of my bread, hath laid great wait for me.
3 47 16 258
10 But be thou merciful un-to me, O Lord : raise thou me
4 15678 23
up again, and I shall re-ward them.
37 4 16 258
11 By this I know thou fa-vour-est me : that mine enemy
457 168 23
doth not tri-umph a-gainst me.
347 258 16
12 And when I am in my health, thou up-hold-est me : &
4 15678 23
shalt set me before thy face for ever.
347 258 16 4 15678
13 Blessed be the Lord God of Is- ra-el : world with- out
23
end. Amen.

Ps. 42 *Quemadmodum* i. 1 *or* 4

37 4 258 16
LIke as the hart de-sir-eth the wa-ter-brooks : so longeth
.4 15678 23
my soul af- ter thee, O God.
37 4 16 258
2 My soul is athirst for God, | yea, even for the liv-ing God :
4 15678 23
when shall I come to appear before the pre-sence of God ?
347 16 258
3 My tears have been my meat, day and night : while they
4 15678 23
daily say unto me, Where is now thy God ?

37 4
4 Now when I think thereupon, I pour out my heart by
16 258
my-self : for I went with the multitude, | and brought them
4 15678 23
forth in- to the house of God.

347 12568 457
5 In the voice of praise and thanks-giv-ing : among such
168 23
as keep holy-day.

37 4 16 258
6 Why art thou so full of hea-viness, O my soul : and why
4 15678 23
art thou disqui-et- ed with-in me ?

37 4 16 258
7 Put thy trust in God : for I will yet give him thanks for
457 168 23
the help of his countenance.

37 4 12568
8 My God, my soul is vex-ed with- in me : therefore will I
4
remember thee concerning the land of Iordan, | and the lit-tle
15678 23
hill of Hermon.

37 4 258
9 One deep calleth another, | because of the noise of the wa-
16 4 15678 23
ter-pipes : all thy waves and storms are gone over me.

347 12568
10 The Lord hath granted his loving-kindness on the day-
time : and in the night-season did I sing of him, | and made
4 15678 23
my prayer unto the God of my life.

347
11 I will say unto the God of my strength, | Why hast thou
258 16 4 15678
for-got-ten me : why go I thus heavily, while the en-e- my
23
op-presseth me ?

37 4 16 258
12 My bones are smitten a-sun-der as with a sword : while
4 15678 23
mine enemies that trouble me cast me in the teeth.

37 4 16 258 4 15678 23
13 Namely, while they say dai-ly un-to me : —Where is
now thy God?
37 4 16 258
14 Why art thou so vex-ed, O my soul : and why art thou
4 15678 23
so disqui-et- ed with-in me?
37 4 16 258
15 O put thy trust in God : for I will yet thank him, |
457 168 23
which is the help of my coun-te-nance, and my God.

Ps. 43 *Judica me, Deus* i. 1 *or* 4

GIve sentence with me, O God, | & defend my cause against
347 12568 457
the un-god-ly peo-ple : O deliver me from the de-ceit-
168 23
ful and wicked man.
347
2 For thou art the God of my strength, | why hast thou put
12568 4 15678
me from thee : and why go I so heavily, | while the en-e- my
23
op-presseth me?
347 12568
3 O send out thy light and thy truth, that they may lead
4 15678 23
me : and bring me unto thy holy hill, and to thy dwelling.
4 And that I may go unto the altar of God, | even unto the
347 12568
God of my joy and glad-ness : and upon the harp will I give
4 15678 23
thanks un-to thee, O God, my God.
37 4 16 258
5 Why art thou so hea-vy, O my soul : and why art thou
4 15678 23
so disqui-et- ed with-in me?
37 4 16 258
6 O put thy trust in God : for I will yet give him thanks, |
457 168 23
which is the help of my coun-te-nance, and my God.

At Mattins

Day 9 Ps. 44 *Deus, auribus* ij. 1 *or* vij. 1

37 4
WE have heard with our ears, O God, | our fa-thers have
12568 4 15678 23
told us : what thou hast done in their time of old.

2 How thou hast driven out the heathen with thy hand, and
37 4 16 258 457 168 23
plant-ed them in : how thou hast destroyed the na-tions, and
cast them out.

37 4 16
3 For they gat not the land in possession through their own
258 ·4 15678 23
sword : neither was it their own arm that helped them.

37 4
4 But thy right hand, and thine arm, and the light of thy
258 16 4 15678 23
coun-te-nance : because thou hadst a fa- vour unto them.

3 47 16 258 4 15678 23
5 Thou art my King, O God : send help un- to Iacob.

347 258 16
6 Through thee will we over-throw our en-e-mies : and in
·4 15678 23
thy Name will we tread them under, that rise up a-gainst us.

37 4 16 258 ·4 15678
7 For I will not trust in my bow : it is not my sword that
23
shall help me.

347 258 16
8 But it is thou that savest us from our en-e-mies : & put-
457 168 23
test them to con-fu-sion that hate us.

347 16 258
9 We make our boast of God all day long : and will praise
4 15678 23
thy Name for ever.

347 12568
10 But now thou art far off, and puttest us to con-fu-sion :
·4 15678 23
and goest not forth with our armies.

347 258 16
11 Thou makest us to turn our backs up-on our en-e-mies :
4 15678 23
so that they which hate us spoil our goods.
3 47 16 258
12 Thou lettest us be eat-en up like sheep : & hast scatter-
4 15678 23
ed us a-mong the heathen.
37 4 16 258 4
13 Thou sellest thy peo-ple for naught : and takest no
15678 23
mo-ney for them.
347 12568
14 Thou makest us to be rebuked of our neigh-bours : to
4 15678
be laughed to scorn, | and had in derision of them that are round
23
a-bout us.
347 12568
15 Thou makest us to be a by-word a-mong the hea-then :
4 15678 23
and that the peo-ple shake their heads at us.
37 4 12568
16 My confusion is dai-ly be-fore me : and the shame of
4 68 157 23
my face hath co-ver-ed me.
347 12568
17 For the voice of the slanderer and blas-phe-mer : for the
4 15678 23
ene-my and a-venger.
347
18 And though all this be come upon us, | yet do we not for-
12568 4 15678 23
get thee : nor behave ourselves froward-ly in thy covenant.
3 47 16 258 4
19 Our heart is not turn-ed back : neither our steps gone
15678 23
out of thy way.
347 12568
20 No, not when thou hast smitten us into the place of dra-
4 15678 23
gons : and covered us with the sha-dow of death.
21 If we have forgotten the Name of our God, | and hol-
37 4 16 258
den up our hands to a-ny strange god : shall not God search it

4 15678 23
out? for he knoweth the ve-ry se- crets of the heart.

37 4 16 258
22 For thy sake also are we killed all the day long : and are
4 15678 23
counted as sheep ap-poin-ted to be slain.

37 4 16 258
23 Up, Lord, why sleep-est thou : awake, | and be not
4 15678 23
absent from us for ever.

37 4 16 258
24 Wherefore hi-dest thou thy face : and forgettest our
4 15678 23
mi-se- ry and trouble?

37 4 16 258
25 For our soul is brought low, | even un-to the dust : our
4 68 157 23
belly cleav-eth un-to the ground.

347 12568 4 15678 23
26 A-rise, and help us : & deliver us for thy mercies' sake.

Ps. 45 *Eructavit cor meum* i. 2 *or* viij. 1

3 4 7 12568
MY heart is inditing of a good mat-ter : I speak of the
4 15678 23
things which I have made un-to the King.

37 4 16 258 4 15678 23
2 My tongue is the pen : of a rea- dy writer.

37 4 16 258
3 Thou art fairer than the chil-dren of men : full of grace
4 15678 23
are thy lips, | because God hath bles-sed thee for ever.

347
4 Gird thee with thy sword upon thy thigh, O thou most
12568 4 15678 23
migh-ty : according to thy wor-ship and renown.

347 12568
5 Good luck have thou with thine ho-nour : ride on, because of the word of truth, of meekness, & righteousness; and
4 68 157 23
thy right hand shall teach thee ter-ri-ble things.

37
6 Thy arrows are very sharp, | & the people shall be sub-du-
4 16 258 · 4 6 123578
ed un-to thee : even in the midst a-mong the Kïng's enemies.

37 4 12568
7 Thy seat, O God, en-dur-eth for ev- er : the sceptre of
4 6 123578
thy kingdom is a rïght sceptre.

37 4 258 16
8 Thou hast loved righteousness, and ha-ted in-i-qui-ty :
wherefore God, even thy God, | hath anointed thee with the
4 15678 23
oil of gladness a-bove thy fellows.

37 4 12568
9 All thy garments smell of myrrh, a-loes, and cas-sia :
4 15678 23
out of the ivory palaces, | where-by they have made thee glad.

347 12568
10 Kings' daughters were among thy honour-a-ble wo-men :
upon thy right hand did stand the Queen in a vesture of gold, |
4 15678 23
wrought about with di- vers colours.

347 16 258
11 Hearken, O daughter, and consider, | in-cline thine ear :
4 15678 23
forget also thine own peo-ple, and thy father's house.

347 12568
12 So shall the King have pleasure in thy beau-ty : for he
4 15678 23
is thy Lord God, and wor-ship thou him.

37 4 16 258
13 And the daughter of Tyre shall be there with a gift :
like as the rich also among the people shall make their suppli-
457 168 23
ca-tion be-fore thee.

37 4 16 258
14 The King's daughter is all glo-ri-ous with-in : her
4 15678 23
clo-thing is of wrought gold.

37 4
15 She shall be brought unto the King in rai-ment of

258 16
nee-dle-work : the virgins that be her fellows shall bear her
4 15678 23
company, | and shall be brought un-to thee.

37 4 16 258
16 With joy and gladness shall they be brought : and shall
4 6 123578
enter in-to the Kïng's palace.

347 12568
17 Instead of thy fathers thou shalt have chil-dren : whom
457 168 23
thou mayest make prin-ces in all lands.

347
18 I will remember thy Name from one generation to an-
12568 ·4
o- ther : therefore shall the people give thanks unto thee,
15678 23
world with-out end.

Ps. 46 *Deus noster refugium* viij. 2

347 16 258 4 15678 23
GOd is our hope and strength : a very pre-sent help in
trouble.

347 12568
2 Therefore will we not fear, though the earth be mov-ed :
4 6 123578
and though the hills be carried in-to the mïdst of the sea.

347 16 258
3 Though the waters thereof rage and swell : and though
4 15678 23
the mountains shake at the tem-pest of the same.

37 4 16
4 The rivers of the flood thereof shall make glad the ci-ty of
258 4 6 123578
God : the holy place of the tabernacle of the möst Highest.

347
5 God is in the midst of her, | therefore shall she not be re-
12568 4 15678 23
mov-ed : God shall help her, and that right early.

37 4
6 The heathen make much ado, and the king-doms are
12568 4 15678 23
mov-ed : but God hath shewed his voice, and the earth shall
melt away.

347 12568 4 15678
7 The Lord of hosts is with us : the God of Ia-cob is
23
our refuge.

37 4 16 258
8 O come hither, and behold the works of the Lord : what
4 15678 23
destruction he hath brought up-on the earth.

37 4 16 258
9 He maketh wars to cease in all the world : he breaketh
the bow, and knappeth the spear in sunder, | and burneth the
457 168 23
cha- ri- ots in the fire.

37 4 16 258
10 Be still then, and know that I am God : I will be ex-
4 15678 23
alted among the heathen, | & I will be ex- al- ted in the earth.

347 12568 4 15678
11 The Lord of hosts is with us : the God of Ia-cob is
23
our refuge.

At Evensong

DAY 9 Ps. 47 *Omnes gentes, plaudite* v. 2 *or* vij. 2

347 12568
O Clap your hands together, all ye peo-ple : O sing unto
4 15678 23
God with the voice of melody.

347 12568
2 For the Lord is high, and to be fear-ed : he is the great
457 168 23
King up-on all the earth.

347 258 16 4
3 He shall subdue the peo-ple un-der us : and the na-tions
15678 23
un- der our feet.

37 4 12568
4 He shall choose out an he-ri-tage for us : even the
4 15678 23
worship of Ia-cob whom he loved.

3 47 16 258 4
5 God is gone up with a mer-ry noise : and the Lord with
6 123578
the soünd of the trump.

37 4 16 258
6 O sing praises, sing praises un-to our God : O sing
4 15678 23
praises, sing prai-ses un- to our King.

37 4 16 258 4
7 For God is the King of all the earth : sing ye praises with
15678 23
un- der-standing.

37 4 12568 4 15678 23
8 God reigneth o-ver the hea-then : God sitteth up- on his
holy seat.

9 The princes of the people are joined unto the people of
347 258 16
the God of A-bra-ham : for God, which is very high exalted, |
4 6 123578
doth defend the earth, as it wëre with a shield.

Ps. 48 *Magnus Dominus* i. 2 *or* vj.

347 12568
GReat is the Lord, and highly to be prai-sed : in the city
4 15678 23
of our God, | even up- on his holy hill.

37 4 16
2 The hill of Syon is a fair place, | and the joy of the whole
258
earth : upon the north-side lieth the city of the great King ;
4 6 123578
God is well known in her palaces as a süre refuge.

37 4 16 258 4
3 For lo, the kings of the earth : are gathered and gone
15678 23
by to-gether.

347 16 258
4 They marvelled to see such things : they were astoni-
457 168 23
shed, and sud-den-ly cast down.

347 12568
5 Fear came there upon them, and sor-row : as upon a
4 15678 23
wo-man in her travail.

37 4 16 258 4 15678 23
6 Thou shalt break the ships of the sea : — through the
east wind.

7 Like as we have heard, so have we seen in the city of the
37 4 16 258 4
Lord of hosts, | in the ci-ty of our God : God upholdeth the
15678 23
same for ever.

37 4 16 258 457
8 We wait for thy loving-kind-ness, O God : in the midst
168 23
of thy temple.

37 4
9 O God, according to thy Name, so is thy praise un-to the
16 258 4 15678 23
world's end : thy right hand is full of righteousness.

37 4
10 Let the mount Syon rejoice, and the daughter of Iu-da
16 258 457 168 23
be glad : be-cause of thy judgements.

347 12568
11 Walk about Syon, and go round a-bout her : and tell the
15678 23
tow-ers thereof.

347 12568
12 Mark well her bulwarks, set up her hou-ses : that ye
4 15678 23
may tell them that come after.

37 4 12568
13 For this God is our God for ev-er and ev-er : he shall
4 15678 23
be our guide un-to death.

Ps. 49 *Audite hæc, omnes* ij. 1 *or* iv. 5

347 12568
O Hear ye this, all ye peo-ple : ponder it with your ears,
4 6 123578
all ye that dwëll in the world.

347 16 258 4 15678 23
2 High and low, rich and poor : one with an-other.

347 12568
3 My mouth shall speak of wis-dom : and my heart shall
4 15678 23
muse of un- der-standing.

347 258 16
4 I will incline mine ear to the pa- ra-ble : and shew my
4 15678 23
dark speech up-on the harp.

347 258 16
5 Wherefore should I fear in the days of wick-ed-ness : and
4 15678 23
when the wickedness of my heels com-pas-seth me round about ?

37 4 16 258
6 There be some that put their trust in their goods : and
4 15678 23
boast themselves in the multi-tude of their riches.

37 4 12568
7 But no man may de-li-ver his bro-ther : nor make agree-
4 15678 23
ment un- to God for him.

3 47 16 258
8 For it cost more to re-deem their souls : so that he must
4 15678 23
let that a- lone for ever.

37 4 16 258 4 6 123578
9 Yea, though he live long : — and sëe not the grave.

37 4 12568
10 For he seeth that wise men also die, and pe-rish to- ge-
ther : as well as the ignorant and foolish, | and leave their
457 168 23
rich-es for other.

37 4
11 And yet they think that their houses shall con-tin-ue

12568
for ev- er : and that their dwelling-places shall endure from
457 168 23
one generation to another ; and call the lands af- ter their
own names.

347 12568
12 Nevertheless, man will not a-bide in ho-nour : seeing he
4 15678 23
may be compared unto the beasts that perish ; this is the way
of them.

347 258 16 4 15678
13 This is their fool-ish-ness : and their posteri-ty praise
23
their saying.

14 They lie in the hell like sheep; death gnaweth upon
347
them, | and the righteous shall have domination over them in
12568 457
the morn-ing : their beauty shall consume in the sepulchre out
168 23
of their dwelling.

3 47 16 258
15 But God hath delivered my soul from the place of hell :
4 15678 23
for he shall re-ceive me.

37 4 16 258
16 Be not thou afraid, though one be made rich : or if the
4 15678 23
glory of his house be in-creased.

347 12568
17 For he shall carry nothing away with him when he di-
4 6 123578
eth : neither shall his pömp follow him.

3 47 16 258
18 For while he lived, he counted him-self an hap-py man :
4 15678 23
and so long as thou dost well unto thyself, men will speak
good of thee.

347 12568
19 He shall follow the generation of his fa- thers : and
4 15678 23
shall ne- ver see light.

347 12568
20 Man being in honour hath no un-der-stand-ing : but is
4 15678 23
compared unto the beasts that perish.

At Mattins

DAY 10 Ps. 50 *Deus deorum* iij. 5

347 12568
THe Lord, even the most high God, hath spo-ken : and
called the world, | from the rising up of the sun, unto
4 15678 23
the go- ing down thereof.

347 12568 4 15678 23
2 Out of Syon hath God ap-pear-ed : in per- fect beauty.

347 12568
3 Our God shall come, and shall not keep si-lence : there
shall go before him a consuming fire, | and a mighty tempest
4 15678 23
shall be stirred up round a-bout him.

37 4 16 258
4 He shall call the hea-ven from a-bove : and the earth that
4 15678 23
he may judge his people.

37 4 16 258
5 Gather my saints to-ge-ther un-to me : those that have
4 15678 23
made a covenant with me with sacrifice.

347 258 16 4
6 And the heavens shall de-clare his righ-teous-ness : for
15678 23
God is Judge himself.

37 4 16 258
7 Hear, O my peo-ple, & I will speak : I myself will testify
4 15678 23
against thee, O Israel, | for I am God, e- ven thy God.

347
8 I will not reprove thee because of thy sacrifices, or for thy
258 16 457 168 23
burnt-of-fer-ings : because they were not al-way be-fore me.

37 4 16 258 4
9 I will take no bullock out of thine house : nor he-goats
15678 23
out of thy folds.

37 4 16 258
10 For all the beasts of the fo-rest are mine : and so are
4 15678 23
the cattle up-on a thousand hills.

347 12568
11 I know all the fowls up-on the moun-tains : and the
4 15678 23
wild beasts of the field are in my sight.

347 12568
12 If I be hungry, I will not tell thee : for the whole world
4 15678 23
is mine, and all that is therein.

37 4 12568 4 15678 23
13 Thinkest thou that I will eat bulls'-flesh : and drink the
blood of goats?

347 12568
14 Offer unto God thanks-giv-ing : and pay thy vows un-
4 6 123578
to the möst Highest.

347 12568
15 And call upon me in the time of trou-ble : so will I
4 15678 23
hear thee, and thou shalt praise me.

37 4 16 258
16 But unto the un-god-ly said God : Why dost thou
457 168 23
preach my laws, | and takest my co- ve-nant in thy mouth?

347 12568
17 Whereas thou hatest to be re-form-ed : and hast cast
4 15678 23
my words be-hind thee.

37 4 16 258
18 When thou sawest a thief, thou con-sen-tedst un-to him :
457 168 23
and hast been partaker with the a-dulterers.

347 258 16
19 Thou hast let thy mouth speak wick-ed-ness : and with
4 15678 23
thy tongue thou hast set forth deceit.

347 12568
20 Thou satest, and spakest a-gainst thy bro-ther : yea, &
4 6 123578
hast slander-ed thine öwn mother's son.

21 These things hast thou done, and I held my tongue, | and
37 4 16 258
thou thoughtest wickedly, that I am even such a one as thy-self :
4 15678 23
but I will reprove thee, | and set before thee the things that
thou hast done.

37 4 16 258
22 O consider this, ye that for-get God : lest I pluck you
457 168 23
away, and there be none to de-liver you.

37 4 16
23 Whoso offereth me thanks and praise, he ho-nour-eth
258
me : and to him that ordereth his conversation right | will I
4 15678 23
shew the sal- va- tion of God.

Ps. 51 *Miserere mei, Deus* ij. I *or* vj.

34 7 12568
HAve mercy upon me, O God, after thy great good-ness :
·4
according to the multitude of thy mercies, do a-way
15678 23
mine of-fences.

347 258 16 4 15678
2 Wash me throughly from my wick-ed-ness : and cleanse
23
me from my sin.

37 4 16 258 457 168 23
3 For I know-ledge my faults : and my sin is e- ver be-
fore me.

37 4 16
4 Against thee only have I sinned, | & done this e-vil in thy
258
sight : that thou mightest be justified in thy saying, | and clear
4 15678 23
when thou art judged.

37 4 258 16
5 Behold, I was sha-pen in wick-ed-ness : and in sin hath
457 168 23
my mo-ther con-ceived me.

3 47 16 258
6 But lo, thou requirest truth in the in-ward parts : and
·4 15678 23
shalt make me to under-stand wis-dom secretly.

37 4 16 258
7 Thou shalt purge me with hyssop, and I shall be clean :
4 15678 23
thou shalt wash me, and I shall be whi- ter than snow.

347 12568
8 Thou shalt make me hear of joy and glad-ness : that the
4 15678 23
bones which thou hast bro-ken may rejoice.

37 4 16 258 4 15678 23
9 Turn thy face from my sins : & put out all my misdeeds.

37 4 16 258
10 Make me a clean heart, O God : and renew a right
457 168 23
spi- rit with-in me.

347 12568
11 Cast me not away from thy pre-sence : and take not
4 15678 23
thy ho-ly spi- rit from me.

3 47 16 258
12 O give me the comfort of thy help a-gain : and stablish
4 15678 23
me with thy free Spirit.

347 12567
13 Then shall I teach thy ways un-to the wick-ed : and
4 15678 23
sinners shall be con-vert-ed unto thee.

14 Deliver me from blood-guiltiness, O God, | thou that art
37 4 16 258 457 168 23
the God of my health : and my tongue shall sing of thy righteousness.

3 47 16 258 4 15678 23
15 Thou shalt o-pen my lips, O Lord : and my mouth shall
shew thy praise.

37 4 16 258
16 For thou desirest no sacrifice, | else would I give it thee :
4 15678 23
but thou delightest not in burnt-offerings.

347 12568
17 The sacrifice of God is a trou-bled spi-rit : a broken and
4 15678 23
contrite heart, O God, shalt thou not despise.

347 12568
18 O be favourable and gracious un-to Sy-on : build thou
457 168 23
the walls of Hie-rusalem.

19 Then shalt thou be pleased with the sacrifice of righ-
347 12568
teousness, | with the burnt-offerings and ob-la-tions : then
4 15678 23
shall they offer young bullocks up-on thine altar.

Ps. 52 *Quid gloriaris* iv. 7 *or* vij. 7

347 12568 4
WHy boastest thou thy-self, thou ty-rant : that thou
15678 23
canst do mischief;

37 4 16 258 457 168 23
2 Whereas the good-ness of God : en-dur-eth yet daily?

37 4 258 16
3 Thy tongue i-ma-gi-neth wick-ed-ness : and with lies
4 6 123578
thou cuttest like a shärp rasor.

347 12568
4 Thou hast loved unrighteousness more than good-ness :
4 15678 23
and to talk of lies more than righteousness.

37 4 16 258 4
5 Thou hast loved to speak all words that may do hurt : —
15678 23
O thou false tongue.

37 4 12568
6 Therefore shall God de-stroy thee for ev-er : he shall
take thee, and pluck thee out of thy dwelling, | and root thee
457 168 23
out of the land of the living.

37 4 16 258 4 15678
7 The righteous also shall see this, and fear : and shall laugh
23
him to scorn ;

37 4 16 258
8 Lo, this is the man that took not God for his strength :
but trusted unto the multitude of his riches, | and strengthened
.4 15678 23
him-self in his wickedness.

3 47 16
9 As for me, I am like a green olive-tree in the house of
258 457 168 23
God : my trust is in the tender mercy of God for ev- er & ever.

37 4 16
10 I will always give thanks unto thee for that thou hast
258 4 6 123578
done : and I will hope in thy Name, for thy saïnts like it well.

At Evensong

DAY 10 Ps. 53 *Dixit insipiens* i. 4 *or* ij. 1

37 4 16 258 4 15678 23
THe foolish body hath said in his heart : — There is no God.
347
2 Corrupt are they, and become abominable in their
258 16 4 15678 23
wick-ed-ness : there is none that doeth good.

37 4 16
3 God looked down from heaven upon the chil-dren of
258 4 6
men : to see if there were any that would under-stand, and
123578
sëek after God.

4 But they are all gone out of the way, | they are altogether
347 12568 4 6 123578
become a-bo-mi-na-ble : there is also none that do-eth gööd,
no not one.

347 258 16
5 Are not they without understanding that work wick-ed-

ness : eating up my people as if they would eat bread ? they
457 168 23
have not call-ed up-on God.
347 16 258
6 They were afraid where no fear was : for God hath bro-
ken the bones of him that besieged thee ; thou hast put them
4 15678 23
to confusion, because God hath de-spised them.
347 12568
7 O that the salvation were given unto Israel out of Sy-on :
457 168 23
O that the Lord would deliver his people out of cap-tivity !
3 47 16 258 4 15678 23
8 Then should Ia-cob re-joice : and Isra-el should be right
glad.

Ps. 54 *Deus, in nomine* vij. 7

37 4 16 258 457 168 23
SAve me, O God, for thy Name's sake : and a-venge me in
thy strength.
347 16 258 4 15678
2 Hear my prayer, O God : and hearken unto the words
23
of my mouth.
347 12568
3 For strangers are risen up a-gainst me : and tyrants,
4 15678 23
which have not God before their eyes, seek af- ter my soul.
347 12568 457 168
4 Behold, God is my help-er : the Lord is with them that
23
up-hold my soul.
347 258 16 4
5 He shall reward evil un-to mine en-e-mies : destroy thou
15678 23
them in thy truth.
3
6 An offering of a free heart will I give thee, and praise thy
47 16 258 4 15678 23
Name, O Lord : because it is so com-fort-able.

347 12568
7 For he hath delivered me out of all my trou-ble : and
4 15678 23
mine eye hath seen his desire up- on mine enemies.

Ps. 55 *Exaudi, Deus* i. 8 *or* iv. 5

347 16 258 4 15678
HEar my prayer, O God : and hide not thyself from my
23
pe-tition.

347 12568
2 Take heed unto me, and hear me : how I mourn in my
4 15678 23
prayer, and am vexed.

3 47 16
3 The enemy crieth so, | and the ungodly com-eth on so
258
fast : for they are minded to do me some mischief; so ma-
4 15678 23
liciously are they set a-gainst me.

347 12568
4 My heart is disquiet-ed with- in me : & the fear of death
457 168 23
is fal- len up-on me.

347 12568
5 Fearfulness and trembling are come up- on me : and an
4 15678 23
horrible dread hath o- ver-whelmed me.

37 4 16 258
6 And I said, O that I had wings like a dove : for then
4 15678 23
would I flee a- way, and be at rest.

3 47 16 258 4 15678
7 Lo, then would I get me a-way far off : and re-main in
23
the wilderness.

37 4 16 258 4
8 I would make haste to es-cape : because of the stor-my
15678 23
wind and tempest.

347 12568
9 Destroy their tongues, O Lord, and di-vide them : for I
4 15678 23
have spied unrighteousness and strife in the city.
37 4 16 258
10 Day and night they go about with-in the walls there-of :
4 15678 23
mischief also and sorrow are in the midst of it.
3 47 16 258 4 15678 23
11 Wick-edness is there-in : deceit and guile go not out of
their streets.
347
12 For it is not an open enemy that hath done me this dis-
12568 4 15678 23
ho-nour : for then I could have borne it.
347
13 Neither was it mine adversary, that did magnify him-self
12568 457 168 23
a-gainst me : for then peradventure I would have hid my-self
from him.
347 12568
14 But it was even thou, my com-pan-ion : my guide, and
4 15678 23
mine own fa-miliar friend.
37 4 12568 4
15 We took sweet coun-sel to-ge-ther : and walked in the
15678 23
house of God as friends.
16 Let death come hastily upon them, | and let them go
37 4 16 258 4
down quick in-to hell : for wickedness is in their dwel-lings,
15678 23
and a-mong them.
37 4 16 258 4 15678 23
17 As for me, I will call up-on God : and the Lord shall
save me.
18 In the evening, and morning, and at noon-day will I
347 258 16 4 15678 23
pray, | and that in-stant-ly : and he shall hear my voice.
19 It is he that hath delivered my soul in peace from the
347 12568 4 15678 23
battle that was a-gainst me : for there were ma- ny with me.

3
20 Yea, even God, that endureth for ever, shall hear me, &
47 16 258 4 15678 23
bring them down : for they will not turn, nor fear God.

37 4 16 258
21 He laid his hands upon such as be at peace with him :
4 15678 23
and he brake his covenant.

22 The words of his mouth were softer than butter, | having
37 4 16 258 4
war in his heart : his words were smoother than oil, | and yet
15678 23
be they very swords.

347 258 16
23 O cast thy burthen upon the Lord, and he shall nou-rish
4 15678 23
thee : and shall not suffer the righteous to fall for ever.
347 16 258
24 And as for them : thou, O God, shalt bring them into
457 168 23
the pit of de-struction.

347
25 The blood-thirsty & deceitful men shall not live out half
16 258 4 15678 23
their days : nevertheless, my trust shall be in thee, O Lord.

At Mattins

DAY 11 Ps. 56 *Miserere mei, Deus* i. 2

37 4
BE merciful unto me, O God, | for man goeth a-bout to de-
12568 457 168 23
vour me : he is daily figh-ting, and troubling me.
37 4 16 258
2 Mine enemies are daily in hand to swal-low me up : for
4 15678 23
they be many that fight against me, O thou most Highest.
37 4 16 258 4 15678
3 Nevertheless, though I am some-time a-fraid : yet put I
23
my trust in thee.

37 4 16 258
4 I will praise God, be-cause of his word : I have put my
4 15678 23
trust in God, | and will not fear what flesh can do un-to me.

3 47 16 258
5 They dai-ly mis-take my words : all that they imagine is
4 15678 23
to do me evil.

37 4 16 258
6 They hold all together, and keep them-selves close : and
4 15678 23
mark my steps, | when they lay wait for my soul.

347 258 16
7 Shall they escape for their wick-ed-ness : thou, O God,
457 168 23
in thy dis-plea-sure shalt cast them down.

347 12568
8 Thou tellest my flittings; put my tears in-to thy bot-tle :
457 168 23
are not these things no- ted in thy book?

3
9 Whensoever I call upon thee, | then shall mine ene-mies
47 16 258 4 15678 23
be put to flight : this I know; for God is on my side.

37 4 16 258 4 15678
10 In God's word will I re-joice : in the Lord's word will
23
I comfort me.

3 47 16 258
11 Yea, in God have I put my trust : I will not be afraid
4 15678 23
what man can do un-to me.

3 47 16 258 4
12 Unto thee, O God, will I pay my vows : unto thee
15678 23
will I give thanks.

347
13 For thou hast delivered my soul from death, and my feet
12568 457 168 23
from fal-ling : that I may walk before God in the light of the
living.

Ps. 57 *Miserere mei, Deus* iv.5 *or* viij.2

BE merciful unto me, O God, be merciful unto me, | for
37 4 16 258
my soul trust-eth in thee : & under the shadow of thy
4 15678 23
wings shall be my refuge, | until this ty-ran-ny be overpast.

347 16 258
2 I will call unto the most high God : even unto the God
4 15678 23
that shall perform the cause which I have in hand.

347 12568
3 He shall send from hea-ven : and save me from the
4 15678 23
reproof of him that would eat me up.

37 4 16 258 4
4 God shall send forth his mer-cy and truth : my soul is
6 123578
a-mön̈g lions.

3 47
5 And I lie even among the children of men, that are set
16 258 4 15678
on fire : whose teeth are spears and arrows, | and their tongue
23
a sharp sword.

347 12568
6 Set up thyself, O God, a-bove the hea-vens : and thy
4 6 123578
glo-ry a- böve all the earth.

37 4 16
7 They have laid a net for my feet, and pres-sed down my
258
soul : they have digged a pit before me, | and are fallen into
4 15678 23
the midst of it themselves.

347 12568 4 15678
8 My heart is fixed, O God, my heart is fix-ed : I will sing,
23
and give praise.

347 16 258
9 Awake up, my glory ; awake, lute and harp : I myself
4 15678 23
will a-wake right early.

347 12568
10 I will give thanks unto thee, O Lord, a-mong the peo-
4 15678 23
ple : and I will sing unto thee a-mong the nations.

347 12568
11 For the greatness of thy mercy reacheth un-to the hea-
4 15678 23
vens : and thy truth un-to the clouds.

347 12568
12 Set up thyself, O God, a-bove the hea-vens : and thy
4 6 123578
glo-ry a- böve all the earth.

Ps. 58 *Si vere utique* ij. 1

347 12568
ARe your minds set upon righteousness, O ye con-gre- ga-
·4 15678 23
tion : and do ye judge the thing that is right, O ye
sons of men ?

37 4 16 258
2 Yea, ye imagine mischief in your heart up-on the earth :
·4 15678 23
and your hands deal with wickedness.

37 4 16
3 The ungodly are froward, even from their mo-ther's
258 4 15678 23
womb : as soon as they are born, they go a-stray, & speak lies.

347 12568
4 They are as venomous as the poison of a ser-pent : even
4 15678 23
like the deaf adder that stop-peth her ears.

37 4 12568
5 Which refuseth to hear the voice of the char-mer : charm
457 168 23
he ne- ver so wisely.

6 Break their teeth, O God, in their mouths; smite the
37 4 16 258
jaw-bones of the li-ons, O Lord : let them fall away like
water that runneth apace; and when they shoot their arrows,
4 15678 23
let them be rooted out.

7 Let them consume away like a snail, | and be like the
37 4 12568 4 15678 23
untimely fruit of a wo-man : and let them not see the sun.
347 16 258
8 Or ever your pots be made hot with thorns : so let indig-
4 15678 23
nation vex him, | even as a thing that is raw.
37 4 12568
9 The righteous shall rejoice when he se-eth the ven-
457 168
geance : he shall wash his footsteps in the blood of the
23
un-godly.

347
10 So that a man shall say, | Verily there is a re-ward for the
12568 4 6 123578
righ-teous : doubtless there is a God that jüdg- eth the earth.

At Evensong

DAY 11 Ps. 59 *Eripe me de inimicis* iij. 5

37 4 16 258
DEliver me from mine en-e-mies, O God : defend me from
.4 15678 23
them that rise up a-gainst me.
347 12568 4
2 O deliver me from the wick-ed do-ers : and save me from
6 123578
the blöod-thirsty men.
37 4 16 258
3 For lo, they lie wait-ing for my soul : the mighty men
4 15678 23
are gathered against me, | without any offence or fault of me,
O Lord.
3 47 16 258
4 They run and prepare them-selves with-out my fault :
4 15678 23
arise thou therefore to help me, and behold.

5 Stand up, O Lord God of hosts, thou God of Israel, | to

347 12568
visit all the hea-then : and be not merciful unto them that
4 15678 23
offend of ma- li- cious wickedness.

347 12568
6 They go to and fro in the eve-ning : they grin like a
4 15678 23
dog, | and run a-bout through the city.

37 4
7 Behold, they speak with their mouth, and swords are in
16 258 4 15678 23
their lips : — — for who doth hear?

347 12568
8 But thou, O Lord, shalt have them in de- ri- sion : and
4 15678 23
thou shalt laugh all the hea-then to scorn.

37 4 16 258
9 My strength will I a-scribe un-to thee : for thou art the
4 15678 23
God of my refuge.

347 258 16
10 God sheweth me his good-ness plen-teous-ly : and God
4 15678 23
shall let me see my desire up-on mine enemies.

37 4 12568
11 Slay them not, lest my peo-ple for-get it : but scatter
4 6 123578
them abroad among the people, | and put them down, O Lörd,
our defence.

12 For the sin of their mouth, and for the words of their
37 4 16 258
lips, | they shall be ta-ken in their pride : and-why their preach-
4 15678 23
ing is of cur-sing and lies.

347
13 Consume them in thy wrath, | consume them, that they
12568
may pe- rish : and know that it is God that ruleth in Iacob, |
4 6 123578
and un-to the ënds of the world.

37 4 16 258
14 And in the eve-ning they will re-turn : grin like a
4 15678 23
dog, | and will go a- bout the city.

37 4 16 258
15 They will run here and there for meat : and grudge if
4 15678 23
they be not sa- tis-fied.

16 As for me, I will sing of thy power, | and will praise thy
347 12568
mercy betimes in the mor-ning : for thou hast been my de-
457 168 23
fence and refuge in the day of my trouble.

37 4 16 258
17 Unto thee, O my strength, will I sing : for thou, O
4 68 157 23
God, art my refuge, and my mer-ci-ful God.

Ps. 60 *Deus, repulisti nos* vj.

37 4 16 258
O God, thou hast cast us out, and scat-tered us a-broad :
4 15678 23
thou hast also been displeased ; O turn thee un- to us
again.

347 258 16
2 Thou hast moved the land, and di-vi-ded it : heal the
4 15678 23
sores there-of, for it shaketh.

37 4 16 258
3 Thou hast shewed thy peo-ple hea-vy things : thou hast
4 15678 23
given us a drink of deadly wine.

347 12568
4 Thou hast given a token for such as fear thee : that they
4 6 123578
may tri-umph be-caüse of the truth.

37 4 258 16
5 Therefore were thy be-lov-ed de-li-ver-ed : help me with
4 15678 23
thy right hand, and hear me.

347 258 16
6 God hath spoken in his ho- li-ness : I will rejoice, and
457 168 23
divide Sy-chem, | and mete out the val-ley of Succoth.

37 4 16 258
7 Gilead is mine, and Ma-nas-ses is mine : Ephraym also is
4 15678 23
the strength of my head ; Iu-da is my lawgiver.

3 47 16
8 Moab is my wash-pot, | over Edom will I cast out my
258 4 15678 23
shoe : Philisti-a, be thou glad of me.

4 37 12568
9 Who will lead me into the strong ci- ty : who will bring
4 15678 23
me in- to Edom ?

3 47 16 258
10 Hast not thou cast us out, O God : wilt not thou, O
4 15678 23
God, go out with our hosts ?

347 12568 4 15678 23
11 O be thou our help in trou-ble : for vain is the help of
man.

3 47 16 258
12 Through God will we do great acts : for it is he that
.4 15678 23
shall tread down our enemies.

Ps. 61 *Exaudi, Deus* vij. 1

37 4 16 258 4 15678 23
HEar my cry-ing, O God : give ear un- to my prayer.
37 4 16 258
2 From the ends of the earth will I call up-on thee :
4 15678 23
when my heart is in heaviness.

37 4 16 258
3 O set me upon the rock that is high-er than I : for thou
4 15678 23
hast been my hope, | and a strong tower for me a-gainst the
enemy.

37 4 12568
4 I will dwell in thy taber-na-cle for ev-er : and my trust
457 168 23
shall be under the co-ver-ing of thy wings.

37 4 16 258
5 For thou, O Lord, hast heard my de-sires : and hast given
4 15678 23
an heritage un-to those that fear thy Name.

37 4 16 258
6 Thou shalt grant the King a long life : that his years
.4 15678 23
may endure throughout all ge- ne-rations.

347 12568
7 He shall dwell before God for ev- er : O prepare thy
4 15678 23
loving mercy and faithfulness, | that they may pre-serve him.
37 4 16 258
8 So will I alway sing praise un-to thy Name : that I may
457 168 23
dai- ly per-form my vows.

At Mattins

DAY 12 Ps. 62 *Nonne Deo* iv. 6 *or* viij. 5

37 4 16 258
MY soul truly waiteth still up-on God : for of him com-
4 15678 23
eth my sal-vation.

347 12568
2 He verily is my strength and my sal-va-tion : he is my
4 15678 23
defence, | so that I shall not greatly fall.

37 4 16 258
3 How long will ye imagine mischief against ev-er-y man :
ye shall be slain all the sort of you; yea, as a tottering wall
4 15678 23
shall ye be, and like a broken hedge.

37 4
4 Their device is only how to put him out whom God will
16 258
ex-alt : their delight is in lies; they give good words with
4 15678 23
their mouth, but curse with their heart.

37 4 16 258
5 Nevertheless, my soul, wait thou still up-on God : for
4 15678 23
my hope is in him.

347 12568
6 He truly is my strength and my sal- va- tion : he is my
4 15678 23
defence, so that I shall not fall.

347 12568
7 In God is my health, and my glo-ry : the rock of my
4 15678 23
might, | and in God is my trust.

347 12568
8 O put your trust in him al-way, ye peo-ple : pour out
4 15678 23
your hearts before him, | for God is our hope.
347 258 16
9 As for the children of men, they are but va-ni-ty : the
children of men are deceitful upon the weights, | they are alto-
4 15678 23
gether lighter than va- ni-ty itself.
347
10 O trust not in wrong & robbery, | give not yourselves un-
258 16 4 15678 23
to va-ni-ty : if riches increase, set not your heart up-on them.
347 16 258
11 God spake once : & twice I have also heard the same, |
4 15678 23
that power be-long-eth unto God.
347 258 16
12 And that thou, Lord, art mer-ci-ful : for thou rewardest
456 168 23
every man ac-cor-ding to his work.

Ps. 63 *Deus, Deus meus* i. 4

37 4 16 258 4 15678 23
O God, thou art my God : ear-ly will I seek thee.
347
2 My soul thirsteth for thee, | my flesh also long-eth
258 16 4 15678 23
af-ter thee : in a barren and dry land, where no water is.
347 258 16
3 Thus have I looked for thee in ho-li-ness : that I might
457 168 23
behold thy pow-er and glory.
3 47 16 258 4
4 For thy loving-kindness is better than the life it-self : my
15678 23
lips shall praise thee.
347 12568
5 As long as I live will I magnify thee on this man-ner :
4 15678 23
and lift up my hands in thy Name.
37 4
6 My soul shall be satisfied, | even as it were with mar-row

12568 4 15678 23
and fat-ness : when my mouth prai-seth thee with joyful lips.

37 4 16 258
7 Have I not remembered thee in my bed : and thought
4 15678 23
upon thee when I was waking?

347 12568
8 Because thou hast been my help-er : therefore under the
4 15678 23
shadow of thy wings will I rejoice.

37 4 12568 4 15678 23
9 My soul hang-eth up- on thee : thy right hand hath up-
holden me.

37 4 16 258 .468
10 These also that seek the hurt of my soul : they shall go
157 23
un-der the earth.

37 4 16 258
11 Let them fall upon the edge of the sword : that they
457 168 23
may be a por-tion for foxes.

12 But the King shall rejoice in God; all they also that
347 12568
swear by him shall be com-men-ded : for the mouth of them
.4 15678 23
that speak lies shall be stopped.

Ps. 64 *Exaudi, Deus* ij. 1 *or* vij. 1

37 4 16 258
HEar my voice, O God, in my prayer : preserve my life
457 168 23
from fear of the enemy.

347 12568
2 Hide me from the gathering together of the fro-ward :
4 15678 23
and from the insurrection of wick-ed doers.

37 4 16 258
3 Who have whet their tongue like a sword : and shoot out
4 15678 23
their ar-rows, e- ven bitter words.

347 12568
4 That they may privily shoot at him that is per-fect : sud-
457 168 23
denly do they hit him, and fear not.

347 12568
5 They encourage them-selves in mis-chief : and commune
457
among themselves how they may lay snares, | and say that no
168 23
man shall see them.

347 258 16
6 They imagine wicked-ness, & prac-tise it : that they keep
4 15678 23
secret among themselves, | every man in the deep of his heart.

3 4 7 12568
7 But God shall suddenly shoot at them with a swift ar-
4 15678 23
row : that they shall be wounded.

3 47 16 258
8 Yea, their own tongues shall make them fall : insomuch
4 15678 23
that whoso seeth them shall laugh them to scorn.

37 4 16 258
9 And all men that see it shall say, | This hath God done :
4 15678 23
for they shall perceive that it is his work.

37 4
10 The righteous shall rejoice in the Lord, and put his trust
16 258 4 15678 23
in him : and all they that are true of heart shall be glad.

At Evensong

DAY 12 Ps. 65 *Te decet hymnus* viij. 1

37 4 12568
THou, O God, art prai-sed in Sy- on : and unto thee shall
4 15678 23
the vow be perform-ed in Hie-rusalem.

37 4 16 258 4 15678 23
2 Thou that hear-est the prayer : un-to thee shall all flesh
come.

347 12568 4
3 My misdeeds pre-vail a-gainst me : O be thou merci-ful
15678 23
un- to our sins.

37
4 Blessed is the man whom thou choosest, and re-cei-vest
4 16 258
un-to thee : he shall dwell in thy court, | and shall be satisfied
4 15678 23
with the pleasures of thy house, | even of thy ho- ly temple.

5 Thou shalt shew us wonderful things in thy righteousness, |
347 12568
O God of our sal-va-tion : thou that art the hope of all the
4 15678 23
ends of the earth, | and of them that re-main in the broad sea.

347 12568
6 Who in his strength setteth fast the moun-tains : and is
4 15678 23
girded a-bout with power.

37 4 16 258
7 Who stilleth the ra-ging of the sea : and the noise of his
4 15678 23
waves, | and the mad-ness of the people.

8 They also that dwell in the uttermost parts of the earth
347 12568
shall be afraid at thy to-kens : thou that makest the outgoings
457 168 23
of the morning and eve-ning to praise thee.

347 258 16 4
9 Thou visitest the earth, and bles-sest it : thou makest it
15678 23
ve- ry plenteous.

347 12568
10 The river of God is full of wa-ter : thou preparest their
4 15678 23
corn, | for so thou pro- vi- dest for the earth.

11 Thou waterest her furrows, | thou sendest rain into the
37 4 16 258
little val-leys there-of : thou makest it soft with the drops of
4 15678 23
rain, | and blessest the in- crease of it.

347 12568 4
12 Thou crownest the year with thy good-ness : and thy
15678 23
clouds drop fatness.

347 258 16
13 They shall drop upon the dwellings of the wil-der-ness :
4 15678 23
and the little hills shall re-joice on every side.

3 47 16 258
14 The folds shall be full of sheep : the valleys also shall
4 15678 23
stand so thick with corn, that they shall laugh and sing.

Ps. 66 *Jubilate Deo* i. 2

347 16 258
O Be joyful in God, all ye lands : sing praises unto the
457 168 23
honour of his Name, | make his praise to be glorious.

37 4 16 258
2 Say unto God, | O how wonderful art thou in thy works :
through the greatness of thy power shall thine enemies be
·4 15678 23
found li- ars unto thee.

37 4 16 258 4 15678 23
3 For all the world shall wor-ship thee : sing of thee, and
praise thy Name.

3 47 16 258
4 O come hither, and be-hold the works of God : how
4 15678 23
wonderful he is in his doing toward the chil-dren of men.

37 4 16 258
5 He turned the sea in-to dry land : so that they went
4 15678 23
through the water on foot ; there did we re-joice thereof.

347
6 He ruleth with his power for ever ; his eyes be-hold the
12568 4 15678
peo-ple : and such as will not believe | shall not be a-ble to
23
ex-alt themselves.

347 12568 4 6
7 O praise our God, ye peo-ple : and make the voice of his
123578
präise to be heard.

3 47 16 258 4 15678 23
8 Who hold-eth our soul in life : and suffer-eth not our
feet to slip.

347 258 16
9 For thou, O God, hast pro-ved us : thou also hast tried
457 168 23
us, like as sil- ver is tried.

37 4 16 258 457 168
10 Thou broughtest us in-to the snare : and laidest trou-ble
23
up-on our loins.

37 4 16 258
11 Thou sufferedst men to ride o-ver our heads : we went
4 15678 23
through fire and water, | and thou broughtest us out in- to a
wealthy place.

347 258 16
12 I will go into thine house with burnt-of-fer-ings : and
will pay thee my vows, | which I promised with my lips, and
4 15678 23
spake with my mouth, | when I was in trouble.

37
13 I will offer unto thee fat burnt-sacrifices, with the in-
4 16 258 4 15678 23
cense of rams : I will of-fer bul-locks and goats.

37 4 16 258
14 O come hither, and hearken, all ye that fear God : and
4 15678 23
I will tell you what he hath done for my soul.

37 4 16 258 4 15678
15 I called unto him with my mouth : and gave him prai-
23
ses with my tongue.

37 4 16 258 4
16 If I incline unto wick-edness with mine heart : the Lord
15678 23
will not hear me.

347 12568 4 15678 23
17 But God hath heard me : and considered the voice of
my prayer.

347 16 258
18 Praised be God who hath not cast out my prayer : nor
4 15678 23
turned his mer- cy from me.

Ps. 67 *Deus misereatur* iv. 11 *or* vij. 5

347 12568
GOd be merciful unto us, and bless us : and shew us the
457 168 23
light of his countenance, and be mer-ci-ful unto us.
37 4 16 258
2 That thy way may be known up-on earth : thy saving
4 15678 23
health a-mong all nations.
37 4 16 258 4 15678
3 Let the people praise thee, O God : yea, let all the peo-
23
ple praise thee.
37 4 16 258
4 O let the nations re-joice and be glad : for thou shalt
457 168 23
judge the folk righteously, | & govern the na-tions up-on earth.
37 4 16 258 4 15678 23
5 Let the people praise thee, O God : let all the peo-ple
praise thee.
347 12568
6 Then shall the earth bring forth her in-crease : and God,
457 168 23
even our own God, shall give us his blessing.
347 12568 4 15678 23
7 God shall bless us : and all the ends of the world shall
fear him.

At Mattins

DAY 13 Ps. 68 *Exurgat Deus* viij. 1 *or* 5

347 258 16
LEt God arise, and let his ene-mies be scat-ter-ed : let
4 15678 23
them also that hate him flee be-fore him.

2 Like as the smoke vanisheth, | so shalt thou [37]drive [4]them [16]a-
[258]way : and like as wax melteth at the fire, | so let the ungodly
perish at [4]the [15678]pre-[23]sence of God.

3 But let the righteous be glad and re-[37]joice [4]be-[16]fore [258]God :
let them also be [457]mer-[168]ry [23]and joyful.

4 O sing unto God, and sing praises [37]un-[4]to [16]his [258]Name : magnify him that rideth upon the heavens, as it were upon an
horse; praise him in his Name IA, | and [4]re-[15678]joice [23]be-fore him.

5 He is a Father of the fatherless, | and defendeth the [37]cause
[4]of the [12568]wi- dows : even God in his ho-[4]ly [15678]ha- [23]bi-tation.

6 He is the God that maketh men to be of one mind in an
house, | and bringeth the prisoners [37]out [4]of cap-[258]ti- [16]vi-ty : but
letteth the runagates con-[457]tin- [168]ue [23]in scarceness.

7 O God, when thou wentest forth be-[347]fore the [12568]peo-ple :
when thou went-[4]est [15678]through [23]the wilderness,

8 The earth shook, | and the heavens dropped at the [37]pre-
[4]sence [16]of [258]God : even as Sinai also was moved at the presence of
God, | who is [4]the [15678]God [23]of Israel.

9 Thou, O God, sentest a gracious rain upon [347]thine in-[258]he-
[16]ri-tance : and refreshedst it [4]when [15678]it [23]was weary.

10 Thy congregation shall [347]dwell [16]there-[258]in : for thou, O
God, hast of thy goodness [4]pre-[15678]par- [23]ed for the poor.

37 4 16 258 4 15678
11 The Lord gave the word : great was the compa-ny of
23
the preachers.

347 258 16
12 Kings with their armies did flee, and were dis-com-fit-ed :
4 6 123578
and they of the house-hold di- vĭ- ded the spoil.

13 Though ye have lien among the pots | yet shall ye be as
37 4 16 258
the wings of a dove : that is covered with silver wings, | and
4 15678 23
her fea-thers like gold.

37 4 16 258
14 When the Almighty scattered kings for their sake : then
4 15678 23
were they as white as snow in Salmon.

347 12568
15 As the hill of Basan, so is God's hill : even an high hill,
4 15678 23
as the hill of Basan.

16 Why hop ye so, ye high hills? this is God's hill, in the
37 4 16 258 4
which it plea-seth him to dwell : yea, the Lord will abide in
15678 23
it for ever.

37
17 The chariots of God are twenty thousand, | even thou-
4 12568 4
sands of an-gels : and the Lord is among them, as in the ho-ly
15678 23
place of Sinai.

18 Thou art gone up on high, | thou hast led captivity cap-
37 4 16 258
tive, | and re-cei-ved gifts for men : yea, even for thine ene-
4 15678 23
mies, | that the Lord God might dwell a-mong them.

4 37 12568
19 Praised be the Lord dai-ly : even the God who helpeth
4 15678 23
us, | and poureth his be-ne- fits up-on us.

37 4
20 He is our God, | even the God of whom com-eth sal-
12568 457 168 23
va-tion : God is the Lord, by whom we es-cape death.

37 4 258 16
21 God shall wound the head of his en- e-mies : and the
457 168 23
hairy scalp of such a one as goeth on still in his wickedness.

22 The Lord hath said, | I will bring my people again, as I
347 12568
did from Ba-san : mine own will I bring again, | as I did some-
4 6 123578
time from the dëep of the sea.

37 4 258 16
23 That thy foot may be dipped in the blood of thine en- e-
4 6 123578
mies : and that the tongue of thy dogs may be rëd through
the same.

347 12568
24 It is well seen, O God, how thou go- est : how thou,
4 15678 23
my God and King, | goest in the sanc- tu-ary.

347 12568
25 The singers go before, | the minstrels fol-low af- ter :
4 15678 23
in the midst are the damsels play-ing with the timbrels.

347
26 Give thanks, O Israel, unto God the Lord in the con-
12568 4 6 123578
gre- ga- tions : from the gröund of the heart.

27 There is little Beniamin their ruler, | and the princes of
37 4 12568 457 168
Iu-da their coun-sel : the princes of Zábulon, and the prin-ces
23
of Nephthali.

3 47 16 258
28 Thy God hath sent forth strength for thee : stablish the
4 15678 23
thing, O God, that thou hast wrought in us.

347 258 16
29 For thy temple's sake at Hie-ru- sa-lem : so shall kings
4 15678 23
bring pre-sents unto thee.

30 When the company of the spear-men, and multitude of
the mighty | are scattered abroad among the beasts of the peo-
37 4 12568
ple, | so that they humbly bring pie-ces of sil-ver : and when
4 15678 23
he hath scattered the peo-ple that de-light in war ;
347 12568
31 Then shall the princes come out of E- gypt : the
4 6 123578
Morians' land shall soon stretch out her händs un-to God.
37 4 16 258
32 Sing unto God, O ye king-doms of the earth : O sing
457 168 23
prai-ses un-to the Lord.
37 4 12568
33 Who sitteth in the heavens over all from the be-gin-ning :
4 15678 23
lo, he doth send out his voice, | yea, and that a mighty voice.
347 258 16
34 Ascribe ye the power to God o-ver Is- ra-el : his worship
4 15678 23
and strength is in the clouds.
347 12568
35 O God, wonderful art thou in thy ho-ly pla- ces : even
the God of Israel ; he will give strength and power unto his
4 15678 23
peo-ple ; bles-sed be God.

At Evensong

DAY 13 Ps. 69 *Salvum me fac* i. 5 *or* 8

37 4 16 258 4 15678 23
SAve me, O God : for the waters are come in, e-ven un-to
my soul.
37 4 16 258
2 I stick fast in the deep mire, where no ground is : I am
4 15678 23
come into deep waters, | so that the floods run over me.

347 16 258
3 I am weary of crying; my throat is dry : my sight faileth
4 15678 23
me for waiting so long up-on my God.

4 They that hate me without a cause are more than the
37 4 16 258
hairs of my head : they that are mine enemies, | and would
457 168 23
destroy me guilt-less, are mighty.

3 47 16 258
5 I paid them the things that I ne-ver took : God, thou
4 15678 23
knowest my simpleness, | and my faults are not hid from thee.

6 Let not them that trust in thee, O Lord God of hosts, |
37 4 16 258
be a-sha-med for my cause : let not those that seek thee be
·4 15678 23
confounded through me, | O Lord God of Israel.

37 4 16 258
7 And-why for thy sake have I suf-fer-ed re-proof : shame
457 168 23
hath co- ver-ed my face.

347 12568
8 I am become a stranger un-to my bre-thren : even an alien
4 15678 23
unto my mo-ther's children.

347 258 16
9 For the zeal of thine house hath e-ven eat-en me : and the
457 168 23
rebukes of them that rebuked thee are fal-len up-on me.

347 12568
10 I wept, and chastened my-self with fas-ting : and that
457 168 23
was turn-ed to my reproof.

347 12568 457 168 23
11 I put on sack-cloth al- so : and they jest- ed up-on me.

347 12568
12 They that sit in the gate speak a-gainst me : and the
4 15678 23
drunkards make songs up-on me.

37 4 16 258 4 68 157
13 But, Lord, I make my prayer un-to thee : in an ac-cep-
23
ta-ble time.

347 12568
14 Hear me, O God, in the multitude of thy mer-cy : even
4 15678 23
in the truth of thy sal-vation.

347 12568
15 Take me out of the mire, that I sink not : O let me be
4 6 123578
delivered from them which hate me, | & out of the dëep waters.

16 Let not the water-flood drown me, | neither let the deep
37 4 16 258 4 15678 23
swal-low me up : & let not the pit shut her mouth up-on me.
347 12568
17 Hear me, O Lord, for thy loving-kindness is com-fort- a-
4 15678 23
ble : turn thee unto me according to the multi-tude of thy

mercies.

347
18 And hide not thy face from thy servant, | for I am in
12568 457 168 23
trou-ble : O haste thee, and hear me.
347 12568
19 Draw nigh unto my soul, and save it : O deliver me, be-
457 168 23
cause of mine enemies.

347
20 Thou hast known my reproof, my shame, and my dis-
12568 4 15678 23
hon-our : mine adversaries are all in thy sight.
347 258 16
21 Thy rebuke hath broken my heart ; I am full of hea-vi-

ness : I looked for some to have pity on me, but there was no
457 168 23
man, | neither found I a- ny to comfort me.
3 47 16 258
22 They gave me gall to eat : & when I was thirsty | they
4 15678 23
gave me vi- ne-gar to drink.

37 4 16
23 Let their table be made a snare to take them-selves with-
258
al : and let the things that should have been for their wealth |
457 168 23
be unto them an oc-ca-sion of falling.

347 12568 4
24 Let their eyes be blinded, that they see not : and ev-er
15678 23
bow thou down their backs.

37 4 12568
25 Pour out thine indig-na-tion up- on them : and let thy
457 168 23
wrathful dis-plea-sure take hold of them.

37 4 16 258 4 15678 23
26 Let their habi-ta-tion be void : and no man to dwell in
their tents.

347 12568
27 For they persecute him whom thou hast smit-ten : and
4 15678 23
they talk how they may vex them whom thou hast wounded.

347 12568
28 Let them fall from one wickedness to an- o- ther : and
4 15678 23
not come in- to thy righteousness.

37 4 12568
29 Let them be wiped out of the book of the liv- ing : and
4 15678 23
not be written a-mong the righteous.

347 258 16
30 As for me, when I am poor and in hea-vi-ness : thy
4 15678 23
help, O God, shall lift me up.

37 4 16 258
31 I will praise the Name of God with a song : and mag-
4 15678 23
nify it with thanks-giving.

3 47 16 258 4
32 This al-so shall please the Lord : better than a bul-lock
15678 23
that hath horns and hoofs.

37 4 16 258
33 The humble shall consider this, and be glad : seek ye
4 15678 23
after God, and your soul shall live.

37 4 16 258 4 15678 23
34 For the Lord hear-eth the poor : and despi-seth not his
prisoners.

4 37 12568 4
35 Let heaven and earth praise him : the sea, and all that
15678 23
mov-eth therein.

37 4 12568
36 For God will save Syon, | & build the ci-ties of Iu- da :
4 15678 23
that men may dwell there, | and have it in pos-session.
347 258 16
37 The posterity also of his servants shall in-he-rit it : and
4 15678 23
they that love his Name shall dwell therein.

Ps. 70 *Deus in adiutorium* iij. 1 *or* iv. 5

347 258 16 4 15678
HAste thee, O God, to de-liv-er me : make haste to help
23
me, O Lord.

37 4 16
2 Let them be ashamed and confounded that seek af-ter my
258 4
soul : let them be turned backward and put to confusion that
15678 23
wish me evil.

347 16 258
3 Let them for their reward be soon brought to shame :
457 168 23
that cry o- ver me, There, there.

3 47 16
4 But let all those that seek thee be joy-ful and glad in
258
thee : and let all such as delight in thy salvation say alway, |
4 15678 23
The Lord be praised.

347 258 16 4 15678 23
5 As for me, I am poor and in mi-se-ry : haste thee un- to
me, O God.

347 12568 4
6 Thou art my helper, and my re-deem-er : O Lord, make
15678 23
no long tarrying.

At Mattins

DAY 14 Ps. 71 *In te, Domine, speravi* vj.

37
IN thee, O Lord, have I put my trust, | let me never be put
4 12568
to con- fu- sion : but rid me and deliver me in thy righ-
4 15678 23
teousness; incline thine ear un-to me, and save me.

37 4 16 258
2 Be thou my strong hold, whereunto I may al-way re-sort :
thou hast promised to help me, | for thou art my house of de-
4 15678 23
fence, and my castle.

37 4 12568
3 Deliver me, O my God, out of the hand of the un-god-
457 168 23
ly : out of the hand of the un-righ-teous and cruel man.

347 12568
4 For thou, O Lord God, art the thing that I long for :
·4 15678 23
thou art my hope, e- ven from my youth.

.37 4 16
5 Through thee have I been holden up ever since I was
258
born : thou art he that took me out of my mother's womb;
4 15678 23
my praise shall be al- ways of thee.

347 12568
6 I am become as it were a monster un-to ma-ny : but my
·4 15678 23
sure trust is in thee.

37 4 16 258
7 O let my mouth be fil-led with thy praise : that I may
4 15678 23
sing of thy glory and hon-our all the day long.

3 47 16 258
8 Cast me not away in the time of age : forsake me not
4 6 123578
when my strĕngth faileth me.

9 For mine enemies speak against me, | and they that lay
347 12568
wait for my soul take their counsel to-ge-ther, say-ing : God

hath forsaken him ; persecute him, and take him, | for there is
457 168 23
none to de-liver him.
37 4 16 258 457 168 23
10 Go not far from me, O God : my God, haste thee to
help me.
3 47 16
11 Let them be confounded and perish that are a-gainst my
258
soul : let them be covered with shame & dishonour | that seek
4 15678 23
to do me evil.
4 37 12568 4
12 As for me, I will patiently a-bide al- way : and will
15678 23
praise thee more and more.
347
13 My mouth shall daily speak of thy righteousness and
12568 4 15678 23
sal-va-tion : for I know no end thereof.
37 4 16 258
14 I will go forth in the strength of the Lord God : and
457 168 23
will make mention of thy righ-teous-ness only.
37 4 16
15 Thou, O God, hast taught me from my youth up un-til
258 457 168 23
now : therefore will I tell of thy wondrous works.
34
16 Forsake me not, O God, in mine old age, | when I am
7 12568
gray-head-ed : until I have shewed thy strength unto this ge-
4 6 123578
neration, | & thy power to all them that are yët for to come.
37 4 16 258
17 Thy righteousness, O God, is ve-ry high : & great things
4 15678 23
are they that thou hast done ; O God, who is like un-to thee ?
18 O what great troubles and adversities hast thou shewed
347 12568
me, | and yet didst thou turn and re-fresh me : yea, and
457 168 23
broughtest me from the deep of the earth again.

4 37 12568
19 Thou hast brought me to great hon- our : and comfort-
4 15678 23
ed me on every side.

20 Therefore will I praise thee in thy faithfulness, O God, |
347 12568
playing upon an instru-ment of mu-sick : unto thee will I sing
4 15678 23
upon the harp, | O thou Ho-ly One of Israel.
37 4 16 258
21 My lips will be fain, when I sing un-to thee : and so
4 15678 23
will my soul whom thou hast de-livered.
37 4 16
22 My tongue also shall talk of thy righteousness all the day
258
long : for they are confounded, and brought unto shame, | that
4 15678 23
seek to do me evil.

Ps. 72 *Deus iudicium* iij. 5

37 4 16 258
GIve the King thy judge-ments, O God : and thy righ-
4 15678 23
teousness un- to the King's son.
37 4 16 258
2 Then shall he judge thy people ac-cor-ding un-to right :
4 15678 23
— and de-fend the poor.
37 4 16 258
3 The mountains al-so shall bring peace : and the little hills
4 15678 23
righteousness un- to the people.
37 4 16 258
4 He shall keep the simple folk by their right : defend the
4 6 123578
children of the poor, | and pun-ish the wrōng doer.
347 12568
5 They shall fear thee, as long as the sun and moon en-dur-
4 15678 23
eth : from one genera-tion to an-other.

3 47 16 258
6 He shall come down like the rain in-to a fleece of wool :
4 68 157 23
even as the drops that wa-ter the earth.

347 12568
7 In his time shall the righ-teous flou-rish : yea, and abun-
4 15678 23
dance of peace, | so long as the moon en-dureth.

347
8 His dominion shall be also from the one sea to the
12568 4 15678 23
o- ther : and from the flood un- to the world's end.

347 12568
9 They that dwell in the wilderness shall kneel be-fore
4 15678 23
him : his en-e-mies shall lick the dust.

347 12568
10 The kings of Tharsis and of the isles shall give pre-
4 15678 23
sents : the kings of Arabia and Sa- ba shall bring gifts.

347 12568 4
11 All kings shall fall down be-fore him : all nations shall
15678 23
do him service.

347 12568
12 For he shall deliver the poor when he cri-eth : the needy
4 15678 23
also, and him that hath no helper.

37 4 12568
13 He shall be favourable to the sim-ple and nee-dy : and
4 6 123578
shall pre-serve the soüls of the poor.

37 4 16 258
14 He shall deliver their souls from false-hood and wrong :
4 15678 23
and dear shall their blood be in his sight.

37 4
15 He shall live, and unto him shall be given of the gold of
258 16
A-ra- bi-a : prayer shall be made ever unto him, | and daily
4 15678 23
shall he be praised.

37 4
16 There shall be an heap of corn in the earth, high up-on

16 258
the hills : his fruit shall shake like Libanus, | and shall be
4 15678 23
green in the city like grass up-on the earth.

17 His Name shall endure for ever; his Name shall remain
37 4 258 16
under the sun a-mong the pos- te- ri-ties : which shall be bles-
457 168 23
sed through him; and all the hea-then shall praise him.

347 258 16
18 Blessed be the Lord God, | even the God of Is- ra-el :
4 15678 23
which on-ly do- eth wondrous things.

347 12568
19 And blessed be the Name of his Majes-ty for ev- er : &
4 15678 23
all the earth shall be filled with his Majes-ty. A- men, Amen.

At Evensong

DAY 14 Ps. 73 *Quam bonus Israel* i. 4 *or* vij. 7

347 258 16 457
TRuly God is loving un-to Is- ra-el : even unto such as are
168 23
of a clean heart.

3 47 16 258 457 168
2 Nevertheless, my feet were al-most gone : my tread-ings
23
had well-nigh slipt.

347 12568
3 And-why I was grieved at the wick-ed : I do also see
4 15678 23
the ungodly in such pros-perity.

37 4 16 258 4 15678 23
4 For they are in no pe-ril of death : but are lus- ty and
strong.

37 4 16 258
5 They come in no mis-for-tune like o-ther folk : neither
457 168 23
are they pla-gued like other men.

37 4 16 258
6 And this is the cause that they are so hold-en with pride :
457 168 23
and over-whelm-ed with cruelty.

347 12568 4 15678 23
7 Their eyes swell with fat-ness : and they do e- ven
what they lust.

347 258 16
8 They corrupt other, and speak of wick-ed blas-phe-my :
4 15678 23
their talking is a-gainst the most High.

347 12568
9 For they stretch forth their mouth un-to the hea-ven :
.4 15678 23
and their tongue go- eth through the world.

347 258 16
10 Therefore fall the peo-ple un-to them : and thereout
4 15678 23
suck they no small ad-vantage.

347 12568
11 Tush, say they, | how should God per-ceive it : is there
4 15678 23
know-ledge in the most High?

12 Lo, these are the ungodly, | these prosper in the world,
347 12568
and these have riches in pos-ses-sion : and I said, | Then have
4 15678
I cleansed my heart in vain, and washed mine hands in in-
23
no-cency.

347 258 16
13 All the day long have I been pun-ish-ed : and chastened
457 168 23
ev- er- y morning.

37 4 16 258
14 Yea, and I had almost said e-ven as they : but lo, then I
4 15678 23
should have condemned the genera-tion of thy children.

37 4 16 258 4 15678 23
15 Then thought I to un-der-stand this : but it was too
hard for me,

37 4 16 258
16 Until I went into the sanc-tua-ry of God : then under-
4 15678 23
stood I the end of these men ;

37 4 12568
17 Namely, how thou dost set them in slip-pe-ry pla-ces :
·4 15678 23
and castest them down, and de-stroyest them.

37 4 16 258 457
18 O how sudden-ly do they con-sume : perish, and come
168 23
to a fearful end !

347 12568
19 Yea, even like as a dream when one a-wa-keth : so shalt
457 168 23
thou make their image to vanish out of the city.

347 12568 4 15678 23
20 Thus my heart was grie-ved : and it went e- ven
through my reins.

347 258 16 4 15678
21 So foolish was I, and ig-no-rant : even as it were a beast
23
be-fore thee.

37 4 16 258
22 Nevertheless, I am al-way by thee : for thou hast holden
4 15678 23
me by my right hand.

347 12568
23 Thou shalt guide me with thy coun-sel : and after that
457 168 23
re-ceive me with glory.

37 4 16 258
24 Whom have I in hea-ven but thee : and there is none
457 168 23
upon earth that I desire in com-pa- ri-son of thee.

4 37 12568
25 My flesh and my heart fail-eth : but God is the strength
457 168 23
of my heart, | and my por-tion for ever.

347 12568
26 For lo, they that forsake thee shall pe-rish : thou hast
457 168 23
destroyed all them that commit forni-ca-tion a-gainst thee.

27 But it is good for me to hold me fast by God, | to put my

37 4 16 258
trust in the Lord God : and to speak of all thy works in the
457 168 23
gates of the daugh-ter of Syon.

Ps. 74 *Ut quid, Deus* ij. 1 *or* iij. 5

37 4 16 258
O God, wherefore art thou absent from us so long : why is
457 168 23
thy wrath so hot against the sheep of thy pasture?

347 12568
2 O think upon thy con-gre-ga-tion : whom thou hast
4 15678 23
purchased, and re-deem-ed of old.

347 258 16
3 Think upon the tribe of thine in-he-ri-tance : and mount
4 15678 23
Syon, where-in thou hast dwelt.

37 4
4 Lift up thy feet, that thou mayest utterly destroy ev-er-y
258 16 4 15678 23
en- e-my : which hath done evil in thy sanc-tu-ary.

347 12568
5 Thine adversaries roar in the midst of thy con-gre-ga-
457 168 23
tions : and set up their ban-ners for tokens.

37 4 16 258
6 He that hewed timber afore out of the thick trees : was
4 68 157 23
known to bring it to an ex-cel-lent work.

37 4 16 258
7 But now they break down all the car-ved work there-of :
457 168 23
with ax- es and hammers.

347 12568
8 They have set fire upon thy ho-ly pla-ces : and have de-
457 168 23
filed the dwelling-place of thy Name, | e- ven un-to the ground.

9 Yea, they said in their hearts, | Let us make havock
347 12568
of them al-to-ge- ther : thus have they burnt up all the hou-
4 6 123578
ses of Göd in the land.

37 4 16 258
10 We see not our tokens, | there is not one pro-phet more :
4 15678 23
no, not one is there among us that un-der-stand-eth any more.

347 12568
11 O God, how long shall the adversary do this dis-hon-our :
4 15678 23
how long shall the enemy blaspheme thy Name, | for ever ?

37 4 16 258
12 Why with-draw-est thou thy hand : why pluckest thou
4 15678 23
not thy right hand out of thy bosom to con-sume the enemy ?

3 47 16 258
13 For God is my King of old : the help that is done upon
4 15678 23
earth, he do- eth it himself.

347 12568
14 Thou didst divide the sea through thy pow-er : thou
4 15678 23
brakest the heads of the dra-gons in the waters.

347 12568
15 Thou smotest the heads of Levia-than in pie-ces : and
4 15678 23
gavest him to be meat for the peo-ple in the wilderness.

37 4
16 Thou broughtest out fountains and waters out of the
16 258 4 15678 23
hard rocks : thou driedst up migh-ty waters.

3 47 16 258
17 The day is thine, and the night is thine : thou hast pre-
4 6 123578
par-ed the light and the sun.

37 4 16 258
18 Thou hast set all the bor-ders of the earth : thou hast
457 168 23
made sum-mer and winter.

347 12568
19 Remember this, O Lord, how the enemy hath re-bu-
4 15678 23
ked : and how the foolish people hath blas-phem-ed thy Name.

20 O deliver not the soul of thy turtle-dove unto the mul-
347 258 16
titude of the en- e-mies : and forget not the congregation of
4 15678 23
the poor for ever.

347 258 16
21 Look up-on the co-ve-nant : for all the earth is full of
4 15678 23
darkness, and cru-el ha- bi-tations.

347 12568
22 O let not the simple go a-way a-sha-med : but let the
·4 15678 23
poor and needy give praise un- to thy Name.

37 4 16 258
23 Arise, O God, main-tain thine own cause : remember
457 168 23
how the foolish man blas-phe-meth thee daily.

37 4 258 16
24 Forget not the voice of thine en- e-mies : the presump-
4 15678 23
tion of them that hate thee increa-seth ev- er more and more.

At Mattins

DAY 15 Ps. 75 *Confitebimur tibi* i. 2 *or* vj.

37 4 16 258 4 15678 23
UNto thee, O God, do we give thanks : yea, un-to thee do
we give thanks.

37 4 16 258 4 15678 23
2 Thy Name al-so is so nigh : and that do thy won-drous
works declare.

347 12568 4
3 When I receive the con-gre-ga- tion : I shall judge ac-
15678 23
cor-ding unto right.

37 4 16 258
4 The earth is weak, and all the in-ha-bi-ters there-of : I
4 15678 23
bear up the pil- lars of it.

347 12568
5 I said unto the fools, | Deal not so mad-ly : and to the
4 15678 23
ungod-ly, Set not up your horn.

37 4 16 258 4 15678 23
6 Set not up your horn on high : and speak not with a stiff
neck.

37 4 16
7 For promotion cometh neither from the east, nor from the
258 4 6 123578
west : — nor yët from the south.

37 4 16 258
8 And-why God is the Judge : he putteth down one, and
4 15678 23
set-teth up an-other.

3 47
9 For in the hand of the Lord there is a cup, and the wine
16 258 4 6 123578
is red : it is full mixt, | and he pour-eth oüt of the same.

37 4 16 258
10 As for the dregs there-of : all the ungodly of the earth
457 168 23
shall drink them, and suck them out.

347 12568 4 15678
11 But I will talk of the God of Ia-cob : and praise him
23
for ever.

37 4 16 258
12 All the horns of the ungodly al-so will I break : and the
4 15678 23
horns of the righteous shall be ex-alted.

Ps. 76 *Notus in Judea* viij. 1 *or* 2

37 4 16 258 4 15678 23
IN Jew-ry is God known : his Name is great in Israel.
347 12568 457 168 23
2 At Salem is his ta-ber-na-cle : and his dwel-ling in
Syon.

37 4 16 258
3 There brake he the ar-rows of the bow : the shield, the
4 15678 23
sword, and the battle.

37 4 16 258 457 168
4 Thou art of more hon-our and might : than the hills of
23
the robbers.

347 16 258
5 The proud are robbed, | they have slept their sleep : and
4 6 123578
all the men whose hands were migh-ty have foünd nothing.

347 12568 4
6 At thy rebuke, O God of Ia- cob : both the chariot and
15678 23
horse are fallen.

347 12568
7 Thou, even thou art to be fear-ed : and who may stand
4 15678 23
in thy sight when thou art angry ?

347 12568
8 Thou didst cause thy judgement to be heard from hea-
.4 15678 23
ven : the earth trem-bled, and was still,

347 12568 4
9 When God a-rose to judge-ment : and to help all the
15678 23
meek up-on earth.

37 4 16 258
10 The fierceness of man shall turn to thy praise : and the
4 15678 23
fierceness of them shalt thou refrain.

11 Promise unto the Lord your God, and keep it, | all ye
347 12568
that are round a-bout him : bring presents unto him that
457 168 23
ought to be feared.

37 4 12568
12 He shall refrain the spi-rit of prin-ces : and is wonderful
4 6 123578
a-mong the kings of the earth.

Ps. 77 *Voce mea ad Dominum* ii. 1

37 4 16 258
I Will cry unto God with my voice : even unto God will
4 15678 23
I cry with my voice, | and he shall hear-ken unto me.

3 47 16 258
2 In the time of my trou-ble I sought the Lord : my sore
4 15678 23
ran, and ceased not in the night-season ; my soul re- fu- sed
comfort.

37 4 16 258
3 When I am in heaviness, I will think up-on God : when
457 168 23
my heart is vex-ed, I will complain.

4 37 12568 4 15678
4 Thou holdest mine eyes wa-king : I am so fee-ble, that
23
I cannot speak.

3 47 16 258 4 15678 23
5 I have consider-ed the days of old : and the years that are
past.

37 4 16 258
6 I call to re-mem-brance my song : and in the night I
·4 15678 23
commune with my own heart, | and search out my spirits.

347 12568
7 Will the Lord absent him-self for ev- er : and will he be
4 15678 23
no more in-treated ?

347 12568
8 Is his mercy clean gone for ev- er : and is his promise
4 15678 23
come utterly to an end for evermore ?

347 12568
9 Hath God forgotten to be gra-cious : and will he shut up
4 15678 23
his loving-kind-ness in dis-pleasure ?

347 258 16
10 And I said, It is mine own in-fir-mi-ty : but I will
4 6 123578
remember the years of the right hand of the möst Highest.

37 4 16 258
11 I will remember the works of the Lord : and call to
457 168 23
mind thy won-ders of old time.

3 47 16 258
12 I will think al-so of all thy works : and my talking
4 15678 23
shall be of thy doings.

347 12568 4 15678
13 Thy way, O God, is ho-ly : who is so great a God
23
as our God ?

347 12568
14 Thou art the God that do-eth won-ders : and hast
4 15678 23
declared thy power a-mong the people.

347 12568
15 Thou hast mightily deliver-ed thy peo- ple : even the
4 15678 23
sons of Ia- cob and Ioseph.

37
16 The waters saw thee, O God, | the waters saw thee, and
4 16 258 4 15678 23
were a-fraid : the depths al- so were troubled.

4 37 258 16
17 The clouds poured out water, | the air thun-der-ed :
4 15678 23
and thine ar-rows went abroad.

37 4 16 258
18 The voice of thy thunder was heard round a-bout : the
457 168 23
lightnings shone upon the ground ; the earth was mov-ed and
shook withal.

3 4 7 12568
19 Thy way is in the sea, and thy paths in the great wa-
4 15678 23
ters : and thy foot-steps are not known.

37 4 16 258
20 Thou leddest thy peo-ple like sheep : by the hand of
457 168 23
Mo-ses and Aäron.

At Evensong

DAY 15 Ps. 78 *Attendite, populo* i.1 *or* ij.1

347 12568 4
HEar my law, O my peo-ple : incline your ears unto the
15678 23
words of my mouth.

347 258 16 4
2 I will open my mouth in a pa- ra-ble : I will declare hard
15678 23
sen-ten-ces of old ;

37 4 16 258
3 Which we have heard and known : and such as our
457 168 23
fa-thers have told us.

4 That we should not hide them from the children of the
37 4 16 258
gene-ra-tions to come : but to shew the honour of the Lord, |
4 15678 23
his mighty and wonder-ful works that he hath done.

37 4 16 258
5 He made a covenant with Iacob, and gave Is-ra-el a law :
4 15678 23
which he commanded their forefathers to teach their children.

347 12568 4
6 That their posteri-ty might know it : and the chil-dren
15678 23
which were yet unborn.

3 47 16 258
7 To the in-tent that when they came up : they might
4 6 123578
shew their chïl-dren the same.

37 4 16 258
8 That they might put their trust in God : and not to for-
4 15678 23
get the works of God, | but to keep his com-mandments.

9 And not to be as their forefathers, | a faithless & stubborn
347 12568
ge-ne-ra-tion : a generation that set not their heart aright, |
457 168 23
and whose spirit cleaveth not stead-fast-ly unto God.

37 4 258 16
10 Like as the chil-dren of Eph-ra-ym : who being harnes-
4 15678 23
sed, & carrying bows, | turned themselves back in the day of
battle.

37 4 16 258 4
11 They kept not the co-ve-nant of God : and would not
15678 23
walk in his law.

37 4 16 258
12 But for-gat what he had done : & the wonderful works
4 15678 23
that he had shew-ed for them.

13 Marvellous things did he in the sight of our forefathers, |
347 12568 4 15678 23
in the land of E-gypt : even in the field of Zoan.
37 4 16 258
14 He divided the sea, and let them go through : he made
4 6 123578
the wa-ters to ständ on an heap.
37 4 16 258
15 In the day-time also he led them with a cloud : and all
4 15678 23
the night through with a light of fire.
347 258 16
16 He clave the hard rocks in the wil-der-ness : and gave
457 168 23
them drink thereof, | as it had been out of the great depth.
37 4 16 258
17 He brought waters out of the sto-ny rock : so that it
4 15678 23
gushed out like the rivers.
347 12568
18 Yet for all this they sinned more a-gainst him : and pro-
4 15678 23
voked the most High-est in the wilderness.
37 4 16 258 4 15678
19 They tempted God in their hearts : and requir-ed meat
23
for their lust.
347 12568
20 They spake against God al-so, say-ing : Shall God pre-
4 15678 23
pare a ta-ble in the wilderness?

21 He smote the stony rock indeed, that the water gushed
37 4 16 258
out, | and the streams flow-ed with-al : but can he give bread
457 168 23
also, | or provide flesh for his people?
37 4 16 258
22 When the Lord heard this, he was wroth : so the fire
4
was kindled in Iacob, | and there came up heavy displea-sure
6 123578
a-gaïnst Israel.

37 4 16 258 4
23 Because they be-lie-ved not in God : and put not their
15678 23
trust in his help.

3 47 16 258 4
24 So he com-man-ded the clouds a-bove : and opened the
15678 23
doors of heaven.

37 4 16 258
25 He rained down manna also up-on them for to eat : and
4 15678 23
gave them food from heaven.

347 16 258 4 15678 23
26 So man did eat an-gels' food : for he sent them meat
enough.

347 12568
27 He caused the east wind to blow un-der hea-ven : and
457 168 23
through his power he brought in the south-west wind.

3 47 16 258
28 He rained flesh up-on them as thick as dust : and fea-
4 6 123578
thered fowls like as the sänd of the sea.

37 4 16 258 4
29 He let it fall a-mong their tents : even round about their
15678 23
ha- bi-tation.

3
30 So they did eat, and were well filled ; for he gave them
47 16 258 457 168 23
their own de-sire : they were not disap-point-ed of their lust.

31 But while the meat was yet in their mouths, | the heavy
37 4 12568
wrath of God came upon them, | & slew the weal-thi-est of
4 15678 23
them : yea, & smote down the chosen men that were in Israel.

37 4 16 258 4
32 But for all this they sin-ned yet more : and belie-ved
15678 23
not his wondrous works.

347 258 16
33 Therefore their days did he con-sume in va-ni-ty : and
4 15678 23
their years in trouble.

37 4 12568
34 When he slew them, they sought him : & turned them
4 15678 23
early, and in-quir-ed after God.

37 4 16 258
35 And they remembered that God was their strength : and
4 15678 23
that the high God was their re-deemer.

37 4 16 258
36 Nevertheless, they did but flat-ter him with their mouth :
4 15678 23
and dissem-bled with him in their tongue.

37 4 16 258
37 For their heart was not whole with him : neither con-
4 15678 23
tinued they sted-fast in his covenant.

347 12568
38 But he was so merciful, that he for-gave their mis-deeds :
4 15678 23
and de-stroy-ed them not.

37 4 16 258
39 Yea, many a time turned he his wrath a-way : & would
4 15678 23
not suffer his whole dis-plea-sure to arise.

3 47 16 258
40 For he considered that they were but flesh : and that
4 15678 23
they were even a wind that passeth away, & com-eth not again.

347 258 16
41 Many a time did they provoke him in the wil-der-ness :
4 15678 23
and grieved him in the desert.

3 47 16 258
42 They turned back, and temp-ted God : and moved the
4 15678 23
Ho-ly One in Israel.

37 4 16 258
43 They thought not of his hand : and of the day when he
457 168 23
delivered them from the hand of the enemy.

347 12568
44 How he had wrought his mira-cles in E- gypt : and his
4 15678 23
wonders in the field of Zoan.

37 4 16 258
45 He turned their wa-ters in-to blood : so that they might
457 168 23
not drink of the rivers.

37 4 16 258
46 He sent lice among them, and de-vour-ed them up : and
4 15678 23
frogs to de-stroy them.

347 12568
47 He gave their fruit unto the ca-ter-pil-ler : and their
4 6 123578
labour un-to the gräss-hopper.

347 12568
48 He destroyed their vines with hail-stones : and their
4 6 123578
mul-ber-ry-trëes with the frost.

37 4 12568
49 He smote their cattle al-so with hail-stones : and their
4 15678 23
flocks with hot thunder-bolts.

50 He cast upon them the furiousness of his wrath, | anger,
37 4 12568 457 168 23
dis-plea-sure, and trou-ble : and sent evil an-gels a-mong them.

3
51 He made a way to his indignation, | and spared not their
47 16 258 4 15678 23
soul from death : but gave their life o-ver to the pestilence.

37 4 12568
52 And smote all the first-born in E- gypt : the most prin-
4 15678 23
cipal and mightiest in the dwel-lings of Ham.

3 47 16 258
53 But as for his own people, he led them forth like sheep :
457 168 23
and carried them in the wil-der-ness like a flock.

3 47 16 258
54 He brought them out safely, that they should not fear :
457 168 23
and overwhelmed their en- e-mies with the sea.

347
55 And brought them within the borders of his sanc-tu-
12568 4 15678 23
a- ry : even to his mountain which he purchas-ed with his
right hand.

37 4 12568
56 He cast out the heathen al-so be-fore them : caused
their land to be divided among them for an heritage, | and
4 15678 23
made the tribes of Israel to dwell in their tents.

347 16 258
57 So they tempted, & displeased the most high God : and
4 15678 23
kept not his tes- ti-monies.

34 7 12568
58 But turned their backs, | & fell away like their fore- fa-
4 15678 23
thers : starting a-side like a broken bow.

34 7 12568
59 For they grieved him with their hill- al- tars : and pro-
4 15678 23
voked him to displea-sure with their images.

37 4 16 258
60 When God heard this, he was wroth : and took sore
457 168 23
dis-plea-sure at Israel.

37 4 12568
61 So that he forsook the taber-na-cle in Sy- lo : even the
457 168 23
tent that he had pitch-ed a-mong men.

37 4 258 16
62 He delivered their power in-to cap-ti- vi-ty : and their
4 68 157 23
beauty in-to the en- e-mies' hand.

37 4 16 258
63 He gave his people over also un-to the sword : and was
4 15678 23
wroth with his in-heritance.

37 4 16 258
64 The fire con-su-med their young men : and their mai-
457 168 23
dens were not giv- en to marriage.

37 4 16 258
65 Their priests were slain with the sword : and there were
.4 15678 23
no widows to make la- men-tation.

37 4 16 258
66 So the Lord awaked as one out of sleep : and like a
4 15678 23
giant re-fresh-ed with wine.

37 4 16 258
67 He smote his enemies in the hind-er parts : and put
4 68 157 23
them to a per-pe- tu-al shame.

37 4 12568
68 He refused the taber-na-cle of Io-seph : and chose not
4 15678 23
the tribe of Ephraym.

347 12568 4
69 But chose the tribe of Iu-da : even the hill of Sy-on
15678 23
which he loved.

37 4 16 258
70 And there he built his tem-ple on high : and laid the
4 15678 23
foundation of it | like the ground which he hath made con-
tinually.

37 4 12568 ·4
71 He chose David al-so his ser-vant : and took him a-way
15678 23
from the sheep-folds.

37 4
72 As he was following the ewes great with young ones he
12568 4
took him : that he might feed Iacob his people, and Isra-el
15768 23
his in-heritance.

37 4 16 258
73 So he fed them with a faith-ful and true heart : and
4 15678 23
ruled them prudently with all his power.

At Mattins

DAY 16 Ps. 79 *Deus, venerunt* i. 4 *or* iv. 6

347 258 16
O God, the heathen are come into thine in-he- ri-tance :
thy holy temple have they defiled, | and made Hieru-
4 15678 23
sa-lem an heap of stones.

2 The dead bodies of thy servants have they given to be

37 4 16 258
meat unto the fowls of the air : and the flesh of thy saints un-
4 6 123578
to the beästs of the land.

37 4
3 Their blood have they shed like water on every side of
258 16 457 168 23
Hie-ru-sa-lem : and there was no man to bury them.

347 258 16
4 We are become an open shame to our en- e-mies : a very
4 15678 23
scorn and derision unto them that are round a-bout us.

347 12568
5 Lord, how long wilt thou be an- gry : shall thy jealousy
4 15678 23
burn like fire for ever?

347
6 Pour out thine indignation upon the heathen that have
12568 457
not known thee : and upon the kingdoms that have not cal-
168 23
led up-on thy Name.

347 12568 4 15678 23
7 For they have de-vour-ed Ia- cob : and laid waste his
dwelling-place.

37
8 O remember not our old sins, | but have mercy up-on us,
4 16 258 4 6 123578
and that soon : for we are come to grëat misery.

37 4 16
9 Help us, O God of our salvation, | for the glo-ry of thy
258 .4 15678 23
Name : O deliver us, and be merciful unto our sins, for thy
Name's sake.

37 4 16 258 4 15678 23
10 Wherefore do the hea-then say : — Where is now
their God?

37 4 16 258
11 O let the vengeance of thy servants' blood that is shed :
457 168 23
be openly shewed upon the hea-then in our sight.

347
12 O let the sorrowful sighing of the prisoners come be-

12568
fore thee : according to the greatness of thy power, | preserve
4 15678 23
thou those that are ap-poin-ted to die.

347
13 And for the blasphemy wherewith our neighbours have
258 16
blas-phe-med thee : reward thou them, O Lord, seven-fold
4 15678 23
in- to their bosom.

14 So we that are thy people, and sheep of thy pasture, |
347 12568
shall give thee thanks for ev- er : and will alway be shewing
4 15678 23
forth thy praise | from generation to ge- ne-ration.

Ps. 80 *Qui regis Israel* iij. 1 *or* 5

HEar, O thou Shepherd of Israel, | thou that leadest
37 4 16 258
Io-seph like a sheep : shew thyself also, thou that sit-
4 15678 23
test up- on the Cherubyn.

347 12568
2 Before Ephraym, Beniamin, and Ma-nas-ses : stir up thy
4 15678 23
strength, and come and help us.

3 47 16 258
3 Turn us a-gain, O God : shew the light of thy counte-
4 15678 23
nance, and we shall be whole.

37 4 16 258
4 O Lord God of hosts : how long wilt thou be angry
457 168 23
with thy peo-ple that prayeth ?

3 47 16 258
5 Thou feedest them with the bread of tears : and givest
4 15678 23
them plen-teous- ness of tears to drink.

347 12568
6 Thou hast made us a very strife un-to our neigh-bours :
4 15768 23
and our ene-mies laugh us to scorn.

37 4 16 258
7 Turn us a-gain, thou God of hosts : shew the light of
4 15678 23
thy countenance, and we shall be whole.

347 12568
8 Thou hast brought a vine out of E-gypt : thou hast cast
457 168 23
out the hea-then, and planted it.

347 258 16 4
9 Thou ma-dest room for it : and when it had taken root
68 157 23
it fill-ed the land.

347 12568
10 The hills were covered with the sha-dow of it : and
4 15678 23
the boughs thereof were like the good-ly cedar-trees.

37 4 16 258
11 She stretched out her branches un-to the sea : and her
4 15678 23
boughs un- to the river.

37 4 16 258
12 Why hast thou then bro-ken down her hedge : that all
4 15678 23
they that go by pluck off her grapes ?

37 4 16 258
13 The wild boar out of the wood doth root it up : and
4 15678 23
the wild beasts of the field de-vour it.

347
14 Turn thee again, thou God of hosts, | look down from
12568 4 15678 23
hea-ven : behold, and vi- sit this vine ;

347
15 And the place of the vineyard that thy right hand hath
12568 4 15678 23
plan-ted : & the branch that thou madest so strong for thyself.

37 4 16 258
16 It is burnt with fire, and cut down : and they shall pe-
457 168 23
rish at the re-buke of thy countenance.

37 4 12568
17 Let thy hand be upon the man of thy right hand : and
457 168 23
upon the son of man, | whom thou madest so strong for thine
own self.

37 4 16 258
18 And so will not we go back from thee : O let us live, |
457 168 23
and we shall call up-on thy Name.

37 4 16 258
19 Turn us again, O Lord God of hosts : shew the light
4 15678 23
of thy countenance, and we shall be whole.

Ps. 81 *Exultate Deo* vij. 7

347 16 258
SIng we merrily unto God our strength : make a cheerful
4 15678 23
noise unto the God of Iacob.

37 4 12568 4 6
2 Take the psalm, bring hi-ther the ta- bret : the mer-ry
123578
härp with the lute.

37 4 16 258
3 Blow up the trumpet in the new moon : even in the
4 15678 23
time appointed, | and upon our so- lemn feast-day.

37 4 258 16
4 For this was made a sta-tute for Is- ra-el : and a law of
4 15678 23
the God of Iacob.

347 12568
5 This he ordained in Ioseph for a tes-ti-mo-ny : when
4 6 123578
he came out of the land of Egypt, | and had heard a stränge
language.

347 12568
6 I eased his shoulder from the bur-then : and his hands
4 68 157 23
were deliver-ed from ma-king the pots.

37 4 16
7 Thou calledst upon me in troubles, and I de-li-ver-ed
258 4 15678 23
thee : and heard thee what time as the storm fell up-on thee.

37 4 12568 4 15678 23
8 I pro-ved thee al- so : at the wa- ters of strife.

37 4 12568
9 Hear, O my people, and I will as-sure thee : O Israel, if
4 15678 23
thou wilt heark-en unto me,

347 12568
10 There shall no strange god be in thee : neither shalt
4 15678 23
thou wor-ship a- ny other god.

11 I am the Lord thy God, | who brought thee out of the
347 12568 4 15678 23
land of E- gypt : open thy mouth wide, and I shall fill it.

37 4 16 258
12 But my people would not hear my voice : and Israel
4 15678 23
would not o-bey me.

347 16 258
13 So I gave them up unto their own hearts' lusts : and
4 15678 23
let them follow their own i- ma- gi-nations.

37 4 16 258
14 O that my people would have hear-kened un-to me :
457 168 23
for if Israel had walk-ed in my ways,

347 258 16
15 I should soon have put down their en- e-mies : and
4 15678 23
turned my hand against their ad-ver-saries.

4 37 12568
16 The haters of the Lord should have been found li-
457 168 23
ars : but their time should have en-dur-ed for ever.

37 4 16
17 He should have fed them also with the fi-nest wheat-
258 4
flour : and with honey out of the stony rock should I have
15678 23
sa- tis-fied thee.

At Evensong

DAY 16 Ps. 82 *Deus stetit* iv. 4 *or* viij. 2

37 4 12568 4
GOd standeth in the congre-ga-tion of prin-ces : he is a
15678 23
Judge a-mong gods.

347 12568
2 How long will ye give wrong judge-ment : and accept
457 168 23
the persons of the un-godly ?

347 258 16
3 Defend the poor and fa-ther-less : see that such as are in
457 168 23
need and ne-ces- si- ty have right.

37 4 16 258
4 Deliver the out-cast and poor : save them from the hand
457 168 23
of the un-godly.

5 They will not be learned nor understand, | but walk on
347 12568 4 15678 23
still in dark-ness : all the foundations of the earth are out of
course.

37 4 16 258 4
6 I have said, Ye are gods : and ye are all the children of
6 123578
the möst Highest.

3 47 16 258 457 168 23
7 But ye shall die like men : & fall like one of the princes.

37 4 16 258
8 Arise, O God, and judge thou the earth : for thou shalt
4 15678 23
take all heathen to thine in-heritance.

Ps. 83 *Deus, quis similis* iij. 5

347 12568
HOld not thy tongue, O God, keep not still si- lence : re-
·4 15678 23
frain not thy-self, O God.

347 258 16
2 For lo, thine enemies make a mur-mur-ing : and they
4 15678 23
that hate thee have lift up their head.

347 12568
3 They have imagined craftily a-gainst thy peo-ple : and
4 15678 23
taken counsel a-gainst thy secret ones.

4 They have said, Come, and let us root them out, | that

347 12568
they be no more a peo- ple : and that the name of Israel may
4 15678 23
be no more in re-membrance.

3 47 16
5 For they have cast their heads to-ge-ther with one con-
258 4 15678 23
sent : and are confe-de-rate a-gainst thee.

347 258 16
6 The tabernacles of the Edomites, and the Is-mael-ites :
4 15678 23
the Mo-ab-ites, and Hagarens.

347 258 16 4
7 Gebal, and Am-mon, and A-ma-lech : the Philistins, with
15678 23
them that dwell at Tyre.

347 12568 4
8 Assur also is join-ed with them : and have holpen the
15678 23
chil-dren of Lot.

37 4 258 16
9 But do thou to them as un-to the Ma-dian-ites : unto
4 15678 23
Sisera, and unto Iabyn at the brook of Kyson.

347 12568 4 6 123578
10 Who perish-ed at En-dor : and became as the düng of
the earth.

37 4 16 258
11 Make them and their princes like O-reb and Zeb : yea,
4 15678 23
make all their princes like as Ze- ba and Sálmana.

37 4 16 258 4
12 Who say, Let us take to our-selves : the houses of God
15678 23
in pos-session.

37 4 16 258
13 O my God, make them like un-to a wheel : and as the
457 168 23
stub-ble be-fore the wind.

37 4 16 258
14 Like as the fire that burn-eth up the wood : and as the
457 168 23
flame that con-su-meth the mountains.

347 12568
15 Persecute them even so with thy tem-pest : and make
4 15678 23
them a-fraid with thy storm.

37 4 16 258 4 15678 23
16 Make their faces a-sha-med, O Lord : that they may
seek thy Name.

37 4 16
17 Let them be confounded and vexed ev-er more and
258 4 15678 23
more : let them be put to shame, and perish.

347 12568
18 And they shall know that thou, whose Name is Ie-ho-
4 15678 23
va : art only the most High-est o- ver all the earth.

Ps. 84 *Quam dilecta* i. 2

347 12568 4 15678 23
O How amiable are thy dwell-ings : — — thou Lord
of hosts !

37
2 My soul hath a desire & longing to enter into the courts
4 16 258 4 15678 23
of the Lord : my heart and my flesh re-joice in the living
God.

3 Yea, the sparrow hath found her an house, | and the
37 4 16 258
swallow a nest where she may lay her young : even thy
4 15678 23
altars, O Lord of hosts, | my King and my God.

37 4 16 258 4
4 Blessed are they that dwell in thy house : they will be
15678 23
al-way praising thee.

37 4 16 258 4
5 Blessed is the man whose strength is in thee : in whose
15678 23
heart are thy ways.

37 4 16 258
6 Who going through the vale of misery use it for a well :
457 168 23
and the pools are fil- led with water.

347 16 258
7 They will go from strength to strength : and unto the
4 15678 23
God of gods appeareth every one of them in Syon.
347 16 258 4 15678
8 O Lord God of hosts, hear my prayer : hearken, O God
23
of Iacob.
347 12568
9 Behold, O God our de-fen-der : and look upon the face
4 15678 23
of thine An-ointed.
37 4 16 258 4 15678 23
10 For one day in thy courts : is bet-ter than a thousand.
37 4 16 258
11 I had rather be a door-keeper in the house of my God :
4 15678 23
than to dwell in the tents of un-godliness.
37 4 16 258
12 For the Lord God is a light and de-fence : the Lord
will give grace and worship, | and no good thing shall he with-
4 15678 23
hold from them that live a godly life.
37 4 16 258 457 168
13 O Lord God of hosts : blessed is the man that put-teth
23
his trust in thee.

Ps. 85 *Benedixisti, Domine* ij.1 *or* viij.1

37 4 16 258
LOrd, thou art become gracious un-to thy land : thou hast
4 15678 23
turned away the capti-vi- ty of Iacob.
347 12568 457
2 Thou hast forgiven the offence of thy peo-ple : and co-
168 23
ver-ed all their sins.
347 12568
3 Thou hast taken away all thy dis-plea-sure : and turned
4 15678 23
thyself from thy wrath-ful in- dig-nation.
347 12568 4 15678 23
4 Turn us then, O God our Sa-viour : & let thine an- ger
cease from us.

347 12568
5 Wilt thou be displeased at us for ev- er : and wilt thou
4 15678 23
stretch out thy wrath from one genera-tion to an-other ?
347 258 16
6 Wilt thou not turn a-gain, and quick-en us : that thy
4 15678 23
peo-ple may re-joice in thee ?
37 4 16 258 4 15678 23
7 Shew us thy mer-cy, O Lord : & grant us thy sal-vation.
347 258 16
8 I will hearken what the Lord God will say con-cer-ning
me : for he shall speak peace unto his people, | and to his
4 6 123578
saints, that they türn not again.
347 12568
9 For his salvation is nigh them that fear him : that glory
4 15678 23
may dwell in our land.
347 12568
10 Mercy and truth are met to-ge- ther : righteousness
457 168 23
and peace have kis-sed each other.
37 4 16 258
11 Truth shall flourish out of the earth : and righteousness
4 15678 23
hath look-ed down from heaven.
347 12568
12 Yea, the Lord shall shew lov-ing-kind-ness : and our
4 15678 23
land shall give her increase.
347 12568
13 Righteousness shall go be-fore him : and he shall direct
4 15678 23
his go- ing in the way.

At Mattins

DAY 17 Ps. 86 *Inclina, Domine* i. 4

347 12568
BOw down thine ear, O Lord, and hear me : for I am
.4 15678 23
poor, and in misery.

347 12568
2 Preserve thou my soul, for I am ho- ly : my God, save
457 168 23
thy servant that put-teth his trust in thee.
3 47 16 258 457 168
3 Be merciful un-to me, O Lord : for I will call dai- ly
23
up-on thee.

37 4 12568
4 Comfort the soul of thy ser-vant : for unto thee, O Lord,
4 15678 23
do I lift up my soul.

347 12568
5 For thou, Lord, art good and gra-cious : and of great
4 15678 23
mercy unto all them that call up-on thee.
37 4 16 258
6 Give ear, Lord, un-to my prayer : and ponder the voice
4 68 157 23
of my hum-ble desires.

37 4 16 258 4 6
7 In the time of my trouble I will call up-on thee : — for
123578
thöu hearest me.

3 47 16 258
8 Among the gods there is none like un-to thee, O Lord :
4 15678 23
there is not one that can do as thou dost.

3
9 All nations whom thou hast made shall come and wor-
47 16 258 457 168 23
ship thee, O Lord : and shall glo- ri- fy thy Name.
37 4 16 258 4
10 For thou art great, and do-est won-drous things : —
15678 23
thou art God alone.

37 4 16
11 Teach me thy way, O Lord, | and I will walk in thy
258 4 15678 23
truth : O knit my heart unto thee, that I may fear thy

Name.

3 47 16 258
12 I will thank thee, O Lord my God, with all my heart :
4 15678 23
and will praise thy Name for evermore.

37 4 12568
13 For great is thy mer-cy to-ward me : and thou hast deli-
4 15678 23
vered my soul from the ne-ther-most hell.

37 4 12568
14 O God, the proud are ri-sen a-gainst me : and the con-
gregations of naughty men have sought after my soul, | and
4 15678 23
have not set thee be-fore their eyes.

37 4
15 But thou, O Lord God, art full of com-pas-sion and
12568 4 15678 23
mer-cy : long-suffering, | plenteous in good-ness and truth.

37 4 12568
16 O turn thee then unto me, | and have mer-cy up-on
457
me : give thy strength unto thy servant, | and help the son
168 23
of thine handmaid.

17 Shew some token upon me for good, | that they who
347 12568
hate me may see it, and be a-sha-med : because thou, Lord,
4 68 157 23
hast holpen me, and com-fort-ed me.

Ps. 87 *Fundamenta eius* iv. 5 *or* v. 2

3 47 16 258
HEr foundations are up-on the ho-ly hills : the Lord
457 168 23
loveth the gates of Syon more than all the dwell-ings of
Iacob.

37 4 16 258 4 15678 23
2 Very excellent things are spo-ken of thee : thou ci- ty
of God.

347 258 16 4 15678
3 I will think upon Ra-hab and Ba-by-lon : with them
23
that know me.

347 12568
4 Behold ye the Phi-lis-tins al-so : and they of Tyre, with
4 15678 23
the Morians ; lo, there was he born.

37 4 16 258
5 And of Syon it shall be reported that he was born in her :
4 15678 23
and the most High shall stablish her.

347 12568
6 The Lord shall rehearse it when he writeth up the peo-
4 15678 23
ple : that he was born there.

37 4 16 258
7 The singers also and trumpeters shall he re-hearse : All
4 15678 23
my fresh springs shall be in thee.

Ps. 88 *Domine Deus* vij. I

347
O Lord God of my salvation, | I have cried day & night be-
12568
fore thee : O let my prayer enter into thy presence, |
4 15678 23
incline thine ear un-to my calling.

347 12568 4
2 For my soul is full of trou-ble : and my life draw-eth
15678 23
nigh un-to hell.

37 4 16 258
3 I am counted as one of them that go down in-to the pit :
4 15678 23
and I have been even as a man that hath no strength.

4 Free among the dead, | like unto them that are wounded,
37 4 16 258
and lie in the grave : who are out of remembrance, | and are
4 15678 23
cut a-way from thy hand.

3 47 16 258 457
5 Thou hast laid me in the low-est pit : in a place of dark-
168 23
ness, and in the deep.

347 12568
6 Thine indignation lieth hard up-on me : and thou hast
4 15678 23
vex-ed me with all thy storms.

3. 47 16 258
7 Thou hast put away mine ac-quain-tance far from me :
4 15678 23
and made me to be ab-hor-red of them.
347 12568 4 15678 23
8 I am so fast in pri-son : that I can-not get forth.
347 12568
9 My sight faileth for ve-ry trou-ble : Lord, I have called
4 15678 23
daily upon thee, | I have stretched forth my hands un-to thee.
37 4 16 258
10 Dost thou shew won-ders a-mong the dead : or shall the
4 15678 23
dead rise up a- gain, and praise thee ?

37 4 16 258
11 Shall thy loving-kindness be shew-ed in the grave : or
4 15678 23
thy faithful-ness in de-struction ?

37 4 16 258
12 Shall thy wondrous works be known in the dark : and
4 15678 23
thy righteousness in the land where all things are for-gotten ?
37 4 16 258
13 Unto thee have I cri-ed, O Lord : and early shall my
4 15678 23
prayer come be-fore thee.
37 4 16 258 4 15678
14 Lord, why ab-hor-rest thou my soul : and hi-dest thou
23
thy face from me ?

3 47
15 I am in misery, | and like unto him that is at the point
16 258 4
to die : even from my youth up | thy terrors have I suffer-ed
15678 23
with a troubled mind.

347 258 16
16 Thy wrathful displeasure go-eth o- ver me : and the fear
4 15678 23
of thee hath un-done me.

37 4 12568
17 They came round about me dai-ly like wa-ter : and com-
457 168 23
passed me to-ge-ther on every side.

37 4 16 258
18 My lovers and friends hast thou put a-way from me :
4 15678 23
and hid mine acquain-tance out of my sight.

At Evensong

DAY 17 PS. 89 *Misericordias Domini* i. 2 *or* vj.

37 4 16
MY song shall be alway of the loving-kind-ness of the
258
Lord : with my mouth will I ever be shewing thy
4 15678 23
truth | from one genera-tion to an-other.

347 12568
2 For I have said, | Mercy shall be set up for ev-er : thy
4 15678 23
truth shalt thou stab-lish in the heavens.

347 12568
3 I have made a covenant with my cho-sen : I have sworn
4 15678 23
unto Da-vid my servant.

37 4 12568
4 Thy seed will I stab-lish for ev-er : and set up thy
4 15678 23
throne from one genera-tion to an-other.

37 4 16
5 O Lord, the very heavens shall praise thy won-drous
258 4 15678 23
works : and thy truth in the con-gre-ga-tion of the saints.

37 4 16 258
6 For who is he a-mong the clouds : that shall be com-
457 168 23
par-ed un-to the Lord ?

37 4 16 258 4 15678 23
7 And what is he a-mong the gods : that shall be like un-
to the Lord ?

37 4 16
8 God is very greatly to be feared in the coun-cil of the
258 4 15678
saints : and to be had in reverence of all them that are round
23
a-bout him.

37 4 16 258
9 O Lord God of hosts, who is like un-to thee : thy truth,
.4 15678 23
most mighty Lord, is on every side.

37 4 16 258
10 Thou rulest the ra-ging of the sea : thou stillest the
4 15678 23
waves there- of when they arise.

347 258 16
11 Thou hast subdued Egypt, and de-stroy-ed it : thou
4 15678 23
hast scattered thine enemies a-broad with thy mighty arm.

37 4 16 258
12 The heavens are thine, | the earth al-so is thine : thou
4 15678 23
hast laid the foundation of the round world, and all that
therein is.

37 4 16 258
13 Thou hast made the north and the south : Tabor and
4 15678 23
Hermon shall re-joice in thy Name.

37 4 16 258 457
14 Thou hast a migh-ty arm : strong is thy hand, and high
168 23
is thy right hand.

37 4 16 258
15 Righteousness & equity are the habi-ta-tion of thy seat :
4 15678 23
mercy and truth shall go be-fore thy face.

37 4 16 258
16 Blessed is the people, O Lord, that can re-joice in thee :
457 168 23
they shall walk in the light of thy countenance.

37 4 16 258
17 Their delight shall be dai-ly in thy Name : and in thy
4 15678 23
righteous-ness shall they make their boast.

37 4 16 258
18 For thou art the glo-ry of their strength : and in thy
4 15678 23
loving-kindness thou shalt lift up our horns.

37 4 16 258
19 For the Lord is our de-fence : the Holy One of Is-
4 15678 23
ra- el is our King.

347
20 Thou spakest sometime in visions unto thy saints, and
12568
said-est : I have laid help upon one that is mighty; I have ex-
457 168 23
alted one chosen out of the people.

347 12568
21 I have found Da-vid my ser-vant : with my holy oil
4 15678 23
have I an-ointed him.

3 47 16 258 4 15678 23
22 My hand shall hold him fast : & my arm shall strength-
en him.

347 258 16
23 The enemy shall not be able to do him vi- o-lence : the
4 15678 23
son of wicked-ness shall not hurt him.

3 47 16 258 ·4
24 I will smite down his foes be-fore his face : and plague
15678 23
them that hate him.

347 12568
25 My truth also and my mercy shall be with him : and in
457 168 23
my Name shall his horn be ex-alted.

37 4 16 258 4 15678
26 I will set his dominion al-so in the sea : and his right
23
hand in the floods.

347 12568
27 He shall call me, | Thou art my Fa-ther : my God,
4 15678 23
and my strong sal-vation.

347 12568 4 6
28 And I will make him my first-born : higher than the
123578
kïngs of the earth.

37 4 16 258
29 My mercy will I keep for him for ev-er-more : and my
4 6 123578
cove-nant shall ständ fast with him.

347 12568
30 His seed also will I make to en-dure for ev-er : and his
4 15678 23
throne as the days of heaven.

347 16 258 4 15678
31 But if his children for-sake my law : and walk not in
23
my judgements ;

347 12568
32 If they break my statutes, | and keep not my com-mand-
4
ments : I will visit their offences with the rod, | and their
15678 23
sin with scourges.

37 4
33 Nevertheless, my loving-kindness will I not ut-terly take
16 258 457 168 23
from him : nor suf-fer my truth to fail.

34 My covenant will I not break, | nor alter the thing
37 4 16 258
that is gone out of my lips : I have sworn once by my holi-
4 15678 23
ness, that I will not fail David.

347 12568
35 His seed shall en-dure for ev- er : and his seat is like as
4 15678 23
the sun be-fore me.

37 4 16 258
36 He shall stand fast for ever-more as the moon : and as
457 168 23
the faithful wit-ness in heaven.

347 12568
37 But thou hast abhorred and forsaken thine An-oin-ted :
4 15678 23
and art dis-plea-sed at him.

347 12568
38 Thou hast broken the covenant of thy ser- vant : and
4 6 123578
cast his cröwn to the ground.

347 12568 4
39 Thou hast overthrown all his hedg-es : and bro-ken
15678 23
down his strong-holds.

347 12568
40 All they that go by spoil him : and he is become a re-
4 15678 23
proach to his neighbours.

347 258 16
41 Thou hast set up the right hand of his en-e-mies : and
4 15678 23
made all his ad-ver-sa- ries to rejoice.

37 4 16 258
42 Thou hast taken away the edge of his sword : & givest
4 15678 23
him not victo-ry in the battle.

347 12568 4 .6 123578
43 Thou hast put out his glo-ry : and cast his throne döwn
to the ground.

347 258 16
44 The days of his youth hast thou shor-ten-ed : & covered
4 15678 23
him with dis-honour.

347 12568
45 Lord, how long wilt thou hide thy-self, for ev- er : and
4 6 123578
shall thy wräth burn like fire ?

347 12568
46 O remember how short my time is : wherefore hast
4 6 123578
thou made äll men for naught ?

37 4 16 258
47 What man is he that liveth, and shall not see death :
4 15678 23
and shall he deliver his soul from the hand of hell ?

347 258 16
48 Lord, where are thy old lov-ing-kind-nes-ses : which
457 168 23
thou swarest unto Da- vid in thy truth ?

3 47 16 258
49 Remember, Lord, the rebuke that thy ser-vants have :
4 15678 23
and how I do bear in my bosom the rebukes of ma-ny
people ;

50 Wherewith thine enemies have blasphemed thee, | and
347 12568
slandered the footsteps of thine An-oin-ted : Praised be the
4 15678 23
Lord for evermore. A-men, and Amen.

At Mattins

DAY 18 Ps. 90 *Domine, refugium* iv. 5 *or* vj.

347 12568 4
O Lord, thou hast been our re- fuge : from one genera-tion
15678 23
to an-other.

2 Before the mountains were brought forth, | or ever the
347 16 258
earth and the world were made : thou art God from everlast-
4 15678 23
ing, and world with-out end.
37 4 12568
3 Thou turnest man to de-struc-tion : again thou sayest, |
4 15678 23
Come a-gain, ye chil-dren of men.
347 258 16
4 For a thousand years in thy sight are but as yes-ter-day :
4 6 123578
seeing that is past as a wätch in the night.
37 4 16 258
5 As soon as thou scatterest them they are e-ven as a sleep :
457 168 23
and fade away sud-den-ly like the grass.
37 4 16 258
6 In the morning it is green, and grow-eth up : but in the
4 15678 23
evening it is cut down, | dri-ed up, and withered.
347 12568
7 For we consume away in thy dis-plea-sure : and are afraid
4 15678 23
at thy wrath-ful in- dig-nation.
347 12568
8 Thou hast set our mis-deeds be-fore thee : and our secret
457 168 23
sins in the light of thy countenance.
3 47 16 258
9 For when thou art angry all our days are gone : we bring
4 68 157 23
our years to an end, | as it were a tale that is told.

10 The days of our age are threescore years and ten ; and
3 47 16 258
though men be so strong that they come to four-score years :

yet is their strength then but labour and sorrow ; so soon
4 15678 23
passeth it a- way, and we are gone.
37 4 16 258
11 But who regardeth the pow-er of thy wrath : for even
4 15678 23
thereafter as a man feareth, | so is thy dis-pleasure.
37 4 16 258
12 So teach us to num-ber our days : that we may apply
4 15678 23
our hearts un- to wisdom.
37 4 16 258
13 Turn thee again, O Lord, at the last : and be gracious
4 15678 23
un- to thy servants.
37 4 16 258
14 O satisfy us with thy mer-cy, and that soon : so shall
4 15678 23
we rejoice and be glad all the days of our life.
347
15 Comfort us again now, after the time that thou hast
258 16 4 15678
pla-gued us : and for the years wherein we have suf-fer- ed
23
ad-versity.
37 4 16 258 457 168 23
16 Shew thy ser-vants thy work : and their chil-dren thy
glory.
347
17 And the glorious Majesty of the Lord our God be up-
12568
on us : prosper thou the work of our hands upon us, | O
4 15678 23
pros-per thou our handiwork.

Ps. 91 *Qui habitat* ij.1 *or* viij.1

37 4 16 258
WHoso dwelleth under the de-fence of the most High :
457 168 23
shall abide under the shadow of the Al-mighty.
347
2 I will say unto the Lord, | Thou art my hope, and my
12568 4 15678 23
strong-hold : my God, in him will I trust.

37 4 12568
3 For he shall deliver thee from the snare of the hun-ter :
4 15678 23
and from the noi- some pestilence.

4 He shall defend thee under his wings, | and thou shalt be
37 4 12568
safe un-der his fea-thers : his faithfulness and truth shall be
4 15678 23
thy shield and buckler.

37 4 16 258
5 Thou shalt not be afraid for any ter-ror by night : nor
4 15678 23
for the arrow that fli- eth by day ;

37 4 12568
6 For the pestilence that walk-eth in dark-ness : nor for
4 15678 23
the sickness that destroy-eth in the noon-day.

37 4
7 A thousand shall fall beside thee, | and ten thousand at thy
16 258 4 15678 23
right hand : but it shall not come nigh thee.

37 4 16 258
8 Yea, with thine eyes shalt thou be-hold : and see the re-
457 168 23
ward of the un-godly.

37 4 16 258
9 For thou, Lord, art my hope : thou hast set thine house
4 6 123578
of de-fënce very high.

37 4 16 258
10 There shall no evil hap-pen un-to thee : neither shall
4 15678 23
any plague come nigh thy dwelling.

37 4 16 258 457
11 For he shall give his angels charge o-ver thee : to keep
168 23
thee in all thy ways.

37 4 16 258
12 They shall bear thee in their hands : that thou hurt not
4 15678 23
thy foot a-gainst a stone.

37 4 12568
13 Thou shalt go upon the li-on and ad- der : the young
·4 15678 23
lion and the dragon shalt thou tread un- der thy feet.

14 Because he hath set his love upon me, | therefore will
347 258 16 457 168 23
I de-li-ver him : I will set him up, be-cause he hath known
my Name.

347 12568
15 He shall call upon me, and I will hear him : yea, I am
457 168 23
with him in trouble; I will deliver him, and bring him to
honour.

347 12568 4 15678
16 With long life will I sa-tis-fy him : and shew him my
23
sal-vation.

Ps. 92 *Bonum est confiteri* v. 2 *or* viij. 2

37 4 16 258
IT is a good thing to give thanks un-to the Lord : and to
.4 15678 23
sing praises un-to thy Name, O most Highest.

347 12568
2 To tell of thy loving-kindness early in the morn-ing :
4 6 123578
and of thy truth in the nïght-season.

37 4 16 258
3 Upon an instrument of ten strings, and up-on the lute :
4 15678 23
upon a loud instru-ment, and up-on the harp.

37 4 16 258
4 For thou, Lord, hast made me glad through thy works : &
457 168 23
I will rejoice in giving praise for the ope-ra-tions of thy hands.

37 4 16 258 4 15678 23
5 O Lord, how glo-rious are thy works : thy thoughts are
very deep.

347 258 16
6 An unwise man doth not well con-si-der this : and a fool
4 15678 23
doth not un-der-stand it.

7 When the ungodly are green as the grass, | and when all
347 12568
the workers of wicked-ness do flou-rish : then shall they be

457 168
destroyed for ever ; but thou, Lord, art the most High-est
23
for evermore.

347
8 For lo, thine enemies, O Lord, | lo, thine ene-mies shall
12568 4 15678 23
pe-rish : and all the workers of wickedness shall be destroyed.

37 4 258 16
9 But mine horn shall be exalted like the horn of an u-ni-
457 168 23
corn : for I am an-oin-ted with fresh oil.

347 258 16
10 Mine eye also shall see his lust of mine en- e- mies : &
·4 15678 23
mine ear shall hear his desire of the wicked that a-rise up a-
gainst me.

347 12568
11 The righteous shall flourish like a palm-tree : and shall
457 168 23
spread abroad like a ce- dar in Libanus.

37 4 16 258
12 Such as are planted in the house of the Lord : shall
4 15678 23
flourish in the courts of the house of our God.

37 4 16 258
13 They also shall bring forth more fruit in their age :
4 6 123578
and shall be fat and wëll-liking.

347 12568
14 That they may shew how true the Lord my strength is :
457 168 23
and that there is no un-righ-teous-ness in him.

At Evensong

DAY 18 Ps. 93 *Dominus regnavit* viij. I *or* 2

37 4 12568
THE Lord is King, and hath put on glo-ri-ous ap- pa-rel :
457 168 23
the Lord hath put on his apparel, and gird-ed him-
self with strength.

347 16 258 457 168
2 He hath made the round world so sure : that it can-not
23
be moved.

347 12568
3 Ever since the world began hath thy seat been pre-par-ed :
4 15678 23
thou art from ev- er-lasting.

37 4
4 The floods are risen, O Lord, | the floods have lift up
16 258 4 15678 23
their voice : the floods lift up their waves.

34 7 258 16
5 The waves of the sea are mighty, and rage hor-ri-bly :
4 15678 23
but yet the Lord, who dwelleth on high, is mightier.

37 4 16 258
6 Thy testimonies, O Lord, are ve-ry sure : holiness be-
4 15678 23
cometh thine house for ever.

Ps. 94 *Deus ultionum* ij. 1 *or* v. 2

37 4 12568
O Lord God, to whom ven-geance be-long-eth : thou
4 15678 23
God, to whom vengeance be-long-eth, shew thyself.

37 4 16 258
2 Arise, thou Judge of the world : and reward the proud
4 15678 23
af-ter their de-serving.

37 4 12568
3 Lord, how long shall the un-god-ly : how long shall the
4 15678 23
un-god- ly triumph ?

347 258 16
4 How long shall all wicked doers speak so dis-dain-ful-ly :
4 6 123578
and make such pröud boasting ?

37 4 16 258 457 168
5 They smite down thy peo-ple, O Lord : and trou-ble
23
thine heritage.

347 12568 4
6 They murder the widow, and the stran-ger : and put the
15678 23
fa- ther-less to death.

37 4 16 258
7 And yet they say, | Tush, the Lord shall not see : nei-
4 15678 23
ther shall the God of Ia- cob re-gard it.

347 12568
8 Take heed, ye unwise a-mong the peo-ple : O ye fools,
4 15678 23
when will ye understand?

37 4 16 258
9 He that planted the ear, shall he not hear : or he that
4 15678 23
made the eye, shall he not see?

347 12568
10 Or he that nurtur-eth the hea-then : it is he that teach-
457 168 23
eth man knowledge, | shall not he punish?

3 47 16 258 4 15678 23
11 The Lord know-eth the thoughts of man : — that they
are but vain.

37 4 16 258
12 Blessed is the man whom thou cha-sten-est, O Lord :
4 15678 23
and teach-est him in thy law.

37 4 258
13 That thou mayest give him patience in time of ad-ver-
16 457 168 23
si-ty : until the pit be digged up for the un-godly.

347 12568
14 For the Lord will not fail his peo-ple : neither will he
4 15678 23
for-sake his in-heritance;

347 12568
15 Until righteousness turn again un-to judge-ment : all
4 15678 23
such as are true in heart shall follow it.

347 12568
16 Who will rise up with me a-gainst the wick-ed : or who
4 15678 23
will take my part against the e- vil-doers?

347 258 16
17 If the Lord had not help-ed me : it had not failed but
4 15678 23
my soul had been put to silence.

347 12568 4 6
18 But when I said, My foot hath slip-ped : thy mer-cy, O
123578
Lörd, held me up.

37 4 16 258
19 In the multitude of the sorrows that I had in my heart :
4 15678 23
thy comforts have re-fresh-ed my soul.

347 258
20 Wilt thou have any thing to do with the stool of wick-
16 4 15678 23
ed-ness : which imagi-neth mis-chief as a law ?

37 4 12568
21 They gather them together against the soul of the righ-
4 68 157 23
teous : and con-demn the in-no-cent blood.

347 12568
22 But the Lord is my re-fuge : and my God is the
457 168 23
strength of my confidence.

23 He shall recompense them their wickedness, | and de-
34 7 12568 4 15678
stroy them in their own ma-lice : yea, the Lord our God shall
23
de-stroy them.

At Mattins

DAY 19 Ps. 95 *Venite, exultemus* iij. 5 *or* vj.

37 4 16 258
O Come, let us sing un-to the Lord : let us heartily rejoice
4 15678 23
in the strength of our sal-vation.

347 12568
2 Let us come before his presence with thanks-giv-ing :
4 15678 23
and shew our-selves glad in him with psalms.

37 4 16 258 457 168 23
3 For the Lord is a great God : and a great King a-bove
all gods.

37 4 16 258
4 In his hand are all the cor-ners of the earth : and the
4 6 123578
strength of the hills is hïs also.
347 12568 457 168
5 The sea is his, and he made it : and his hands pre-par-ed
23
the dry land.
37 4 16 258
6 O come, let us wor-ship and fall down : and kneel before
4 15678 23
the Lord our Maker.
3 47 16 258
7 For he is the Lord our God : and we are the people of
4 15678 23
his pasture, | and the sheep of his hand.
37 4 16 258
8 To-day if ye will hear his voice, hard-en not your hearts :
4 15678 23
as in the provocation, | and as in the day of tempta-tion in the
wilderness;
347 258 16 4 15678 23
9 When your fa-thers temp-ted me : prov-ed me, and saw
my works.
37 4
10 Forty years long was I grieved with this gene-ra-tion,
16 258 4
and said : It is a people that do err in their hearts, | for they
15678 23
have not known my ways.
37 4 16 258
11 Unto whom I sware in my wrath : that they should not
4 15678 23
en-ter in- to my rest.

Ps. 96 *Cantate Domino* viij.1

37 4 16 258 ·4
O Sing unto the Lord a new song : sing unto the Lord,
15678 23
all the whole earth.
3 47 16 258
2 Sing unto the Lord, and praise his Name : be telling of
457 168 23
his sal-va-tion from day to day.

347 12568
3 Declare his honour un-to the hea-then : and his wonders
4 6 123578
un-to äll people.

347 12568
4 For the Lord is great, and cannot worthi-ly be prai-sed :
457 168 23
he is more to be fear-ed than all gods.

347 12568
5 As for all the gods of the heathen, they are but i- dols :
4 15678 23
but it is the Lord that made the heavens.

347 12568
6 Glory and worship are be-fore him : power and honour
4 15678 23
are in his sanc-tu-ary.

347 12568
7 Ascribe unto the Lord, O ye kindreds of the peo-ple :
457 168 23
ascribe unto the Lord wor-ship and power.

37 4 16 258
8 Ascribe unto the Lord the honour due un-to his Name :
4 15678 23
bring presents, and come in-to his courts.

37 4 258 16
9 O worship the Lord in the beau-ty of ho- li-ness : let the
4 15678 23
whole earth stand in awe of him.

347 16 258
10 Tell it out among the heathen that the Lord is King :
and that it is he who hath made the round world so fast
4
that it cannot be moved ; and how that he shall judge the
15678 23
peo- ple righteously.

347 16 258
11 Let the heavens rejoice, and let the earth be glad : let
4 15678 23
the sea make a noise, and all that therein is.

37 4 12568
12 Let the field be joyful, and all that is in it : then shall
4 15678 23
all the trees of the wood re-joice be-fore the Lord.

3 47 16 258
13 For he cometh, | for he com-eth to judge the earth :

4 15678 23
and with righteousness to judge the world, | and the peo-ple
with his truth.

Ps. 97 *Dominus regnavit* i. 2

37 4 16 258
THe Lord is King, the earth may be glad there-of : yea,
.4 15678 23
the multitude of the isles may be glad thereof.

347 12568
2 Clouds and darkness are round a-bout him : righteousness
4 15678 23
and judgement are the ha-bi- ta- tion of his seat.

347 12568 4
3 There shall go a fire be-fore him : and burn up his en-e-
15678 23
mies on every side.

37 4 16 258 457
4 His lightnings gave shine un-to the world : the earth saw
168 23
it, and was afraid.

37 4 16 258
5 The hills melted like wax at the pre-sence of the Lord :
457 168 23
at the presence of the Lord of the whole earth.

37 4 258 16
6 The heavens have de-clar-ed his righ-teous-ness : and all
4 15678 23
the people have seen his glory.

7 Confounded be all they that worship carved images, | and
37 4 16 258 4 6 123578
that de-light in vain gods : wor-ship hïm, all ye gods.

347 12568
8 Syon heard of it, and re-joi-ced : and the daughters of
4 15678 23
Iuda were glad, | because of thy judge-ments, O Lord.

37 4 16 258
9 For thou, Lord, art higher than all that are in the earth :
457 168 23
thou art exalted far a-bove all gods.

37
10 O ye that love the Lord, | see that ye hate the thing
4 12568
which is e- vil : the Lord preserveth the souls of his saints;

457 168 23
he shall deliver them from the hand of the un-godly.

37 4 12568
11 There is sprung up a light for the righ-teous : and joy-
4 6 123578
ful gladness for such as are trüe-hearted.

347 12568
12 Rejoice in the Lord, ye righ-teous : and give thanks for
4 15678 23
a remem-brance of his holiness.

At Evensong

DAY 19 Ps. 98 *Cantate Domino* i. 4 *or* vj.

37 4 16 258 4 68 157
O Sing unto the Lord a new song : for he hath done mar-
23
vel-lous things.

3 47 16 258
2 With his own right hand, and with his ho-ly arm : hath
4 15678 23
he gotten him-self the victory.

347 12568
3 The Lord declared his sal-va-tion : his righteousness hath
457 168 23
he openly shewed in the sight of the heathen.

4 He hath remembered his mercy and truth toward the
347 258 16
house of Is- ra-el : and all the ends of the world have seen the
457 168 23
sal-va-tion of our God.

347 16 258
5 Shew yourselves joyful unto the Lord, all ye lands : sing,
4 15678 23
re-joice, and give thanks.

37 4 16 258
6 Praise the Lord up-on the harp : sing to the harp with a
4 15678 23
psalm of thanks-giving.

37 4 16 258
7 With trumpets al-so, and shawms : O shew yourselves
4 15678 23
joyful be-fore the Lord the King.

37 4 16 258
8 Let the sea make a noise, and all that there-in is : the
4 15678 23
round world, and they that dwell therein.

9 Let the floods clap their hands, | & let the hills be joyful
37 4 16 258 4 15678 23
to-ge-ther be-fore the Lord : for he is come to judge the earth.
3 47 16 258
10 With righteousness shall he judge the world : and the
457 168 23
peo-ple with equity.

Ps. 99 *Dominus regnavit* iij. 2 *or* iv. 1

347 12568
THe Lord is King, be the people never so un- pa- tient :
4
he sitteth between the Cherubyn, | be the earth ne-ver
15678 23
so un-quiet.
347 12568 4 15678 23
2 The Lord is great in Sy-on : and high a-bove all people.
37 4 16 258
3 They shall give thanks un-to thy Name : which is great,
4 15678 23
won-der-ful, and holy.
347
4 The King's power loveth judgement ; thou hast pre-par-
258 16 4
ed e-qui-ty : thou hast executed judgement and righ-teous-
15678 23
ness in Iacob.
347 16 258
5 O magnify the Lord our God : and fall down before his
4 15678 23
foot-stool, for he is holy.

6 Moses and Aäron among his priests, | and Samuel among
37 4 16 258 ·4 15678
such as call up-on his Name : these called upon the Lord, and
23
he heard them.
347 12568
7 He spake unto them out of the clou-dy pil-lar : for

457 168 23
they kept his testimonies, | and the law that he gave them.

347 16 258
8 Thou heardest them, O Lord our God : thou forgavest
4 15678 23
them, O God, | and punishedst their own in-ventions.

37
9 O magnify the Lord our God, | and worship him up-on
4 16 258 4 15678 23
his ho-ly hill : for the Lord our God is holy.

Ps. 100 *Jubilate Deo* v. 2 *or* viij. 2

347 16 258
O Be joyful in the Lord, all ye lands : serve the Lord with
4 15678 23
gladness, | and come before his pre- sence with a song.

2 Be ye sure that the Lord he is God ; it is he that hath
37 4 16 258
made us, and not we our-selves : we are his people, | and the
457 168 23
sheep of his pasture.

3 O go your way into his gates with thanksgiving, | and
3 47 16 258 ·4
in-to his courts with praise : be thankful unto him, and speak
15678 23
good of his Name.

347 12568
4 For the Lord is gracious, | his mercy is ev-er-last-ing :
4 15678 23
and his truth endureth from generation to ge- ne-ration.

Ps. 101 *Misericordiam et iudicium* i. 2 *or* vij. 2

37 4 12568
MY song shall be of mer-cy and judge-ment : unto thee,
4 15678 23
O Lord, will I sing.

347 12568 4 15678 23
2 O let me have un-der-stan-ding : in the way of godliness.

37 4 16 258
3 When wilt thou come un-to me : I will walk in my
4 15678 23
house with a perfect heart.

37 4
4 I will take no wicked thing in hand ; I hate the sins of
258 16 4 15678 23
un-faith-ful-ness : there shall no such cleave un-to me.

347 16 258
5 A froward heart shall de-part from me : I will not know
4 15678 23
a wick-ed person.

347 12568 4 15678 23
6 Whoso privily slander-eth his neigh-bour : — him will
I destroy.

4 37 12568 4
7 Whoso hath also a proud look and high sto-mach : I
15678 23
will not suffer him.

37 4 16 258
8 Mine eyes look upon such as are faith-ful in the land :
4 15678 23
that they may dwell with me.

3 47 16 258 4 15678 23
9 Whoso lead-eth a god-ly life : he shall be my servant.

37 4 16 258
10 There shall no deceitful person dwell in my house : he
457 168 23
that telleth lies shall not tar- ry in my sight.

37 4 16
11 I shall soon destroy all the ungodly that are in the
258 4 15678 23
land : that I may root out all wicked doers from the ci- ty
of the Lord.

At Mattins

DAY 20 Ps. 102 *Domine, exaudi* ij. 1

347 16 258 4 15678 23
HEar my prayer, O Lord : and let my cry-ing come un-
to thee.

37 4 12568
2 Hide not thy face from me in the time of my trou-ble :
457 168 23
incline thine ear unto me when I call ; O hear me, and that
right soon.

3 47 16 258
3 For my days are con-su-med a-way like smoke : and my
4 15678 23
bones are burnt up as it were a fire-brand.

37 4 16 258
4 My heart is smitten down, and wi-ther-ed like grass : so
4 15678 23
that I for-get to eat my bread.

37 4 12568 ·4
5 For the voice of my groan-ing : my bones will scarce
15678 23
cleave to my flesh.

347 258 16
6 I am become like a pelican in the wil-der-ness : and like
4 15678 23
an owl that is in the desert.

347 12568
7 I have watched, | and am even as it were a spar-row :
4 15678 23
that sitteth alone up- on the house-top.

37 4 16 258
8 Mine enemies revile me all the day long : and they that
457 168 23
are mad upon me are sworn to-ge-ther a-gainst me.

37 4 16 258
9 For I have eaten ashes as it were bread : and mingled
4 15678 23
my drink with weeping.

37 4 16 258
10 And that because of thine indig-na-tion and wrath : for
4 15678 23
thou hast taken me up, and cast me down.

347 12568 457 168 23
11 My days are gone like a sha-dow : and I am wi-ther-ed
like grass.

347 12568
12 But thou, O Lord, shalt en-dure for ev-er : and thy
·4 15678 23
remembrance throughout all ge- ne-rations.

347 12568
13 Thou shalt arise, and have mer-cy up-on Sy-on : for it
4 15678 23
is time that thou have mercy upon her, | yea, the time is come.

37 4 16 258
14 And-why thy servants think up-on her stones : and it
4 15678 23
pitieth them to see her in the dust.

37 4 16 258
15 The heathen shall fear thy Name, O Lord : and all the
4 15678 23
kings of the earth thy Majesty ;

347 12568 4
16 When the Lord shall build up Sy-on : and when his
15678 23
glo- ry shall appear ;

4 37 258
17 When he turneth him unto the prayer of the poor de-
16 457 168 23
sti-tute : and de-spi-seth not their desire.

347 12568
18 This shall be written for those that come af- ter : and
4 15678 23
the people which shall be born shall praise the Lord.

347 12568
19 For he hath looked down from his sanc-tu- a- ry : out
4 15678 23
of the heaven did the Lord be-hold the earth ;

347
20 That he might hear the mournings of such as are in
258 16 4 15678 23
cap- ti- vi-ty : and deliver the children ap-point-ed unto death.

347 12568
21 That they may declare the Name of the Lord in Sy-on :
4 15678 23
and his wor-ship at Hie-rusalem ;

347 12568
22 When the people are gather-ed to-ge- ther : and the
457 168 23
kingdoms al- so, to serve the Lord.

347 12568
23 He brought down my strength in my jour-ney : and
457 168 23
shor-ten-ed my days.

37
24 But I said, | O my God, take me not away in the midst
4 16 258 4
of mine age : as for thy years, | they endure throughout all
15678 23
ge- ne-rations.

37
25 Thou, Lord, in the beginning hast laid the foun-da-tion
4 16 258 4 15678 23
of the earth : and the heavens are the work of thy hands.
37 4 16 258
26 They shall perish, but thou shalt en-dure : they all shall
4 15678 23
wax old as doth a garment ;

27 And as a vesture shalt thou change them, | and they
347 12568 4 15678
shall be chan-ged : but thou art the same, | and thy years
23
shall not fail.
347 12568
28 The children of thy servants shall con-tin-ue : and
4 15678 23
their seed shall stand fast in thy sight.

Ps. 103 *Benedic, anima mea* vj. *or* viij. 2

347 16 258 4
PRaise the Lord, O my soul : and all that is within me
15678 23
praise his holy Name.
347 16 258 4 15678 23
2 Praise the Lord, O my soul : and forget not all his
benefits ;
3 47 16 258 457 168
3 Who for-giv-eth all thy sin : and healeth all thine
23
in-firmities ;
347 12568
4 Who saveth thy life from de-struc-tion : and crowneth
4 15678 23
thee with mercy and lov-ing-kindness ;
37 4 16 258
5 Who satisfieth thy mouth with good things : making
4 15678 23
thee young and lus-ty as an eagle.
347 12568
6 The Lord executeth righteous-ness and judge-ment : for
4 15678 23
all them that are op-pres-sed with wrong.

347 12568
7 He shewed his ways un-to Mo-ses : his works unto the
457 168 23
chil-dren of Israel.

37 4 12568
8 The Lord is full of com-pas-sion and mer-cy : long-suf-
4 6 123578
fering, and of grëat goodness.

37 4 12568
9 He will not al-way be chi-ding : neither keepeth he his
457 168 23
an-ger for ever.

37 4 16 258
10 He hath not dealt with us af-ter our sins : nor rewarded
4 15678 23
us according to our wick-ed-nesses.

37 4 16
11 For look how high the heaven is in com-pa-rison of the
258 4 15678 23
earth : so great is his mercy also to-ward them that fear him.

37 4 16 258
12 Look how wide also the east is from the west : so far
4 15678 23
hath he set our sins from us.

4 37 12568
13 Yea, like as a father pitieth his own chil-dren : even so
4 15678 23
is the Lord merciful un-to them that fear him.

37 4 16 258
14 For he knoweth where-of we are made : he remember-
4 15678 23
eth that we are but dust.

37 4 16 258
15 The days of man are but as grass : for he flourisheth as
4 15678 23
a flow-er of the field.

37 4 16 258
16 For as soon as the wind goeth o-ver it, it is gone : and
4 15678 23
the place thereof shall know it no more.

17 But the merciful goodness of the Lord endureth for ever
347 12568
and ever upon them that fear him : and his righteousness up-
4 15678 23
on chil-dren's children.

347 258 16
18 Even upon such as keep his co-ve-nant : and think up-
457 168 23
on his com-mand-ments to do them.

347 12568
19 The Lord hath prepared his seat in hea-ven : and his
4 15678 23
king-dom ru-leth over all.

3 47 16
20 O praise the Lord, ye angels of his, | ye that ex-cel in
258
strength : ye that fulfil his commandment, | and hearken un-
4 15678 23
to the voice of his words.

37 4 16 258
21 O praise the Lord, all ye his hosts : ye servants of his
4 15678 23
that do his pleasure.

22 O speak good of the Lord, all ye works of his, | in all
347 12568 4 6 123578
places of his do-min-ion : praise thou the Lörd, O my soul.

At Evensong

DAY 20 Ps. 104 *Benedic, anima mea* i. 2 *or* ij.

347 16 258
PRaise the Lord, O my soul : O Lord my God, thou art
become exceeding glorious ; thou art clothed with ma-
4 15678 23
jes-ty and honour.

347 12568
2 Thou deckest thyself with light, as it were with a gar-
4 15678 23
ment : and spreadest out the hea-vens like a curtain.

347 12568
3 Who layeth the beams of his chambers in the wa-ters :
4 6
and maketh the clouds his chariot, | and walketh up-on the
123578
wïngs of the wind.

347 12568 4 15678 23
4 He maketh his an-gels spi-rits : and his mi-ni-sters a
flaming fire.

37 4 16 258
5 He laid the foun-da-tions of the earth : that it never
4 15678 23
should move at any time.

347 12568
6 Thou coveredst it with the deep, | like as with a gar-
4 6 123578
ment : the wa-ters ständ in the hills.

3 47 16 258 457 168
7 At thy re-buke they flee : at the voice of thy thun-der
23
they are afraid.

37
8 They go up as high as the hills, | and down to the val-
4 16 258 4 15678
leys be-neath : even unto the place which thou hast ap-point-
23
ed for them.

3 47 16
9 Thou hast set them their bounds which they shall not
258 4 68 157 23
pass : neither turn a-gain to co-ver the earth.

347 12568 4 15678
10 He sendeth the springs in-to the ri- vers : which run
23
a-mong the hills.

347 16 258 4 15678 23
11 All beasts of the field drink there-of : & the wild ass- es
quench their thirst.

347
12 Beside them shall the fowls of the air have their ha-bi-
12568 4 15678 23
ta- tion : and sing a-mong the branches.

37 4 16 258
13 He watereth the hills from a-bove : the earth is filled
4 15678 23
with the fruit of thy works.

347 12568
14 He bringeth forth grass for the cat-tle : and green herb
4 15678 23
for the ser- vice of men ;

15 That he may bring food out of the earth, | and wine
37 4 16 258
that maketh glad the heart of man : and oil to make him a
4 15678 23
cheerful countenance, | and bread to streng-then man's heart.
3 47 16 258
16 The trees of the Lord al-so are full of sap : even the
4 15678 23
cedars of Libanus which he hath planted ;
37 4 16 258
17 Wherein the birds make their nests : and the fir-trees
4 15678 23
are a dwell-ing for the stork.
37 4 16 258
18 The high hills are a refuge for the wild goats : and so
4 15678 23
are the stony rocks for the conies.
347 12568
19 He appointed the moon for cer-tain sea-sons : and the
457 168 23
sun know-eth his going down.
37 4 16 258
20 Thou makest darkness that it may be night : wherein
4 15678 23
all the beasts of the for- est do move.
37 4 16 258 4 15678 23
21 The lions roaring af-ter their prey : do seek their meat
from God.
347 12568
22 The sun ariseth, and they get them a-way to-ge- ther :
4 15678 23
and lay them down in their dens.
347 12568 4
23 Man goeth forth to his work, and to his la-bour : un-
15678 23
til the evening.
37 4 16 258
24 O Lord, how ma-nifold are thy works : in wisdom
457 168 23
hast thou made them all ; the earth is full of thy riches.
347 12568
25 So is the great and wide sea al-so : wherein are things
4 15678 23
creeping innumerable, | both small and great beasts.

347 258 10
26 There go the ships, and there is that Le-vi- a-than :
4 15678 23
whom thou hast made to take his pas-time therein.

37 4 16 258
27 These wait all up-on thee : that thou mayest give them
4 6 123578
meat in düe season.

347 258 16
28 When thou givest it them they ga-ther it : and when
4 15678 23
thou openest thy hand, they are fil- led with good.

347 12568
29 When thou hidest thy face, they are trou-bled : when
4 15678
thou takest away their breath they die, | & are turned a-gain
23
to their dust.

37 4 17
30 When thou lettest thy breath go forth they shall be
258 4 6 123578
made : and thou shalt re-new the fäce of the earth.

347 12568
31 The glorious Majesty of the Lord shall en-dure for ev-
4 15678 23
er : the Lord shall re-joice in his works.

37 4 16 258
32 The earth shall tremble at the look of him : if he do
4 6 123578
but touch the hïlls, they shall smoke.

37 4 16 258
33 I will sing unto the Lord as long as I live : I will praise
4 15678 23
my God while I have my being.

4 37 12568 4 6 123578
34 And so shall my words please him : my joy shall bë in
the Lord.

35 As for sinners, they shall be consumed out of the
37 4 16 258
earth, | and the ungodly shall come to an end : praise thou
4 6 123578
the Lord, O my söul, praise the Lord.

At Mattins

DAY 21 Ps. 105 *Confitemini Domino* iij. 1 *or* 5

37 4 16 258
O Give thanks unto the Lord, and call up-on his Name :
4 15678 23
tell the people what things he hath done.

347 12568
2 O let your songs be of him, and praise him : and let
4 15678 23
your talking be of all his wondrous works.

37 4 16 258 4
3 Rejoice in his ho-ly Name : let the heart of them re-
15678 23
joice that seek the Lord.

37 4 16 258 4 6 123578
4 Seek the Lord and his strength : seek his fäce evermore.

37 4 16 258
5 Remember the marvellous works that he hath done : his
4 15678 23
wonders, and the judge-ments of his mouth,

347 12568 4
6 O ye seed of Abra-ham his ser- vant : ye children of Ia-
15678 23
cob his chosen.

347 16 258 4 15678 23
7 He is the Lord our God : his judge-ments are in all
the world.

347 12568
8 He hath been alway mindful of his cove-nant and pro-
4 15678 23
mise : that he made to a thou-sand ge- ne-rations ;

347 258 16
9 Even the covenant that he made with A-bra-ham : and
4 15678 23
the oath that he sware un- to Isaac ;

37 4 16 258
10 And appointed the same unto Ia-cob for a law : and to
4 15678 23
Israel for an ev-er-last-ing testament ;

347 258 16
11 Saying, Unto thee will I give the land of Cha-na-an :
4 15678 23
the lot of your in-heritance ;

347 258 16 .4
12 When there were yet but a few of them : and they
15678 23
stran-gers in the land ;

347 12568
13 What time as they went from one nation to an-o-
4 15678 23
ther : from one kingdom to an- o- ther people ;

3 47 16 258
14 He suffered no man to do them wrong : but reproved
4 15678 23
e-ven kings for their sakes ;

347 12568 4 15678 23
15 Touch not mine An-oin-ted : and do my pro-phets
no harm.

37 4 16 258
16 Moreover, he called for a dearth up-on the land : and
4 15678 23
destroyed all the pro- vi- sion of bread.

347 12568
17 But he had sent a man be-fore them : even Ioseph, who
4 6 123578
was sold to be a bönd-servant ;

37 4 16 258 4
18 Whose feet they hurt in the stocks : the iron enter-ed
15678 23
in- to his soul ;

3 47 16 258
19 Until the time came that his cause was known : the
4 6 123578
word of the Lörd tried him.

37 4 16 258
20 The king sent, and de-li-ver-ed him : the prince of the
4 15678 23
peo-ple let him go free.

37 4 16 258 4 15678
21 He made him lord al-so of his house : and ruler of all
23
his substance ;

37 4 16 258
22 That he might inform his princes af-ter his will : and
457 168 23
teach his se- na-tors wisdom.

347 12568
23 Israel also came in-to E-gypt : and Iacob was a stran-
4 15678 23
ger in the land of Ham.

37 4 258 16
24 And he increased his peo-ple ex-ceed-ing-ly : and made
4 15678 23
them strong-er than their enemies ;

37 4 12568
25 Whose heart turned, | so that they ha-ted his peo-ple :
4 15678 23
and dealt untru-ly with his servants.

37 4 12568 4
26 Then sent he Mo-ses his ser-vant : and Aäron whom
15678 23
he had chosen.

37 4 12568
27 And these shewed his to-kens a-mong them : and won-
4 15678 23
ders in the land of Ham.

3 47 16 258
28 He sent dark-ness, and it was dark : and they were not
4 15678 23
obedi-ent un- to his word.

37 4 16 258 4 15678 23
29 He turned their wa-ters in-to blood : — — and slew
their fish.

3 47 16 258 4 6
30 Their land brought forth frogs : yea, even in their
123578
kïngs' chambers.

37 4 16 258
31 He spake the word, and there came all man-ner of flies :
4 15678 23
and lice in all their quarters.

37 4 16 258 4 15678
32 He gave them hail-stones for rain : and flames of fire
23
in their land.

37 4 12568
33 He smote their vines al-so and fig-trees : and destroyed
4 15678 23
the trees that were in their coasts.

34 He spake the word, and the grass-hoppers came, | and
347 12568
caterpillers in-nu-me- ra- ble : and did eat up all the grass in
4 15678 23
their land, | and devoured the fruit of their ground.

37 4 16 258 4
35 He smote all the first-born in their land : even the
15678 23
chief of all their strength.

37 4 16 258
36 He brought them forth also with sil-ver and gold :
457 168 23
there was not one feeble per-son a-mong their tribes.

347 12568 4 15678
37 Egypt was glad at their de-part-ing : for they were
23
a-fraid of them.

347 258 16
38 He spread out a cloud to be a co-ver-ing : and fire to
4 6 123578
give light in the nïght-season.

37 4 16 258
39 At their de-sire he brought quails : and he filled them
4 15678 23
with the bread of heaven.

37 4
40 He opened the rock of stone, | and the wa-ters flow-
16 258 4 6 123578
ed out : so that rivers ran in the drÿ places.

347 12568
41 For-why he remembered his ho-ly pro-mise : and A-
4 15678 23
bra-ham his servant.

37 4 16 258
42 And he brought forth his peo-ple with joy : and his
457 168 23
cho-sen with gladness ;

37 4 12568
43 And gave them the lands of the hea-then : and they
4 15678 23
took the labours of the peo-ple in pos-session ;

347 12568 4 15678 23
44 That they might keep his sta- tutes : — and ob-serve
his laws.

At Evensong

DAY 21 Ps. 106 *Confitemini Domino.* ij.1 *or* vj.

347 12568
O Give thanks unto the Lord, for he is gra-cious : and
457 168 23
his mercy en-dur-eth for ever.

37 4 16 258 4 15678
2 Who can express the noble acts of the Lord : or shew
23
forth all his praise ?

37 4 12568 4 6
3 Blessed are they that al-way keep judge-ment : — and
123578
dö righteousness.

4 Remember me, O Lord, | according to the favour that
347 12568 4 15678 23
thou bearest un-to thy peo-ple : O visit me with thy sal-
vation ;

347 12568
5 That I may see the felicity of thy cho-sen : and rejoice
4 15678
in the gladness of thy people, | and give thanks with thine
23
in-heritance.

347 12568
6 We have sinned with our fa- thers : we have done
4 6 123578
a-miss, and deält wickedly.

7 Our fathers regarded not thy wonders in Egypt, | neither
347 12568
kept they thy great goodness in re-mem-brance : but were
4 15678 23
disobedient at the sea, | e-ven at the Red sea.

37 4 16 258
8 Nevertheless, he helped them for his Name's sake : that
4 15678 23
he might make his pow- er to be known.

37 4 16 258
9 He rebuked the Red sea also, and it was dri-ed up : so

4 15678 23
he led them through the deep, as through a wilderness.

37 4 16 258
10 And he saved them from the ad-ver-sa-ries' hand : and
457 168 23
delivered them from the hand of the enemy.

347
11 As for those that troubled them, the waters o-ver-
258 16 4 15678 23
whel-med them : there was not one of them left.

37 4 16 258 ·4 15678 23
12 Then be-lie-ved they his words : and sang praise un-to
him.

3 47 16 258
13 But within a while they for-gat his works : and would
4 15678 23
not a-bide his counsel.

347 258 16
14 But lust came upon them in the wil-der-ness : and they
4 15678 23
tempted God in the desert.

37 4 16 258
15 And he gave them their de-sire : and sent leanness
4 15678 23
with-al in- to their soul.

37 4 16 258 4 6
16 They angered Moses al-so in the tents : and Aä-ron the
123578
saïnt of the Lord.

347 12568
17 So the earth opened, and swallow-ed up Da-than : and
4 15678 23
covered the congrega-tion of A-biram.

347 258 16
18 And the fire was kindled in their com-pa-ny : the flame
457 168 23
burnt up the un-godly.

347 12568 4 15678
19 They made a calf in Ho-reb : and worshipped the mol-
23
ten image.

37 4 12568
20 Thus they turn-ed their glo-ry : into the similitude of
4 15678 23
a calf that eateth hay.

347 12568
21 And they forgat God their Sa-viour : who had done so
4 15678 23
great things in Egypt ;

3 47 16 258
22 Wondrous works in the land of Ham : and fearful
4 15678 23
things by the Red sea.

23 So he said he would have destroyed them, | had not
37 4 16 258
Moses his chosen stood be-fore him in the gap : to turn away
4 15678 23
his wrathful indignation, | lest he should de-stroy them.

3 47 16 258
24 Yea, they thought scorn of that plea-sant land : and
4 15678 23
gave no cre-dence un- to his word ;

37 4 16 258 4
25 But mur-mured in their tents : and hearkened not un-to
6 123578
the voïce of the Lord.

347 12568
26 Then lift he up his hand a-gainst them : to overthrow
4 15678 23
them in the wilderness ;

347 12568
27 To cast out their seed a-mong the na- tions : and to
457 168 23
scat-ter them in the lands.

347 12568
28 They joined themselves unto Ba-al-pe-or : and ate the
457 168 23
of- fer-ings of the dead.

347
29 Thus they provoked him to anger with their own in-
12568 4 15678 23
ven-tions : and the plague was great a-mong them.

347 12568 4 6 123578
30 Then stood up Phine-es and pray-ed : and so the plägue
ceased.

347 258 16
31 And that was counted unto him for righ-teous-ness :
4 15678 23
among all poste-ri- ties for evermore.

37 4 16 258
32 They angered him also at the wa-ters of strife : so that
457 168 23
he punished Mo-ses for their sakes ;
37 4 12568
33 Because they pro-vo-ked his spi-rit : so that he spake
457 168 23
unad-vi- sed-ly with his lips.
347 12568 4 15678 23
34 Neither destroyed they the hea-then : as the Lord com-
manded them ;
347 12568 4 15678 23
35 But were mingled a-mong the hea-then : and learn-ed
their works.

36 Insomuch that they worshipped their idols, | which
3 47 16 258
turned to their own de-cay : yea, they offered their sons and
4 15678 23
their daugh-ters un- to devils ;

37 And shed innocent blood, | even the blood of their sons
347 12568
and of their daugh-ters : whom they offered unto the idols
4 15678 23
of Chanaan ; and the land was de- fi- led with blood.
37 4 16 258
38 Thus were they stained with their own works : and
4 15678 23
went a-whoring with their own in-ventions.
347
39 Therefore was the wrath of the Lord kindled a-gainst
12568 4 15678 23
his peo-ple : insomuch that he abhorred his own in-heritance.
37 4 12568
40 And he gave them over into the hand of the hea-then :
4 6 123578
and they that hated them were lörds o-ver them.
347 258 16 4 15678
41 Their ene-mies op-pres-sed them : and had them in
23
sub-jection.
347 258 16
42 Many a time did he de-li-ver them : but they rebelled

against him with their own inventions, | and were brought
4 15678 23
down in their wickedness.

347 258 16 4 6
43 Nevertheless, when he saw their ad-ver-si-ty : — he
123578
heärd their complaint.

44 He thought upon his covenant, | and pitied them, ac-
347 12568
cording unto the multitude of his mer-cies : yea, he made all
457 168 23
those that led them away cap-tive to pity them.

45 Deliver us, O Lord our God, | and gather us from
347 12568
a-mong the hea-then : that we may give thanks unto thy
4 15678 23
holy Name, | and make our boast of thy praise.

46 Blessed be the Lord God of Israel from everlasting, and
37 4 16 258 457 168 23
world with-out end : and let all the peo-ple say, Amen.

At Mattins

DAY 22 Ps. 107 *Confitemini Domino* ij.1 *or* viij.1

347 12568
O Give thanks unto the Lord, for he is gra-cious : and his
457 168 23
mercy en-dur-eth for ever.

347 12568
2 Let them give thanks whom the Lord hath re-deem-ed :
457 168 23
and delivered from the hand of the enemy ;

37
3 And gathered them out of the lands, | from the east, and
4 16 258 4 15678 23
from the west : from the north, and from the south.

37 4 16 258
4 They went astray in the wilderness out of the way : and
457 168 23
found no ci- ty to dwell in.

37 4 12568 .4 15678 23
5 Hun-gry and thirs-ty : their soul faint-ed in them.

347 12568
6 So they cried unto the Lord in their trou-ble : and he
4 15678 23
deliver-ed them from their distress.

37 4 16 258
7 He led them forth by the right way : that they might go
4 15678 23
to the ci- ty where they dwelt.

347
8 O that men would therefore praise the Lord for his
12568 4
good-ness : and declare the wonders that he doeth for the
15678 23
chil-dren of men !

3 47 16 258
9 For he satis-fi-eth the emp-ty soul : and filleth the hun-
4 15678 23
gry soul with goodness.

37 4 16 258
10 Such as sit in darkness, and in the sha-dow of death :
4 15678 23
being fast bound in mi-se- ry and iron ;

37 4 16 258
11 Because they rebelled against the words of the Lord :
4 6 123578
and lightly regarded the counsel of the möst Highest ;

347 258 16
12 He also brought down their heart through hea-vi-ness :
4 15678 23
they fell down, and there was none to help them.

347 12568
13 So when they cried unto the Lord in their trou-ble : he
4 15678 23
delivered them out of their distress.

14 For he brought them out of darkness, | and out of the
37 4 16 258 4 15678 23
sha-dow of death : and brake their bonds in sunder.

347
15 O that men would therefore praise the Lord for his
12568 4
good-ness : and declare the wonders that he doeth for the
15678 23
chil-dren of men !

3 47 16 258
16 For he hath bro-ken the gates of brass : and smitten
457 168 23
the bars of i- ron in sunder.

37 4 16 258
17 Foolish men are pla-gued for their of-fence : and be-
457 168 23
cause of their wickedness.

37 4 16 258
18 Their soul abhorred all man-ner of meat : and they
4 15678 23
were e-ven hard at death's door.

347 12568
19 So when they cried un-to the Lord in their trou-ble :
4 15678 23
he delivered them out of their distress.

347 258 16
20 He sent his word, and heal-ed them : and they were
4 15678 23
saved from their de-struction.

347
21 O that men would therefore praise the Lord for his
12568 4
good-ness : and declare the wonders that he doeth for the
15678 23
chil-dren of men !

347
22 That they would offer unto him the sacrifice of thanks-
12568 4 15678 23
giv-ing : and tell out his works with gladness !

347 16 258
23 They that go down to the sea in ships : and occupy
4 15678 23
their busi-ness in great waters ;

37 4 16 258 4 15678
24 These men see the works of the Lord : and his won-
23
ders in the deep.

347 12568
25 For at his word the stormy wind a-ri-seth : which
4 15678 23
lift-eth up the waves thereof.

37
26 They are carried up to the heaven, | and down a-gain
4 16 258 457 168 23
to the deep : their soul melteth away be-cause of the trouble.

27 They reel to & fro, | and stagger [3]like a [47]drunk-[16]en [258]man :
and [4]are [15678]at [23]their wit's end.

28 So when they cry unto the Lord [347]in their [12568]trou-ble : he
delivereth [4]them [15678]out [23]of their distress.

29 For he [3]ma-keth the [47]storm [16]to [258]cease : so that [4]the [15678]waves
[23]there-of are still.

30 Then are they glad, be-[37]cause they [4]are [16]at [258]rest : and so
he bringeth them unto the ha-[4]ven [15678]where [23]they would be.

31 O that men would therefore praise the Lord [347]for his
[12568]good-ness : & declare the wonders that he doeth for [4]the [15678]chil-
[23]dren of men !

32 That they would exalt him also in the congregation [347]of
the [12568]peo-ple : and praise him in the [457]seat [168]of [23]the elders !

33 Who turneth the floods in-[347]to a [258]wil-[16]der-ness : and dri-
[4]eth [15678]up [23]the water-springs.

34 A fruitful land [37]ma-[4]keth he [12568]bar-ren : for the wickedness
[4]of [15678]them [23]that dwell therein.

35 Again, he maketh the wilderness a [347]stand-ing [12568]wa-ter :
and water-[4]springs [15678]of [23]a dry ground.

36 And there he [37]set-[4]teth the [12568]hun-gry : that they may
build them a [457]ci- [168]ty [23]to dwell in ;

37 That they may sow their land, [34]and [7]plant [12568]vine-yards .
to yield [4]them [15678]fruits [23]of increase.

347 258 16
38 He blesseth them, so that they multi-ply ex-ceed-ing-
4 15678 23
ly : and suffereth not their cat- tle to decrease.
37 4 16 258
39 And again, when they are minish-ed, and brought low :
4 15678 23
through oppression, | through a-ny plague, or trouble ;
37 4
40 Though he suffer them to be evil in-treat-ed through
12568 .4 15678 23
ty- rants : and let them wander out of the way in the wilderness ;
347 258 16
41 Yet helpeth he the poor out of mi-se-ry : and maketh
4 15678 23
him house-holds like a flock of sheep.
37 4 16 258
42 The righteous will consider this, and re-joice : and the
4 15678 23
mouth of all wicked-ness shall be stopped.
37 4 16 258
43 Whoso is wise will pon-der these things : and they
4 15678 23
shall understand the lov-ing-kind-ness of the Lord.

At Evensong

DAY 22 PS. 108 *Paratum cor meum* vij.6 *or* viij.2

347 12568
O God, my heart is ready, my heart is rea-dy : I will sing
4 15678 23
and give praise with the best mem-ber that I have.
3 47 16 258 4 15678 23
2 A-wake, thou lute and harp : I myself will a-wake right
early.
347 12568
3 I will give thanks unto thee, O Lord, a-mong the peo-
4 15678 23
ple : I will sing praises unto thee a-mong the nations.
347 12568
4 For thy mercy is greater than the hea-vens : and thy
457 168 23
truth reach-eth un-to the clouds.

347 12568
5 Set up thyself, O God, a-bove the hea-vens : and thy
4 6 123578
glo-ry a- böve all the earth.

347 258 16
6 That thy beloved may be de-li-ver-ed : let thy right
457 168 23
hand save them, and hear thou me.

347 258 16
7 God hath spoken in his ho- li-ness : I will rejoice there-
457 168 23
fore, and divide Sychem, | & mete out the val-ley of Succoth.

37 4 16 258
8 Gilead is mine, and Ma-nas-ses is mine : Ephraym also
4 15678 23
is the strength of my head.

347 12568
9 Iuda is my law-giver, Moab is my wash-pot : over Edom
4 15678 23
will I cast out my shoe ; upon Philisti-a will I triumph.

4 37 12568
10 Who will lead me into the strong ci- ty : and who will
4 15678 23
bring me in- to E-dom ?

37 4 16 258
11 Hast not thou for-sa-ken us, O God : and wilt not
4 15678 23
thou, O God, go forth with our hosts ?

347 258 16 4 15678 23
12 O help us a-gainst the en- e-my : for vain is the help
of man.

3 47 16 258
13 Through God we shall do great acts : and it is he that
·4 15678 23
shall tread down our enemies.

Ps. 109 *Deus, laudem* i. 4 *or* vij. 7

37 4 16 258
HOld not thy tongue, O God, of my praise : for the
mouth of the ungodly, | yea, the mouth of the deceit-
4 15678 23
ful is o-pen-ed up-on me.

37 4 16 258
2 And they have spoken a-gainst me with false tongues :
they compassed me about also with words of hatred, | and
457 168 23
fought a-gainst me with-out a cause.

3 For the love that I had unto them, | lo, they take now
37 4 16 258 4 15678 23
my con-tra-ry part : but I give my-self un-to prayer.
37 4 16 258 4
4 Thus have they rewarded me e-vil for good : and ha-tred
15678 23
for my good will.
347 258 16
5 Set thou an ungodly man to be ru-ler o-ver him : and let
4 15678 23
Satan stand at his right hand.
347 12568
6 When sentence is given upon him, let him be con-dem-
4 15678 23
ned : and let his prayer be turn-ed into sin.
347 16 258 4 15678 23
7 Let his days be few : and let ano-ther take his office.
37 4 258 16 4 15678 23
8 Let his chil-dren be fa-ther-less : and his wife a widow.
347 16 258
9 Let his children be vagabonds, and beg their bread : let
457 168 23
them seek it also out of de- so-late places.
37 4 16 258
10 Let the extortioner consume all that he hath : and let
4 15678 23
the stran-ger spoil his labour.
37 4 258 16
11 Let there be no man to pi-ty him : nor to have com-
457 168 23
passion upon his fa-ther-less children.
347 12568
12 Let his posterity be de-stroy-ed : and in the next gene-
4 15678 23
ration let his name be clean put out.

13 Let the wickedness of his fathers be had in remem-

37 4 16 258
brance in the sight of the Lord : and let not the sin of his
457 168 23
mo-ther be done away.

3 47 16 258
14 Let them alway be be-fore the Lord : that he may root
4 15678 23
out the memorial of them from off the earth.

37 4 16 258
15 And that, because his mind was not to do good : but
persecuted the poor helpless man, | that he might slay him
4 15678 23
that was vex- ed at the heart.

37 4
16 His delight was in cursing, | and it shall hap-pen un-
16 258
4 15678 23
to him : he loved not blessing, | therefore shall it be far
from him.

347 12568
17 He clothed himself with cursing, like as with a rai-
4
ment : and it shall come into his bowels like water, | and like
15678 23
oil in-to his bones.

347 12568
18 Let it be unto him as the cloke that he hath up-on
4 68 157 23
him : and as the girdle that he is al-way gird-ed withal.

347 258 16
19 Let it thus happen from the Lord un-to mine en-e-
457 168 23
mies : and to those that speak e- vil a-gainst my soul.

37 4
20 But deal thou with me, O Lord God, according un-to
16 258 457 168 23
thy Name : for sweet is thy mercy.

37 4 16 258
21 O deliver me, for I am help-less and poor : and my
457 168 23
heart is wound-ed with-in me.

347 12568
22 I go hence like the shadow that de-part-eth : and am
4 6 123578
driven away as the gräss-hopper.

347 12568
23 My knees are weak through fast-ing : my flesh is dried
4 15678 23
up for want of fatness.

37 4 16 258
24 I became also a re-proach un-to them : they that look-
4 15678 23
ed upon me sha-ked their heads.

347 16 258 4 15678
25 Help me, O Lord my God : O save me accor-ding to
23
thy mercy.

37 4 16 258
26 And they shall know, how that this is thy hand : and
.4 15678 23
that thou, Lord, hast done it.

37 4 16 258
27 Though they curse, yet bless thou : & let them be con-
4 68 157 23
founded that rise up against me; but let thy ser-vant rejoice.

37 4 16 258
28 Let mine adversaries be clo-thed with shame : and let
457 168 23
them cover themselves with their own con-fu-sion, as with a
cloke.

37 4
29 As for me, I will give great thanks unto the Lord with
16 258 4 15678 23
my mouth : and praise him a-mong the multitude;

37 4 16 258
30 For he shall stand at the right hand of the poor : to
4 15678 23
save his soul from un-righ-teous judges.

At Mattins

DAY 23 Ps. 110 *Dixit Dominus* iij.1 *or* vij.1

37 4 16 258
THe Lord said un-to my Lord : Sit thou on my right
4 15678 23
hand, | until I make thine en-e-mies thy foot-stool.

347 12568
2 The Lord shall send the rod of thy power out of Sy-on :

4 15678 23
be thou ruler, | even in the midst a-mong thine enemies.

3 In the day of thy power shall the people offer thee free-
347 12568
will offerings with an ho-ly wor-ship : the dew of thy birth
457 168 23
is of the womb of the morning.

3 47 16 258
4 The Lord sware, & will not re-pent : Thou art a Priest
4 15678 23
for ever after the or-der of Mel-chisedech.

37 4 16 258
5 The Lord up-on thy right hand : shall wound even
4 15678 23
kings in the day of his wrath.

347 12568
6 He shall judge a-mong the hea-then : he shall fill the
places with the dead bodies; and smite in sunder the heads
4 15678 23
o-ver di- vers countries.

37 4 16 258 4
7 He shall drink of the brook in the way : therefore shall
15678 23
he lift up his head.

Ps. 111 *Confitebor tibi* viij. 2

37 4 16 258
I Will give thanks unto the Lord with my whole heart :
4 15678 23
secretly among the faithful, | and in the con-gre-gation.
3 47 16 258
2 The works of the Lord are great : sought out of all
4 15678 23
them that have plea-sure therein.

347 12568
3 His work is worthy to be praised, and had in ho- nour :
457 168 23
and his righteousness en-dur-eth for ever.

37
4 The merciful and gracious Lord hath so done his mar-
4 16 258 457 168 23
vel-lous works : that they ought to be had in re-membrance.

347 12568
5 He hath given meat unto them that fear him : he shall
4 15678 23
ever be mind-ful of his covenant.

37 4 16 258
6 He hath shewed his people the pow-er of his works : that
4 15678 23
he may give them the heri-tage of the heathen.

347 12568
7 The works of his hands are veri-ty and judge-ment : all
4 15678 23
his com-mand-ments are true.

37 4 12568 4
8 They stand fast for ev-er and ev-er : and are done in
15678 23
truth and equity.

347 12568
9 He sent redemption un-to his peo-ple : he hath com-
457 168 23
manded his covenant for ever ; holy & re- ve-rend is his Name.

37 4 12568
10 The fear of the Lord is the be-gin-ning of wis-dom : a
good understanding have all they that do thereafter ; the praise
457 168 23
of it en-dur-eth for ever.

Ps. 112 *Beatus vir* i. 1 *or* iv. 4

37 4 16 258
BLessed is the man that fear-eth the Lord : he hath great
4 15678 23
delight in his com-mandments.

37 4 16 258
2 His seed shall be migh-ty up-on earth : the generation of
4 15678 23
the faith-ful shall be blessed.

37 4 16 258
3 Riches and plenteousness shall be in his house : and his
457 168 23
righteousness en-dur-eth for ever.

347 12568
4 Unto the godly there ariseth up light in the dark-ness :
457 168 23
he is merciful, lov-ing, and righteous.

347 12568
5 A good man is merci-ful, and len-deth : and will guide
·4 15678 23
his words with dis-cretion.

37 4 12568
6 For he shall nev-er be mov-ed : and the righteous shall
457 168 23
be had in ever-last-ing re-membrance.

347 12568
7 He will not be afraid of any e-vil ti- dings : for his heart
4 15678 23
standeth fast, and be- lie-veth in the Lord.

3 47 16 258
8 His heart is establish-ed, and will not shrink : until he
4 15678 23
see his desire up- on his enemies.

37 4 16 258
9 He hath dispersed abroad, and giv-en to the poor : and
457
his righteousness remaineth for ever ; his horn shall be ex-al-
168 23
ted with honour.

347 12568
10 The ungodly shall see it, and it shall grieve him : he
shall gnash with his teeth, and consume away ; the desire of
457 168 23
the un-god-ly shall perish.

Ps. 113 *Laudate, pueri* viij. 1

347 12568 4 6 123578
PRaise the Lord, ye ser-vants : O praise the Näme of
the Lord.

37 4 16 258 4 15678
2 Blessed be the Name of the Lord : from this time forth
23
for evermore.

347 12568
3 The Lord's Name is prai-sed : from the rising up of the
4 6 123578
sun unto the go-ing döwn of the same.

347 12568 4
4 The Lord is high a-bove all hea-then : and his glory a-
15678 23
bove the heavens.

5 Who is like unto the Lord our God, | that hath his
37 4 16 258
dwel-ling so high : and yet humbleth himself to behold the
4 15678 23
things that are in hea-ven and earth ?

37 4 16 258 4
6 He taketh up the simple out of the dust : and lifteth the
.6 123578
poor oüt of the mire ;

347 12568
7 That he may set him with the prin-ces : even with the
4 15678 23
prin-ces of his people.

37 4 16 258
8 He maketh the barren wo-man to keep house : and to be
457 168 23
a joyful mo-ther of children.

At Evensong

DAY 23 Ps. 114 *In exitu Israel** vij.1 *or* 6

347 12568
WHen Israel came out of E- gypt : and the house of
4 6 123578
Iacob from a-mong the stränge people.
347 12568 4 15678 23
2 Iuda was his sanc-tu- a- ry : and Isra-el his do-minion.
37 4 16 258 4 15678 23
3 The sea saw that, and fled : Ior-dan was driven back.
37 4 16 258 4 15678
4 The mountains skip-ped like rams : and the lit-tle hills,
23
like young sheep.

347 12568
5 What aileth thee, O thou sea, that thou fled-dest : and
4 15678 23
thou Iordan, that thou wast driven back ?

---

* This and the following Psalm will be found noted to the *Irregular* or *Peregrine Tone* at the end of the Psalter.

37 4 16 258 4
6 Ye mountains, that ye skip-ped like rams : and ye lit-tle
15678 23
hills, like young sheep?

37 4 16 258
7 Tremble, thou earth, at the pre-sence of the Lord : at
4 15678 23
the presence of the God of Iacob.

347 12568
8 Who turned the hard rock into a stan-ding wa- ter : and
4 15678 23
the flint-stone in- to a springing well.

Ps. 115 *Non nobis, Domine* vij.1 *or* 6

37
NOt unto us, O Lord, not unto us, | but unto thy Name
4 16 258 4 15678 23
give the praise : for thy loving mercy, and for thy
truth's sake.

37 4 16 258 4 15678 23
2 Wherefore shall the hea-then say : — Where is now
their God?

347 12568 4
3 As for our God, he is in hea-ven : he hath done what-so-
15678 23
ev- er pleased him.

37 4 16 258 4 15678 23
4 Their idols are sil-ver and gold : even the work of men's
hands.

347 12568 4 15678 23
5 They have mouths, and speak not : eyes have they, and
see not.

347 12568 4 15678 23
6 They have ears, and hear not : noses have they, and
smell not.

347
7 They have hands, and handle not; feet have they, and
12568 4 15678 23
walk not : nei-ther speak they through their throat.

37 4 16 258
8 They that make them are like un-to them : and so are
4 15678 23
all such as put their trust in them.

37 4 16 258
9 But thou, house of Israel, trust thou in the Lord : he is
4 15678 23
their suc-cour and defence.

37 4 16 258
10 Ye house of Aäron, | put your trust in the Lord : he is
4 15678 23
their help-er and de-fender.

37 4 16 258
11 Ye that fear the Lord, | put your trust in the Lord : he
4 15678 23
is their help-er and de-fender.

347 12568
12 The Lord hath been mindful of us, and he shall bless
4
us : even he shall bless the house of Israel, | he shall bless the
15678 23
house of Aäron.

37 4 16 258 4 15678 23
13 He shall bless them that fear the Lord : — — both
small and great.

37 4 16 258 4 15678
14 The Lord shall in-crease you more and more : you and
23
your children.

37 4 16 258 4 15678 23
15 Ye are the bles-sed of the Lord : who made hea-ven
and earth.

37 4 16 258
16 All the whole hea-vens are the Lord's : the earth hath
4 15678 23
he given to the chil-dren of men.

37 4 16 258
17 The dead praise not thee, O Lord : neither all they
4 15678 23
that go down in- to silence.

37 4 16 258
18 But we will praise the Lord : from this time forth for
457 168 23
ev- er-more. Praise the Lord.

At Mattins

DAY 24 Ps. 116 *Dilexi, quoniam* ij. I

4 37 12568 4 15678 23
I Am well plea-sed : that the Lord hath heard the voice of
my prayer.

37 4 16 258
2 That he hath inclined his ear un-to me : therefore will
4 15678 23
I call upon him as long as I live.

3 47 16 258
3 The snares of death compas-sed me round a-bout : and
4 15678 23
the pains of hell gat hold up-on me.

4 I shall find trouble and heaviness, | and I will call upon
37 4 16 258 4 15678 23
the Name of the Lord : O Lord, I beseech thee, de- li- ver
my soul.

347 12568 4 15678 23
5 Gracious is the Lord, and righ-teous : yea, our God is
merciful.

37 4 12568 4
6 The Lord pre-ser-veth the sim-ple : I was in mise-ry,
15678 23
and he helped me.

347 16 258
7 Turn again then unto thy rest, O my soul : for the
4 15678 23
Lord hath re-warded thee.

3 47 16 258
8 And-why thou hast deliver-ed my soul from death : mine
4 15678 23
eyes from tears, and my feet from falling.

37 4 16 258 457 168 23
9 I will walk be-fore the Lord : in the land of the living.

4 37
10 I believed, and therefore will I speak ; but I was sore
12568 4 15678 23
trou-bled : I said in my haste, All men are liars.

37 4 16 258
11 What reward shall I give un-to the Lord : for all the
4 15678 23
benefits that he hath done un-to me?
37 4 12568 4
12 I will receive the cup of sal-va-tion : and call up-on
6 123578
the Näme of the Lord.
347 12568
13 I will pay my vows now in the presence of all his peo-
4 15678 23
ple : right dear in the sight of the Lord is the death of his
saints.
347 12568
14 Behold, O Lord, how that I am thy ser-vant : I am
thy servant, and the son of thine handmaid; thou hast broken
4 15678 23
my bonds in sunder.
347 12568
15 I will offer to thee the sacrifice of thanks-giv-ing : and
4 6 123578
will call up-on the Näme of the Lord.
347
16 I will pay my vows unto the Lord, in the sight of all
12568
his peo-ple : in the courts of the Lord's house, | even in the
457 168 23
midst of thee, O Hie-ru- sa-lem. Praise the Lord.

Ps. 117 *Laudate Dominum* v.1 *or* vij. 5

347 12568 4 15678 23
O Praise the Lord, all ye hea-then : praise him, all ye
nations.
347
2 For his merciful kindness is ever more and more to-
12568 4 15678 23
wards us : and the truth of the Lord endureth for ev- er.
Praise the Lord.

Ps. 118 *Confitemini Domino* i. 4 *or* vj.

347 12568
O Give thanks unto the Lord, for he is gra-cious : because
457 168 23
his mercy en-dur-eth for ever.

347 12568
2 Let Israel now confess that he is gra-cious : and that his
457 168 23
mercy en-dur-eth for ever.

37 4 16 258
3 Let the house of A-aron now con-fess : that his mercy
457 168 23
en-dur-eth for ever.

3 47 16 258
4 Yea, let them now that fear the Lord con-fess : that his
457 168 23
mercy en-dur-eth for ever.

347 12568 4 .6 123578
5 I called upon the Lord in trou-ble : and the Lord heärd
me at large.

37 4 16 258 .4 15678
6 The Lord is on my side : I will not fear what man do-
23
eth unto me.

347 12568
7 The Lord taketh my part with them that help me :
4 15678 23
therefore shall I see my desire up-on mine enemies.

37 4 16 258 4 15678
8 It is better to trust in the Lord : than to put a-ny con-
23
fi-dence in man.

37 4 16 258 4
9 It is better to trust in the Lord : than to put any con-fi-
15678 23
dence in princes.

3 47 16 258
10 All nations compas-sed me round a-bout : but in the
4 15678 23
Name of the Lord will I de-stroy them.

11 They kept me in on every side, | they kept me in, I
37 4 16 258 4 15678 23
say, on ev-e-ry side : but in the Name of the Lord will I de-
stroy them.

12 They came about me like bees, | & are extinct, even as
37 4 16 258 4
the fire a-mong the thorns : for in the Name of the Lord I
15678 23
will de-stroy them.

37 4 16 258 4
13 Thou hast thrust sore at me, that I might fall : but the
15678 23
Lord was my help.

37 4 16 258
14 The Lord is my strength, and my song : and is be-
.4 15678 23
come my sal-vation.

347
15 The voice of joy and health is in the dwellings of the
12568 4 15678 23
righ-teous : the right hand of the Lord bring-eth migh-ty
things to pass.

37 4 258 16
16 The right hand of the Lord hath the pre-em- i-nence :
4 15678 23
the right hand of the Lord bring-eth migh-ty things to pass.

3 47 16 258 4 6 123578
17 I shall not die, but live : and de-clare the wörks of the
Lord.

347 258 16
18 The Lord hath chastened and cor-rect-ed me : but he
4 15678 23
hath not given me o- ver unto death.

347 258 16
19 Open me the gates of righ-teous-ness : that I may go
4 15678 23
into them, | and give thanks un-to the Lord.

37 4 16 258 4 15678 23
20 This is the gate of the Lord : the righteous shall en- ter
into it.

347 12568
21 I will thank thee, for thou hast heard me : and art be-
.4 15678 23
come my sal-vation.

37 4 12568
22 The same stone which the buil-ders re-fu-sed : is be-
4 15678 23
come the head-stone in the corner.

4 37 12568 4 15678 23
23 This is the Lord's do-ing : and it is mar-vel-lous in
our eyes.

3 47 16 258
24 This is the day which the Lord hath made : we will
4 15678 23
re-joice and be glad in it.

37 4 16 258 4 15678 23
25 Help me now, O Lord : O Lord, send us now pros-
perity.

37 4 16 258
26 Blessed be he that cometh in the Name of the Lord :
4 6 123578
we have wished you good luck, | ye that are of the hoüse of
the Lord.

37 4 16 258
27 God is the Lord who hath shew-ed us light : bind the
457 168 23
sacrifice with cords, | yea, even unto the horns of the altar.

347 12568
28 Thou art my God, and I will thank thee : thou art my
4 15678 23
God, and I will praise thee.

347 12568
29 O give thanks unto the Lord, for he is gra-cious : and
457 168 23
his mercy en-dur-eth for ever.

At Evensong

DAY 24 Ps. 119 *Beati immaculati* iij. 5

37 4 16 258
BLessed are those that are unde-fi-led in the way : and
4 6 123578
walk in the läw of the Lord.

347 12568
2 Blessed are they that keep his tes-ti-mo-nies : and seek
4 15678 23
him with their whole heart.

347 258 16 4 15678 23
3 For they who do no wick-ed-ness : — walk in his ways.

347 12568 4 15678
4 Thou hast char-ged : that we shall diligently keep thy
23
com-mandments.

3 47 16 258 4
5 O that my ways were made so di-rect : that I might
15678 23
keep thy statutes !

347 12568
6 So shall I not be con-found-ed : while I have respect
4 15678 23
unto all thy com-mandments.

3 47 16 258
7 I will thank thee with an un-feign-ed heart : when I
4 15678 23
shall have learned the judge-ments of thy righteousness.

347 12568 457 168 23
8 I will keep thy ce-re-mo-nies : O for-sake me not
utterly.

In quo corriget iij. 5

3 47 16 258
WHerewithal shall a young man cleanse his way : even
.4 15678 23
by ruling him-self af- ter thy word.

347 12568
10 With my whole heart have I sought thee : O let me
4 15678 23
not go wrong out of thy com-mandments.

37 4 16 258
11 Thy words have I hid with-in my heart : that I should
4 15678 23
not sin a-gainst thee.

3 47 16 258 457 168 23
12 Bles-sed art thou, O Lord : O teach me thy statutes.

347 12568 457
13 With my lips have I been tell-ing : of all the judge-
168 23
ments of thy mouth.

347 12568
14 I have had as great delight in the way of thy tes-ti-mo-
457 168 23
nies : as in all man-ner of riches.

347 12568 4
15 I will talk of thy com-mand-ments : and have re-spect
15678 23
un- to thy ways.

347 12568 4 15678
16 My delight shall be in thy sta-tutes : and I will not
23
for-get thy word.

Retribue servo tuo i. 1

347 12568 4 15678 23
O Do well un-to thy ser- vant : that I may live, and keep
thy word.

37 4 16 258 4
18 O-pen thou mine eyes : that I may see the won-drous
15678 23
things of thy law.

37 4 16 258 4
19 I am a stran-ger up-on earth : O hide not thy com-
15678 23
mand-ments from me.

37 4 16 258
20 My soul breaketh out for the very fer-vent de-sire : that
4 15678 23
it hath alway un- to thy judgements.

37 4 16 258
21 Thou hast re-bu-ked the proud : and cursed are they
4 15678 23
that do err from thy com-mandments.

37 4 16 258
22 O turn from me shame and re-buke : for I have kept
4 15678 23
thy tes- ti-monies.

347 12568
23 Princes also did sit and speak a-gainst me : but thy ser-
4 15678 23
vant is occupi-ed in thy statutes.

3 47 16 258 4 15678 23
24 For thy testimonies are my de-light : — and my coun-
sellors.

Adhæsit pavimento i. 1

37 4 16 258
MY soul clea-veth to the dust : O quicken thou me, ac-
457 168 23
cord-ing to thy word.

347 258 16
26 I have knowledged my ways, and thou heard-est me :
457 168 23
O teach me thy statutes.

347 12568
27 Make me to understand the way of thy com-mand-
457 168 23
ments : and so shall I talk of thy wondrous works.

347 258 16
28 My soul melteth away for ve-ry hea-vi-ness : comfort
4 15678 23
thou me accord-ing un- to thy word.

347 12568
29 Take from me the way of ly- ing : and cause thou me
·4 15678 23
to make much of thy law.

3 47 16 258
30 I have cho-sen the way of truth : and thy judgements
4 15678 23
have I laid be-fore me.

347 12568 4 15678 23
31 I have stuck unto thy tes-ti-mo-nies : O Lord, con-
found me not.

347 12568
32 I will run the way of thy com-mand-ments : when
4 15678 23
thou hast set my heart at liberty.

At Mattins

DAY 25 *Legem pone* i. 4 *or* iv. 6

37 4 12568
TEach me, O Lord, the way of thy sta- tutes : and I shall
4 68 157 23
keep it un- to the end.

3 47 16 258
34 Give me understanding, and I shall keep thy law : yea,
4 15678 23
I shall keep it with my whole heart.

347 12568
35 Make me to go in the path of thy com-mand-ments :
4 15678 23
for there- in is my desire.

347 12568 4 68
36 Incline my heart unto thy tes-ti-mo-nies : and not to
157 23
co- ve-tousness.

4 37 258 16
37 O turn away mine eyes, lest they be-hold va-ni-ty : and
4 15678 23
quicken thou me in thy way.

347 12568 4 15678 23
38 O stablish thy word in thy ser-vant : that I may
fear thee.

37 4 12568 4
39 Take away the rebuke that I am a-fraid of : for thy
15678 23
judge-ments are good.

347 12568
40 Behold, my delight is in thy com-mand-ments : O
4 15678 23
quicken me in thy righteousness.

Et veniat super me i. 4 *or* iv. 6

37 4 16 258
LEt thy loving mercy come also un-to me, O Lord : even
4 15678 23
thy salvation, accord-ing un- to thy word.

347 12568
42 So shall I make answer unto my blas-phe-mers : for my
457 168 23
trust is in thy word.

37 4 16
43 O take not the word of thy truth utterly out of my
258 4 15678 23
mouth : for my hope is in thy judgements.

3 47 16 258 457 168 23
44 So shall I al-way keep thy law : yea, for ev- er and
ever.

347 258 16 4 15678 23
45 And I will walk at li-ber-ty : for I seek thy com-mand-
ments.

37 4 16 258
46 I will speak of thy testimonies also, e-ven be-fore kings :
457 168 23
and will not be a-shamed.

347 12568
47 And my delight shall be in thy com-mand-ments :
4 15678 23
which I have loved.

48 My hands also will I lift up unto thy commandments,
347 12568 4 15678 23
which I have lov-ed : & my study shall be in thy statutes.

Memor esto servi tui ij. I

37 4 16 258
O Think upon thy servant, as con-cer-ning thy word :
4 15678 23
wherein thou hast caus-ed me to put my trust.
347 12568 4
50 The same is my comfort in my trou-ble : for thy word
68 157 23
hath quick-en-ed me.

347 12568
51 The proud have had me exceedingly in de- ri- sion :
457 168 23
yet have I not shrink-ed from thy law.
37 4 16
52 For I remembered thine everlasting judge-ments, O
258 4 15678 23
Lord : and re- cei-ved comfort.
37 4 16 258 4 15678 23
53 I am hor-ri-bly a-fraid : for the ungod-ly that for-sake
thy law.
3 47 16 258 457 168 23
54 Thy sta-tutes have been my songs : in the house of my
pilgrimage.

3 4 7
55 I have thought upon thy Name, O Lord, in the night-
12568 4 15678 23
sea-son : — and have kept thy law.
347 16 258 4 15678 23
56 This I had : because I kept thy com-mandments.

Portio mea, Domine ij. I

37 4 16 258 4 15678 23
THou art my por-tion, O Lord : I have pro-mi-sed to
keep thy law.

37 4
58 I made my humble petition in thy presence with my
16 258 457 168 23
whole heart : O be merciful unto me, ac-cord-ing to thy
word.

347 12568
59 I called mine own ways to re-mem-brance : and turned
4 15678 23
my feet unto thy tes- ti-monies.

37 4 16 258 4
60 I made haste, and pro-long-ed not the time : to keep
15678 23
thy com-mandments.

37 4 258 16
61 The congregations of the un-god-ly have rob-bed me :
4 15678 23
but I have not for-got-ten thy law.

37 4 16 258
62 At midnight I will rise to give thanks un-to thee :
4 15678 23
because of thy righ-teous judgements.

347 12568 4
63 I am a companion of all them that fear thee : and keep
15678 23
thy com-mandments.

37 4 12568 457 168
64 The earth, O Lord, is full of thy mer-cy : O teach me
23
thy statutes.

Bonitatem fecisti ij. I

347 12568
O Lord, thou hast dealt graciously with thy ser-vant :
4 15678 23
accord-ing un- to thy word.

37 4 12568
66 O learn me true under-stand-ing and know-ledge : for
4 15678 23
I have belie-ved thy com-mandments.

37 4 16 258 457 168
67 Before I was trou-bled, I went wrong : but now have
23
I kept thy word.
347 12568 457 168 23
68 Thou art good and gra-cious : O teach me thy statutes.
347 12568
69 The proud have imagined a lie a-gainst me : but I will
4 15678 23
keep thy command-ments with my whole heart.
3 47 16 258 4
70 Their heart is as fat as brawn : but my delight hath
15678 23
been in thy law.
347 12568
71 It is good for me that I have been in trou-ble : that I
4 15678 23
may learn thy statutes.
37 4 16 258
72 The law of thy mouth is dear-er un-to me : than thou-
4 15678 23
sands of gold and silver.

At Evensong

DAY 25 *Manus tuæ fecerunt* i. 10 *or* vij. 8

37 4 16 258
THy hands have made me and fa-shion-ed me : O
4 15678 23
give me understanding, | that I may learn thy com-
mandments.
347 12568
74 They that fear thee will be glad when they see me :
4 15678 23
because I have put my trust in thy word.
37 4 16 258
75 I know, O Lord, that thy judge-ments are right : and
4 15678 23
that thou of very faithfulness hast caused me to be troubled.
347 12568
76 O let thy merciful kindness be my com-fort : according
4 15678 23
to thy word un- to thy servant.

37 4 16
77 O let thy loving mercies come unto me, that I may
258 4 15678 23
live : for thy law is my delight.

78 Let the proud be confounded, | for they go wickedly
347 12568 4 15678 23
about to de-stroy me : but I will be occupied in thy com-
mandments.

347 12568
79 Let such as fear thee, and have known thy tes-ti-mo-
4 15678 23
nies : be turn-ed unto me.

347 12568 4
80 O let my heart be sound in thy sta-tutes : that I be
15678 23
not a-shamed.

Defecit in salutare tuum i. 10 *or* vij. 8

347 12568
MY soul hath longed for thy sal-va-tion : and I have a
4 15678 23
good hope be-cause of thy word.

37 4 16 258 4
82 Mine eyes long sore for thy word : saying, | O when
15678 23
wilt thou comfort me?

37 4 16 258
83 For I am become like a bot-tle in the smoke : yet do I
4 15678 23
not for-get thy statutes.

37 4 12568
84 How many are the days of thy ser-vant : when wilt
4 15678 23
thou be avenged of them that per-se-cute me?

37 4 16 258 4
85 The proud have dig-ged pits for me : which are not
15678 23
af-ter thy law.

37 4 16 258
86 All thy com-mand-ments are true : they persecute me
4 15678 23
false-ly ; O be thou my help.

37 4 16 258
87 They had almost made an end of me up-on earth : but
4 15678 23
I forsook not thy com-mandments.

347 12568
88 O quicken me after thy lov-ing-kind-ness : and so shall
457 168 23
I keep the testi-mo-nies of thy mouth.

In eternum, Domine iv. 6

347 16 258 457 168 23
O Lord, thy word : endureth for ev- er in heaven.
347
90 Thy truth also remaineth from one generation to
12568 4
an- o- ther : thou hast laid the foundation of the earth, and
15678 23
it a-bideth.

347 258 16
91 They continue this day according to thine or- di-nance :
4 15678 23
for all things serve thee.

37 4 16 258
92 If my delight had not been in thy law : I should have
4 15678 23
perish-ed in my trouble.

347 12568
93 I will never forget thy com-mand-ments : for with
4 68 157 23
them thou hast quick-en-ed me.

347 12568 4 15678 23
94 I am thine, O save me : for I have sought thy com-
mandments.

347 12568
95 The ungodly laid wait for me to de-stroy me : but I
4 15678 23
will consider thy tes- ti-monies.

37 4 16 258
96 I see that all things come to an end : but thy com-
4 15678 23
mand-ment is ex-ceeding broad.

Quomodo dilexi iv. 6

37 4 16 258
LOrd, what love have I un-to thy law : all the day long is
4 15678 23
my stu- dy in it.

98 Thou through thy commandments hast made me wiser
347 258 16 4 15678 23
than mine en- e-mies : for they are ev- er with me.

347 12568
99 I have more understanding than my teach-ers : for thy
4 15678 23
testimo-nies are my study.

347 12568 4 15678
100 I am wiser than the a- ged : because I keep thy
23
com-mandments.

37 4 16 258 4
101 I have refrained my feet from ev-ery e-vil way : that
15678 23
I may keep thy word.

347 12568 4 15678
102 I have not shrunk from thy judge-ments : — for
23
thou teachest me.

37 4 16 258
103 O how sweet are thy words un-to my throat : yea,
4 15678 23
sweeter than ho-ney un- to my mouth.

347 12568
104 Through thy commandments I get un-der-stand-ing :
4 15678 23
therefore I hate all evil ways.

At Mattins

DAY 26 *Lucerna pedibus meis* i. 1 *or* 4

37 4 16 258 4 15678
THy word is a lantern un-to my feet : and a light un-
23
to my paths.

37 4 258 16
106 I have sworn, and am sted-fast-ly pur-pos-ed : to keep
4 15678 23
thy righ-teous judgements.

4 37 12568
107 I am troubled a-bove mea-sure : quicken me, O Lord,
457 168 23
ac-cord-ing to thy word.

37 4
108 Let the free-will offerings of my mouth please thee,
16 258 457 168 23
O Lord : and teach me thy judgements.

37 4 16 258 4 15678 23
109 My soul is al-way in my hand : yet do I not for-
get thy law.

37 4 16 258
110 The ungodly have laid a snare for me : but yet I
4 15678 23
swerved not from thy com-mandments.

347
111 Thy testimonies have I claimed as mine heri-tage for
12568 4 15678 23
ev-er : and-why they are the ve-ry joy of my heart.

347 12568
112 I have applied my heart to fulfil thy sta-tutes al-way :
457 168 23
e- ven un-to the end.

Iniquos odio habui i. 1 *or* 4

3 47 16 258 4 15678 23
I Hate them that i-ma-gine e-vil things : but thy law do
I love.

347 16 258 457 168 23
114 Thou art my de-fence and shield : and my trust is in
thy word.

347 12568
115 Away from me, ye wick-ed : I will keep the com-
457 168 23
mand-ments of my God.

37 4 16
116 O stablish me according to thy word, that I may
258 457 168 23
live : and let me not be disap-poin-ted of my hope.

37 4 16 258
117 Hold thou me up, and I shall be safe : yea, my de-
4 15678 23
light shall be ev-er in thy statutes.

347
118 Thou hast trodden down all them that depart from
12568 4 15678 23
thy sta-tutes : for they i- ma-gine but deceit.

347 16
119 Thou puttest away all the ungodly of the earth like
258 4 15678 23
dross : therefore I love thy tes- ti-monies.

3 47 16 258 457
120 My flesh trem-bleth for fear of thee : and I am a-fraid
168 23
of thy judgements.

Feci iudicium i. 1 *or* 4

37 4 16 258
I Deal with the thing that is law-ful and right : O give
4 15678 23
me not over un-to mine op-pressors.

37 4 16
122 Make thou thy servant to delight in that which is
258 .4 15678 23
good : that the proud do me no wrong.

37 4 16
123 Mine eyes are wasted away with look-ing for thy
258 457 168 23
health : and for the word of thy righteousness.

347
124 O deal with thy servant according unto thy lov-ing
12568 457 168 23
mer-cy : and teach me thy statutes.

347 12568
125 I am thy servant, | O grant me un-der-stand-ing :
4 15678 23
that I may know thy tes- ti-monies.

3 47 16 258
126 It is time for thee, Lord, to lay tó thine hand : for
4 15678 23
they have de-stroy-ed thy law.

347 12568 .4 15678 23
127 For I love thy com-mand-ments : a-bove gold and
precious stone.

347 12568
128 Therefore hold I strait all thy com-mand-ments : and
4 15678 23
all false ways I ut- ter-ly abhor.

Mirabilia ij. 1

4 23578 16 4 6
THy testimo-nies are won-der-ful : therefore doth my
123578
söul keep them.

37 4 16 258
130 When thy word go-eth forth : it giveth light and un-
457 168 23
derstanding un- to the simple.

37 4 16 258
131 I opened my mouth, and drew in my breath : for my
4 15678 23
delight was in thy com-mandments.

37 4 16 258
132 O look thou upon me, | and be merci-ful un-to me :
4 15678 23
as thou usest to do un-to those that love thy Name.

37 4 16 258
133 Order my steps in thy word : and so shall no wick-
4 15678 23
edness have do-min-ion over me.

37 4 16 258
134 O deliver me from the wrongful deal-ings of men :
4 15678 23
and so shall I keep thy com-mandments.

347 12568
135 Shew the light of thy countenance up-on thy ser-
457 168 23
vant : and teach me thy statutes.

347 12568 4 15678
136 Mine eyes gush out with wa-ter : because men keep
23
not thy law.

Justus es, Domine ij. 1

3 47 16 258 457 168 23
RIgh-teous art thou, O Lord : and true is thy judge-
ment.

347 12568
138 The testimonies that thou hast com-mand-ed : are
4 15678 23
exceed-ing righ-teous and true.

37 4 258 16
139 My zeal hath e-ven con-su-med me : because mine
4 15678 23
enemies have for-got-ten thy words.

347 258 16 4 15678
140 Thy word is tried to the ut-ter-most : and thy ser-
23
vant loveth it.

37 4 12568
141 I am small, and of no re-pu- ta- tion : yet do I not
4 15678 23
for-get thy com-mandments.

347 258 16
142 Thy righteousness is an ever-last-ing righ-teous-ness :
4 6 123578
and thy läw is the truth.

347 12568
143 Trouble & heaviness have taken hold up-on me : yet
4 15678 23
is my delight in thy com-mandments.

347 12568
144 The righteousness of thy testimonies is ev-er-last-ing :
457 168 23
O grant me under-stand-ing, and I shall live.

At Evensong

DAY 26 *Clamavi in toto corde meo* i. 4 *or* iv. 6

37 4 16 258 4
I Call with my whole heart : hear me, O Lord, | I will
15678 23
keep thy statutes.

37 4 16 258
146 Yea, even unto thee do I call : help me, and I shall
4 15678 23
keep thy tes- ti-monies.

37 4 16 258 4
147 Early in the morning do I cry un-to thee : for in thy
15678 23
word is my trust.

37 4 12568
148 Mine eyes pre-vent the night-watch-es : that I might
457 168 23
be occu-pi- ed in thy words.

347
149 Hear my voice, O Lord, according unto thy lov-ing-
12568 457 168 23
kind-ness : quicken me, ac-cord-ing as thou art wont.

347 12568
150 They draw nigh that of malice per-se-cute me : and
4 15678 23
are far from thy law.

3 47 16 258 4
151 Be thou nigh at hand, O Lord : for all thy com-
15678 23
mand-ments are true.

347 16
152 As concerning thy testimonies, I have known long
258 4 15678 23
since : that thou hast ground-ed them for ever.

Vide humilitatem i. 4 *or* iv. 6

347 258 16 4
O Consider mine adversity, and de-li- ver me : for I do
15678 23
not for-get thy law.

347 258 16
154 Avenge thou my cause, and de-li-ver me : quicken
457 168 23
me ac-cord-ing to thy word.

37 4 12568 4
155 Health is far from the un-god-ly : for they re-gard
15678 23
not thy statutes.

37 4 16 258 4 15678 23
156 Great is thy mer-cy, O Lord : quick-en me, as thou
art wont.

347 12568
157 Many there are that trouble me, and per-se-cute me :
4 15678 23
yet do I not swerve from thy tes- ti-monies.

37 4 12568
158 It grieveth me when I see the trans-gres-sors : because
4 15678 23
they keep not thy law.

347 12568
159 Consider, O Lord, how I love thy com-mand-ments :
4 15678 23
O quicken me, according to thy lov-ing-kindness.

347 12568
160 Thy word is true from ev-er-last-ing : all the judge-
4 15678 23
ments of thy righteousness en-dure for evermore.

Principes persecuti sunt iij. 5

37 4 16 258
PRinces have persecuted me with-out a cause : but my
4 15678 23
heart standeth in awe of thy word.

37 4 16 258 4 15678 23
162 I am as glad of thy word : as one that find-eth great
spoils.

347 12568 4 15678 23
163 As for lies, I hate and ab-hor them : but thy law do
I love.

347 12568 4
164 Seven times a day do I praise thee : because of thy
15678 23
righ-teous judgements.

3 47 16 258
165 Great is the peace that they have who love thy law :
4 15678 23
and they are not of-fend-ed at it.

3 47 16 258
166 Lord, I have looked for thy sa-ving health : & done
4 15678 23
af-ter thy com-mandments.

347 12568 4
167 My soul hath kept thy tes-ti-mo-nies : and lov-ed
15678 23
them ex-ceedingly.

347 12568
168 I have kept thy commandments and tes-ti-mo-nies :
4 15678 23
for all my ways are be-fore thee.

Appropinquet deprecatio iij. 5

37 4 16 258
LEt my complaint come be-fore thee, O Lord : give me
457 168 23
understanding, ac-cord-ing to thy word.

347 12568
170 Let my supplication come be-fore thee : deliver me,
457 168 23
ac-cord-ing to thy word.

37 4 16 258
171 My lips shall speak of thy praise : when thou hast
457 168 23
taught me thy statutes.

37 4 16 258
172 Yea, my tongue shall sing of thy word : for all thy
457 168 23
com-mand-ments are righteous.

347 12568 4 15678 23
173 Let thine hand help me : for I have cho-sen thy com-
mandments.

3 47 16 258
174 I have longed for thy sa-ving health, O Lord : and in
4 15678 23
thy law is my delight.

347 12568
175 O let my soul live, and it shall praise thee : and thy
457 168 23
judge-ments shall help me.

37 4 16 258
176 I have gone astray like a sheep that is lost : O seek
4 15678 23
thy servant, | for I do not for-get thy com-mandments.

At Mattins

DAY 27 Ps. 120 *Ad Dominum* i. 10 *or* vj.

37 4 16 258 4 15678
WHen I was in trouble I call-ed up-on the Lord : — and
23
he heard me.

3 47 16 258 457
2 Deliver my soul, O Lord, from ly-ing lips : and from
168 2
a de-ceitful tongue.

37 4 16
3 What reward shall be given or done unto thee, thou false
258
4 15678 23
tongue : even mighty and sharp ar-rows, with hot burning
coals.

347 12568
4 Wo is me, that I am constrained to dwell with Me-
4 15678 23
sech : and to have my habitation among the tents of Cedar.

37 4 16 258 457
5 My soul hath long dwelt a-mong them : that are en-
168 23
e-mies unto peace.

37 4 16
6 I labour for peace, | but when I speak un-to them there-
258
457 168 23
of : they make them rea- dy to battle.

Ps. 121 *Levavi oculos* v. 2 *or* viij. 2

37 4 16 258 ·4
I Will lift up mine eyes un-to the hills : from whence
15678 23
com-eth my help.

37 4 16 258 ·4
2 My help cometh e-ven from the Lord : who hath made
15678 23
hea-ven and earth.

37 4 12568
3 He will not suffer thy foot to be mov-ed : and he that
4 15678 23
keep-eth thee will not sleep.

347 258 16 4 15678
4 Behold, he that keep-eth Is- ra-el : shall nei-ther slum-
23
ber nor sleep.

347 12568
5 The Lord himself is thy keep-er : the Lord is thy de-
4 15678 23
fence up-on thy right hand ;

37 4 16 258 457 168 23
6 So that the sun shall not burn thee by day : nei-ther the
moon by night.

34 7 12568
7 The Lord shall preserve thee from all e- vil : yea, it is
4 15678 23
even he that shall keep thy soul.

3 47 16
8 The Lord shall preserve thy going out, and thy com-ing
258 4 15678 23
in : from this time forth for evermore.

Ps. 122 *Lætatus sum* i. 2 *or* iv. 6

37 4 16 258 4
I Was glad when they said un-to me : We will go in-to
6 123578
the höuse of the Lord.

37 4 16 258 4 15678 23
2 Our feet shall stand in thy gates : — O Hie-rusalem.

347 12568 457 168 23
3 Hierusalem is built as a ci- ty : that is at u- ni- ty in
itself.

37 4 16
4 For thither the tribes go up, | even the tribes of the
258 4 6 123578
Lord : to testify unto Israel, | to give thanks un-to the Näme
of the Lord.

347 12568
5 For there is the seat of judge-ment ; even the seat of
4 15678 23
the house of David.

37 4 258 16 457
6 O pray for the peace of Hie-ru-sa-lem : they shall pros-
168 23
per that love thee.

3 47 16 258 4 15678
7 Peace be with-in thy walls : and plenteousness with- in
23
thy palaces.

3 47 16 258 457
8 For my brethren and com-pan-ions' sakes : I will wish
168 23
thee pros-perity.

3 47 16 258 4
9 Yea, because of the house of the Lord our God : I will
15678 23
seek to do thee good.

Ps. 123 *Ad te levavi* ij. I *or* viij. I

3 47 16 258 4
UNto thee lift I up mine eyes : O thou that dwel-lest
15678 23
in the heavens.

2 Behold, even as the eyes of servants look unto the hand
37
of their masters, | and as the eyes of a maiden unto the hand
4 12568
of her mis-tress : even so our eyes wait upon the Lord our
457 168 23
God, | until he have mer-cy up-on us.

37 4 12568
3 Have mercy upon us, O Lord, have mer-cy up-on us :
4 15678 23
for we are ut-ter- ly de-spised.

37 4 12568
4 Our soul is filled with the scornful re-proof of the weal-
457 168 23
thy : and with the de-spite-ful-ness of the proud.

Ps. 124 *Nisi quia Dominus* i. 3 *or* iij. I

IF the Lord himself had not been on our side, | now may
37 4 16 258
Is-ra-el say : if the Lord himself had not been on our
4 15678 23
side, | when men rose up a-gainst us;

37 4 16 258
2 They had swal-lowed us up quick : when they were so
4 15678 23
wrathfully dis-plea-sed at us.

37 4 258 16
3 Yea, the wa-ters had drown--ed us : and the stream had
4 15678 23
gone o- ver our soul.

37 4 16 258 4 15678 23
4 The deep wa-ters of the proud : had gone e-ven o- ver
our soul.

37 4 16 258
5 But prai-sed be the Lord : who hath not given us over
4 15678 23
for a prey un-to their teeth.

37 4
6 Our soul is escaped | even as a bird out of the snare of
12568 457 168 23
the fow-ler : the snare is broken, and we are de-livered.

37 4 16 258
7 Our help standeth in the Name of the Lord : who hath
·4 15678 23
made hea-ven and earth.

Ps. 125 *Qui confidunt* viij. 1 *or* 2

37
THey that put their trust in the Lord shall be even as
4 12568
the mount Sy-on : which may not be removed, | but
4 15678 23
stand-eth fast for ever.

347 258 16
2 The hills stand a-bout Hie-ru- sa-lem : even so stand-
4 15678
eth the Lord round about his people, | from this time forth
23
for evermore.

37 4
3 For the rod of the ungodly cometh not into the lot of
12568 ·4 15678 23
the righ-teous : lest the righteous put their hand un- to
wickedness.

347 16 258 4 15678 23
4 Do well, O Lord : unto those that are good and true
of heart.

347 258 16
5 As for such as turn back unto their own wick-ed-ness :
the Lord shall lead them forth with the evil-doers ; but peace
457 168 23
shall be up-on Israel.

At Evensong

DAY 27 Ps. 126 *In convertendo* i. 2 *or* 4

347 12568
WHen the Lord turned again the captivi-ty of Sy-on :
4 15678 23
then were we like un- to them that dream.

37 4 12568 4 15678 23
2 Then was our mouth fil-led with laugh-ter : — and our
tongue with joy.

347 12568
3 Then said they a-mong the hea-then : The Lord hath
4 15678 23
done great things for them.

347 12568
4 Yea, the Lord hath done great things for us al-rea-dy :
4 6 123578
— where- öf we rejoice.

37 4 16 258 4 15678 23
5 Turn our cap-ti-vi-ty, O Lord : as the ri- vers in the
south.

3 47 16 258 4 15678 23
6 They that sow in tears : — — shall reap in joy.

37
7 He that now goeth on his way weeping, | and bear-eth
4 16 258 4
forth good seed : shall doubtless come again with joy, | and
15678 23
bring his sheaves with him.

Ps. 127 *Nisi Dominus* ij. 1 *or* viij. 2

347 16 258 4
EXcept the Lord build the house : their labour is but
15678 23
lost that build it.

347 12568 4 15678
2 Except the Lord keep the ci- ty : the watch-man wa-
23
keth but in vain.

3 It is but lost labour that ye haste to rise up early, | and

347 258 16
so late take rest, and eat the bread of care-ful-ness : for so
4 15678 23
he giv-eth his be-loved sleep.
37 4 16 258
4 Lo, children and the fruit of the womb : are an heritage
4 15678 23
and gift that com-eth of the Lord.
37 4 12568
5 Like as the arrows in the hand of the gi- ant : even so
4 6 123578
are the yöung children.
37 4 16 258
6 Happy is the man that hath his qui-ver full of them :
457
they shall not be ashamed when they speak with their en-
168 23
e-mies in the gate.

Ps. 128 *Beati omnes* i. 1 *or* viij. 2

3 47 16 258 4 15678 23
BLessed are all they that fear the Lord : and walk in his
ways.
37 4 16 258
2 For thou shalt eat the la-bours of thine hands : O well
4 15678 23
is thee, and hap-py shalt thou be.
3 47 16 258 4 15678
3 Thy wife shall be as the fruit-ful vine : upon the walls
23
of thine house.
347 12568 4 15678
4 Thy children like the o-live branch-es : round a-bout
23
thy table.
347 12568 4 6 123578
5 Lo, thus shall the man be bles-sed : — that feär-eth
the Lord.
347 12568
6 The Lord from out of Syon shall so bless thee : that
4 15678 23
thou shalt see Hierusalem in prosperi-ty all thy life long.

347 12568
7 Yea, that thou shalt see thy chil-dren's chil-dren : and
457 168 23
peace up-on Israel.

Ps. 129 *Sæpe expugnaverunt* iij. 5 *or* vij. 7

37 4
MAny a time have they fought against me from my
16 258 457 168 23
youth up : may Is- ra- el now say.

37 4 16
2 Yea, many a time have they vexed me from my youth
258 457 168 23
up : but they have not pre-vail-ed a-gainst me.

3 47 16 258 4 15678 23
3 The plowers plow-ed up-on my back : and made long
furrows.

347 16 258
4 But the righ-teous Lord : hath hewn the snares of the
457 168 23
un-god-ly in pieces.

347 12568
5 Let them be confounded & turn-ed back-ward : as ma-
4 15678 23
ny as have e-vil will at Syon.

347 12568
6 Let them be even as the grass growing up-on the house-
4 15678 23
tops : which withereth a-fore it be plucked up ;

37 4 16 258
7 Whereof the mower fil-leth not his hand : neither he
4 15678 23
that bindeth up the sheaves his bosom.

4
8 So that they who go by say not so much as, | The Lord
23578 16 4 6 123578
pros-per you : we wish you good luck in the Näme of the
Lord.

Ps. 130 *De profundis* i. 6

37 4 16 258 4 6
OUt of the deep have I called un-to thee, O Lord : — —
123578
Lörd, hear my voice.

37 4 16 258 4 15678 23
2 O let thine ears con-si-der well : the voice of my com-
plaint.

37 4 16
3 If thou, Lord, wilt be extreme to mark what is done a-
258 457 168 23
miss : O Lord, who may a-bide it ?
37 4 16 258 4 15678 23
4 For there is mer-cy with thee : therefore shalt thou be
feared.

37 4 16 258 4
5 I look for the Lord ; my soul doth wait for him : in his
15678 23
word is my trust.

37 4 16 258
6 My soul fleeth un-to the Lord : before the morning
4 15678 23
watch, | I say, be-fore the morning watch.

347
7 O Israel, trust in the Lord, | for with the Lord there is
12568 457 168 23
mer-cy : and with him is plen-teous re-demption.
4 23578 16 4 15678 23
8 And he shall re-deem Is- ra-el : — — from all his sins.

Ps. 131 *Domine, non est* ij. 1 *or* viij. 1

347 12568 4 15678 23
LOrd, I am not high-mind-ed : I have no proud looks.
34 7 12568 4
2 I do not exercise myself in great mat-ters : which
15678 23
are too high for me.

3 But I refrain my soul, and keep it low, | like as a child
347 12568 4 15678
that is weaned from his mo-ther : yea, my soul is e-ven as
23
a weaned child.
37 4 16 258 4 15678 23
4 O Israel, trust in the Lord : from this time forth for
evermore.

At Mattins

DAY 28 Ps. 132 *Memento, Domine* viij. 1

347 12568 4 15678 23
LOrd, re-mem-ber Da-vid : and all his trouble.
37 4 16 258
2 How he sware un-to the Lord : and vowed a vow
4 15678 23
un-to the Almigh-ty God of Iacob ;
37 4 16 258
3 I will not come within the taber-na-cle of mine house :
4 15678 23
nor climb up in-to my bed ;
37 4
4 I will not suffer mine eyes to sleep, | nor mine eye-lids
12568 4 6 123578
to slum-ber : neither the temples of my head to täke any
rest ;
37 4 16 258
5 Until I find out a place for the tem-ple of the Lord : an
4 15678 23
habitation for the migh-ty God of Iacob.
347 258 16 4 15678 23
6 Lo, we heard of the same at Eph-ra-ta : and found it in
the wood.
347 12568
7 We will go into his ta-ber-na-cle : and fall low on our
4 15678 23
knees be-fore his foot-stool.
347 258 16 4
8 Arise, O Lord, in-to thy rest-ing-place : thou, and the
15678 23
ark of thy strength.
37 4 258 16
9 Let thy priests be cloth-ed with righ-teous-ness : and let
.4 15678 23
thy saints sing with joyfulness.
3 47 16 258
10 For thy ser-vant Da-vid's sake : turn not away the
4 15678 23
presence of thine An-ointed.
347 12568
11 The Lord hath made a faithful oath un-to Da-vid : &
4 15678 23
he shall not shrink from it ;

37 4 12568 457 168 23
12 Of the fruit of thy bo-dy : shall I set up-on thy seat.

13 If thy children will keep my covenant, | and my tes-
347 12568
timonies that I shall learn them : their children also shall
4 15678 23
sit upon thy seat for evermore.

37
14 For the Lord hath chosen Syon to be an habi-ta-tion
4 16 258 4 15678 23
for him-self : he hath long-ed for her.

347 12568
15 This shall be my rest for ev-er : here will I dwell,
457 168 23
for I have a de-light therein.

37 4 12568
16 I will bless her vic-tuals with in-crease : and will
4 15678 23
sa-tis- fy her poor with bread.

3 47 16 258 ·4
17 I will deck her priests with health : and her saints
15678 23
shall re-joice and sing.

347 12568
18 There shall I make the horn of Da-vid to flou-rish : I
4 15678 23
have ordained a lantern for mine An-ointed.

37 4 16 258
19 As for his enemies, I shall clothe them with shame :
4 6 123578
but upon himself shall his cröwn flourish.

Ps. 133 *Ecce quam bonum* iv. 4 *or* v. 1

37 4 16 258
BEhold, how good and joy-ful a thing it is : brethren, to
457 168 23
dwell to-ge-ther in unity !

2 It is like the precious ointment upon the head | that ran
37 4 16 258
down un-to the beard : even unto Aäron's beard, | and went
457 168 23
down to the skirts of his clothing.

347 12568 4 15678
3 Like as the dew of Her-mon : which fell upon the hill
23
of Syon.

347 12568 4 15678
4 For there the Lord promi-sed his bles-sing : and life
23
for evermore.

Ps. 134 *Ecce nunc* 1. 2 *or* vij. 6

3 47 16 258 4 15678 23
BE-hold now, praise the Lord : all ye ser-vants of the
Lord ;

37 4 16 258
2 Ye that by night stand in the house of the Lord : even
4 15678 23
in the courts of the house of our God.

347 12568 4 15678 23
3 Lift up your hands in the sanc-tu- a- ry : — — and
praise the Lord.

37 4 16 258
4 The Lord that made hea-ven and earth : give thee bles-
4 15678 23
sing out of Syon.

Ps. 135 *Laudate nomen* iij. 6 *or* vij. 6

37 4 16 258
O Praise the Lord, | laud ye the Name of the Lord :
4 15678 23
praise it, O ye ser-vants of the Lord.

37 4 16 258
2 Ye that stand in the house of the Lord : in the courts
4 15678 23
of the house of our God.

347 12568
3 O praise the Lord, for the Lord is gra-cious : O sing
4 15678 23
praises unto his Name, for it is lovely.

37 4 16 258
4 For-why the Lord hath chosen Iacob un-to him-self :
4 15678 23
and Israel for his own pos-session.

3 47 16 258
5 For I know that the Lord is great : and that our Lord
457 168 23
is a-bove all gods.

37
6 Whatsoever the Lord pleased, | that did he in hea-ven,
4 16 258 4 15678 23
and in earth : and in the sea, and in all deep places.
37 4 16
7 He bringeth forth the clouds from the ends of the
258
world : and sendeth forth lightnings with the rain, | bring-
457 168 23
ing the winds out of his treasures.
37 4 12568 4 15678 23
8 He smote the first-born of E- gypt : — both of man
and beast.

9 He hath sent tokens & wonders into the midst of thee, |
347 12568 4 15678 23
O thou land of E- gypt : upon Pharaö, and all his servants.
347 12568 4 6 123578
10 He smote di-vers na- tions : — and slĕw mighty kings.
347
11 Sehon king of the Amorites, and Og the king of
12568 457 168 23
Ba-san : and all the king-doms of Chanaän.
347 258 16
12 And gave their land to be an he- ri-tage : even an
4 15678 23
heritage unto Is-ra- el his people.
37 4 12568
13 Thy Name, O Lord, en-dur-eth for ev-er : so doth
4 15678 23
thy memorial, O Lord, | from one genera-tion to an-other.
347 12568
14 For the Lord will a-venge his peo-ple : and be gra-
4 15678 23
cious un- to his servants.
37 4
15 As for the images of the heathen, | they are but sil-ver
16 258 4 15678 23
and gold : the work of men's hands.

347 12568 4
16 They have mouths, and speak not : eyes have they,
15678 23
but they see not.

347 12568
17 They have ears, and yet they hear not : neither is there
4 15678 23
a-ny breath in their mouths.

37 4 16 258
18 They that make them are like un-to them : and so
4 15678 23
are all they that put their trust in them.

347 258 16
19 Praise the Lord, ye house of Is- ra-el : praise the Lord,
4 15678 23
ye house of Aäron.

347 12568 4 6
20 Praise the Lord, ye house of Le-vi : ye that fear the
123578
Lörd, praise the Lord.

347 12568 4 15678
21 Praised be the Lord out of Sy-on : who dwel-leth at
23
Hie-rusalem.

At Evensong

DAY 28 Ps. 136 *Confitemini* iij. 6 *or* v. 1

347 12568
O Give thanks unto the Lord, for he is gra-cious : and
457 168 23
his mercy en-dur-eth for ever.

37 4 16 258
2 O give thanks unto the God of all gods : for his mercy
457 168 23
en-dur-eth for ever.

37 4 16 258
3 O thank the Lord of all lords : for &c.

37 4 12568
4 Who only do-eth great won-ders : for &c.

347 12568
5 Who by his excellent wisdom made the hea-vens : for &c.

347 12568
6 Who laid out the earth a-bove the wa-ters : for &c.

347 16 258
7 Who hath made great lights : for &c.

37 4 16 258
8 The sun to rule the day : for &c.

37 4 16 258
9 The moon and the stars to gov-ern the night : for &c.

347 12568
10 Who smote Egypt with their first-born : for &c.

347 12568
11 And brought out Israel from a-mong them : for &c.

37 4 16 258
12 With a mighty hand, and stretch-ed out arm : for &c.

37 4 16 258
13 Who divided the Red sea in two parts : for &c.

347 258 16
14 And made Israel to go through the midst of it : for &c.

37
15 But as for Pharaö and his host, | he overthrew them in
4 16 258
the Red sea : for &c.

347 258 16
16 Who led his people through the wil-der-ness : for &c.

347 16 258
17 Who smote great kings : for &c.

3 47 16 258
18 Yea, and slew migh-ty kings : for &c.

37 4 258 16
19 Sehon king of the A-mor-ites : for &c.

347 12568
20 And Og the king of Ba-san : for &c.

347 258 16
21 And gave away their land for an he- ri-tage : for &c.

347 12568
22 Even for an heritage unto Isra-el his ser-vant : for &c.

347 12568
23 Who remembered us when we were in trou-ble : for &c.

347 258 16
24 And hath delivered us from our en- e-mies : for &c.

37 4 16 258
25 Who giveth food to all flesh : for &c.

347 12568
26 O give thanks unto the God of hea-ven : for &c.

347 16 258
27 O give thanks unto the Lord of lords : for his mercy
457 168 23
en-dur-eth for ever.

Ps. 137 *Super flumina* i. 2 *or* ij. 1

347 16 258
BY the waters of Babylon we sat down and wept : when
4 15678 23
we remember-ed thee, O Syon.

37 4 16 258 4 15678
2 As for our harps, we hang-ed them up : upon the trees
23
that are therein.

3 For they that led us away captive | required of us then
347 258 16 4
a song and melody in our hea-vi-ness : Sing us one of the
15678 23
songs of Syon.

37 4 16 258 4 15678 23
4 How shall we sing the Lord's song : — in a strange
land?

347 258 16
5 If I forget thee, O Hie-ru-sa-lem : let my right hand
4 15678 23
for-get her cunning.

6 If I do not remember thee, | let my tongue cleave to
37 4 16 258 457 168 23
the roof of my mouth : yea, if I prefer not Hie-ru- sa-lem
in my mirth.

37 4
7 Remember the children of Edom, O Lord, in the day of
258 16
Hie-ru-sa-lem : how they said, | Down with it, down with
4 15678 23
it, e- ven to the ground.

37 4 258 16
8 O daughter of Babylon, wast-ed with mi-se-ry : yea,
4 15678 23
happy shall he be that rewardeth thee, as thou hast served us.

37 4 12568
9 Blessed shall he be that ta-keth thy chil-dren : and
4 15678 23
throw-eth them a-gainst the stones.

Ps. 138 *Confitebor tibi* vij. 2 *or* 6

37 4 16
I Will give thanks unto thee, O Lord, with my whole
258 4 15678 23
heart : even before the gods will I sing praise un-to
thee.

2 I will worship toward thy holy temple, and praise thy
37 4 16 258
Name, | because of thy loving-kind-ness and truth : for thou
457 168 23
hast magnified thy Name, and thy Word a-bove all things.

347 258 16
3 When I called upon thee, thou heard-est me : and endu-
4 15678 23
edst my soul with much strength.

37 4 16 258
4 All the kings of the earth shall praise thee, O Lord :
4 15678 23
for they have heard the words of thy mouth.

37 4 16 258
5 Yea, they shall sing in the ways of the Lord : that
4 15678 23
great is the glo- ry of the Lord.

347
6 For though the Lord be high, | yet hath he respect un-to
12568 4 15678 23
the low-ly : as for the proud, he behold-eth them a-far off.

347
7 Though I walk in the midst of trouble, | yet shalt thou
12568
re-fresh me : thou shalt stretch forth thy hand upon the furi-
4 15678 23
ousness of mine enemies, | and thy right hand shall save
me.

37 4
8 The Lord shall make good his loving-kind-ness to-
12568
ward me : yea, thy mercy, O Lord, endureth for ever;
457 168 23
despise not then the works of thine own hands.

At Mattins

DAY 29 Ps. 139 *Domine, probasti* iij. 5 *or* viij. 5

O Lord, thou hast searched me [347]out, and [12568]known me : thou
knowest my down-sitting, and mine uprising ; thou
understan-[4]dest [6]my [123578]thoüghts long before.

2 Thou art about my path, [3]and a-[47]bout [16]my [258]bed : and
[457]spi-[168]est [23]out all my ways.

3 For lo, there is not a [37]word [4]in [16]my [258]tongue : but thou,
O Lord, knowest [4]it [15678]al- [23]to-gether.

4 Thou hast fashioned me be-[37]hind [4]and [16]be-[258]fore : and laid
[4]thine [15678]hand [23]up-on me.

5 Such knowledge is too wonderful and [37]ex-[4]cel-lent [12568]for
me : I cannot [4]at-[15678]tain [23]un-to it.

6 Whither shall I go then [347]from thy [12568]Spi-rit : or whither
shall I go [4]then [15678]from [23]thy presence ?

7 If I climb up into [37]hea-ven, [4]thou [16]art [258]there : if I go
down to hell, [4]thou [6]art [123578]thëre also.

8 If I take the [37]wings [4]of the [12568]morn-ing : and remain in the
ut-[4]ter-[6]most [123578]pärts of the sea ;

9 Even there also shall [347]thy hand [12568]lead me : and thy [4]right
[15678]hand [23]shall hold me.

10 If I say, | Peradventure the [37]dark-[4]ness shall [258]co-[16]ver me :
then shall my night [4]be [15678]turn-[23]ed to day.

11 Yea, the darkness is no darkness with thee, | but the
37 4 16 258 4 15678 23
night is as clear as the day : the darkness & light to thee are
both alike.

347 16 258 4 15678
12 For my reins are thine : thou hast covered me in
23
my mother's womb.

13 I will give thanks unto thee, | for I am fearfully and
37 4 16 258
won-der-ful-ly made : marvellous are thy works, | and that
.4 15678 23
my soul know-eth right well.

37 4 16 258
14 My bones are not hid from thee : though I be made
4 6 123578
secretly, | and fashion-ed be-nëath in the earth.

37 4 12568
15 Thine eyes did see my substance, | yet be-ing un-per-
4 15678 23
fect : and in thy book were all my mem-bers written ;

347 258 16 4
16 Which day by day were fa-shion-ed : when as yet
15678 23
there was none of them.

37 4 16 258
17 How dear are thy counsels un-to me, O God : O how
457 168 23
great is the sum of them !

37 4 16 258
18 If I tell them, they are more in num-ber than the sand :
4 15678 23
when I wake up, I am pre-sent with thee.

37 4 16 258
19 Wilt thou not slay the wick-ed, O God : depart from
4 6 123578
me, ye blöod-thirsty men.

347 12568
20 For they speak unrighteous-ly a-gainst thee : and thine
4 15678 23
ene-mies take thy Name in vain.

37 4 16 258
21 Do not I hate them, O Lord, that hate thee : and am
·4 15678 23
not I grieved with those that rise up a-gainst thee?

37 4 16 258 4
22 Yea, I hate them right sore : even as though they
15678 23
were mine enemies.

37 4 16 258
23 Try me, O God, and seek the ground of my heart :
4 15678 23
prove me, and ex-am-ine my thoughts.

37 4 12568
24 Look well if there be any way of wick-ed-ness in me :
·4 15678 23
and lead me in the way ev- er-lasting.

Ps. 140 *Eripe me, Domine* i. 1 *or* 4

37 4 16 258
DEliver me, O Lord, from the e-vil man : and preserve
4 15678 23
me from the wicked man.

37 4 16 258 ·4
2 Who imagine mis-chief in their hearts : and stir up strife
15678 23
all the day long.

347 12568
3 They have sharpened their tongues like a ser-pent : ad-
4 15678 23
ders' poison is un- der their lips.

37 4 12568
4 Keep me, O Lord, from the hands of the un-god-ly :
preserve me from the wicked men, | who are purposed to
4 15678 23
o-ver-throw my goings.

3
5 The proud have laid a snare for me, | and spread a net
47 16 258 4 15678 23
a-broad with cords : yea, and set traps in my way.

37 4 16 258
6 I said unto the Lord, | Thou art my God : hear the
457 168 23
voice of my prayers, O Lord.

37 4 16 258
7 O Lord God, thou strength of my health : thou hast
4 15678 23
covered my head in the day of battle.

347 16 258
8 Let not the ungodly have his de-sire, O Lord : let not
4 15678 23
his mischievous imagination prosper, lest they be too proud.

37 4 16
9 Let the mischief of their own lips fall up-on the head of
258 4 15678 23
them : that com-pass me about.

347 12568
10 Let hot burning coals fall up-on them : let them be
457 168 23
cast into the fire, and into the pit, | that they ne- ver rise
up again.

37 4 16 258
11 A man full of words shall not pros-per up-on the earth :
4 15678 23
evil shall hunt the wicked person to o- ver-throw him.

3 47 16 258
12 Sure I am that the Lord will a-venge the poor : and
457 168 23
maintain the cause of the helpless.

37 4 16 258
13 The righteous also shall give thanks un-to thy Name :
457 168 23
and the just shall con-tin- ue in thy sight.

Ps. 141 *Domine, clamavi* iv. 7 *or* vj.

37 4 16 258
LOrd, I call upon thee, haste thee un-to me : and consider
4 15678 23
my voice when I cry un-to thee.

347 12568
2 Let my prayer be set forth in thy sight as the in- cense :
4 15678 23
and let the lifting up of my hands be an eve-ning sacrifice.

3 47 16 258
3 Set a watch, O Lord, be-fore my mouth : and keep
4 15678 23
the door of my lips.

3 47 16 258
4 O let not mine heart be inclined to a-ny e-vil thing :
let me not be occupied in ungodly works with the men that
4 15678 23
work wickedness, | lest I eat of such things as please them.

347 12568 4 15678 23
5 Let the righteous rather smite me friend-ly : — and reprove me.

347 16 258
6 But let not their precious balms break my head : yea, I
4 15678 23
will pray yet a-gainst their wickedness.

347 12568
7 Let their judges be overthrown in sto-ny pla-ces : that
4 15678 23
they may hear my words, for they are sweet.

3 47 16 258
8 Our bones lie scatter-ed be-fore the pit : like as when
4 15678 23
one breaketh and hew-eth wood up-on the earth.

37 4 16 258
9 But mine eyes look unto thee, O Lord God : in thee is
4 15678 23
my trust, | O cast not out my soul.

37 4 16 258
10 Keep me from the snare that they have laid for me :
4 15678 23
and from the traps of the wick-ed doers.

347 12568
11 Let the ungodly fall into their own nets to- ge- ther :
457 168 23
and let me ev- er es-cape them.

At Evensong

DAY 29 Ps. 142 *Voce mea ad Dominum* i. 8 *or* iij. 4

37 4 16 258
I Cried unto the Lord with my voice : yea, even unto the
4 15678 23
Lord did I make my sup-pli-cation.

347 12568
2 I poured out my com-plaints be-fore him : and shewed
4 15678 23
him of my trouble.

37 4 16
3 When my spirit was in heaviness | thou knew-est my
258 4 15678 23
path : in the way wherein I walked have they privi-ly laid a
snare for me.
37 4 16 258
4 I looked also up-on my right hand : and saw there was
4 15678 23
no man that would know me.
37 4 16 258 457 168 23
5 I had no place to flee un-to : and no man car-ed for my
soul.
37 4 16 258
6 I cried unto thee, O Lord, and said : Thou art my
457 168 23
hope, | and my portion in the land of the living.
37 4 16 258 4 6 123578
7 Con-si-der my com-plaint : for I am brŏught very low.
347 12568 4 15678 23
8 O deliver me from my per-se-cu-tors : for they are too
strong for me.
9 Bring my soul out of prison, | that I may give thanks
37 4 16 258
un-to thy Name : which thing if thou wilt grant me, | then
4 15678 23
shall the righteous resort un- to my company.

Ps. 143 *Domine, exaudi* vij. 1 *or* 7

37 4 16 258
HEar my prayer, O Lord, and con-si-der my de-sire :
4 15678 23
hearken unto me for thy truth, & righ-teous-ness' sake.
347 12568
2 And enter not into judgement with thy ser-vant : for in
4 15678 23
thy sight shall no man living be jus- ti-fied.
3 For the enemy hath persecuted my soul ; he hath smit-

37 4 16 258
ten my life down to the ground : he hath laid me in the
4 15678 23
darkness, | as the men that have been long dead.

37 4 12568
4 Therefore is my spirit vex-ed with-in me : & my heart
457 168 23
with-in me is desolate.

3 47 16
5 Yet do I remember the time past; I muse upon all thy
258 4 15678 23
works : yea, I exercise myself in the works of thy hands.

37 4 16 258
6 I stretch forth my hands un-to thee : my soul gaspeth
4 15678 23
unto thee as a thirsty land.

3 47
7 Hear me, O Lord, and that soon, | for my spi-rit wax-
16 258
eth faint : hide not thy face from me, | lest I be like unto
4 15678 23
them that go down in-to the pit.

8 O let me hear thy loving-kindness betimes in the morn-
37 4 16 258
ing, | for in thee is my trust : shew thou me the way that
4 15678 23
I should walk in, | for I lift up my soul un-to thee.

347 258 16
9 Deliver me, O Lord, from mine en- e-mies : for I flee
4 15678 23
un-to thee to hide me.

37
10 Teach me to do the thing that pleaseth thee, | for thou
4 16 258 4 15678
art my God : let thy loving Spirit lead me forth into the land
23
of righteousness.

37 4 16 258
11 Quicken me, O Lord, for thy Name's sake : & for thy
4 15678 23
righteousness' sake | bring my soul out of trouble.

347 258 16
12 And of thy goodness slay mine en- e-mies : and destroy
4 15678 23
all them that vex my soul; for I am thy servant.

At Mattins

DAY 30 PS. 144 *Benedictus Dominus* i. 4 *or* vj.

347 16 258
BLessed be the Lord my strength : who teacheth my
4 15678 23
hands to war, and my fin-gers to fight;

2 My hope and my fortress, my castle and deliverer, | my
3 47 16 258 4
de-fend-er, in whom I trust : who subdueth my peo-ple
15678 23
that is under me.

37 4 16
3 Lord, what is man, that thou hast such re-spect un-to
258 4 15678 23
him : or the son of man, that thou so re-gardest him?

37 4 16 258 ·4
4 Man is like a thing of naught : his time passeth a-way
15678 23
like a shadow.

37 4 16 258
5 Bow thy heavens, O Lord, and come down : touch the
457 168 23
moun-tains, and they shall smoke.

37 4 12568
6 Cast forth thy light-ning, and tear them : shoot out
4 15678 23
thine ar-rows, and con-sume them.

37 4 16 258
7 Send down thine hand from a-bove : deliver me, and
4 6 123578
take me out of the great waters, | from the hand of stränge
children.

37 4 258 16
8 Whose mouth talk-eth of va-ni-ty : and their right hand
4 15678 23
is a right hand of wickedness.

3 47 16 258
9 I will sing a new song un-to thee, O God : and sing
4 6 123578
praises un-to thee up-on a tën-stringed lute.

37 4 16 258
10 Thou hast given vic-tory un-to kings : and hast

4 15678 23
delivered David thy servant from the pe- ril of the sword.

3 4 7 12568
11 Save me, and deliver me from the hand of strange chil-
dren : whose mouth talketh of vanity, | and their right hand
457 168 23
is a right hand of in-iquity.

37 4 16 258
12 That our sons may grow up as the young plants : and
4 15678 23
that our daughters may be as the polished cor-ners of the
temple.

13 That our garners may be full, | and plenteous with all
37 4 16 258
man-ner of store : that our sheep may bring forth thousands
457 168 23
and ten thou-sands in our streets.

37
14 That our oxen may be strong to labour, | that there be
4 16 258
457 168 23
no de-cay : no leading into captivity, | & no com-plain-ing in
our streets.

37 4 16 258
15 Happy are the people that are in such a case : yea, bles-
4 15678 23
sed are the people who have the Lord for their God.

Ps. 145 *Exaltabo te, Deus* v. 2 *or* vij. 5

3 47 16 258
I Will magnify thee, O God, my King : and I will praise
457 168 23
thy Name for ev- er and ever.

37 4 16 258
2 Every day will I give thanks un-to thee : and praise thy
457 168 23
Name for ev- er and ever.

347 12568
3 Great is the Lord, | and marvellous-worthy to be prai-
457 168 23
sed : there is no end of his greatness.

347 12568
4 One generation shall praise thy works un-to an- o- ther :
4 15678 23
and de-clare thy power.

347 12568
5 As for me, I will be talking of thy wor-ship : thy glory,
4 15678 23
thy praise, and wondrous works ;

37 4
6 So that men shall speak of the might of thy mar-vel-
16 258 457 168 23
lous acts : and I will also tell of thy greatness.

347 12568
7 The memorial of thine abundant kindness shall be shew-
457 168 23
ed : and men shall sing of thy righteousness.

37 4 258 16
8 The Lord is gra-cious and mer-ci-ful : long-suffering,
4 6 123578
and of grëat goodness.

37 4 16 258 4
9 The Lord is loving unto ev-e-ry man : and his mercy is
15678 23
o- ver all his works.

37 4 16 258 4
10 All thy works praise thee, O Lord : and thy saints give
15678 23
thanks un-to thee.

347 12568 457 168
11 They shew the glory of thy king-dom : and talk of
23
thy power.

347 12568
12 That thy power, thy glory, and mightiness of thy king-
4 15678 23
dom : might be known un-to men.

347 12568
13 Thy kingdom is an ever-last-ing king-dom : and thy
4 15678 23
dominion endureth through-out all ages.

37 4 16 258 4
14 The Lord upholdeth all such as fall : and lifteth up all
15678 23
those that are down.

3 47 16 258
15 The eyes of all wait upon thee, O Lord : and thou
4 6 123578
givest them their meat in düe season.

37 4 16 258 457
16 Thou o-pen-est thine hand : and fillest all things liv-
168 23
ing with plenteousness.

3 47 16 258 457 168 23
17 The Lord is righ-teous in all his ways : and ho-ly in
all his works.

347 12568
18 The Lord is nigh unto all them that call up- on him :
4 15678 23
yea, all such as call up- on him faithfully.

347 12568
19 He will fulfil the desire of them that fear him : he also
·4 15678 23
will hear their cry, and will help them.

347 12568
20 The Lord preserveth all them that love him : but scat-
457 168 23
tereth abroad all the un-godly.

37 4 16 258
21 My mouth shall speak the praise of the Lord : and let
457 168 23
all flesh give thanks unto his holy Name for ev- er and ever.

Ps. 146 *Lauda, anima mea* iij. 5 *or* iv. 5

3 47 16
PRaise the Lord, O my soul; while I live will I praise the
258
Lord : yea, as long as I have any being, | I will sing
4 15678 23
prai-ses un- to my God.

37 4 16
2 O put not your trust in princes, nor in a-ny child of
258 4 15678 23
man : for there is no help in them.

3 For when the breath of man goeth forth | he shall turn
37 4 16 258 4 6 123578
a-gain to his earth : and then all his thoüghts perish.

37 4 16 258
4 Blessed is he that hath the God of Ia-cob for his help :
4 15678 23
and whose hope is in the Lord his God ;

37 4
5 Who made heaven & earth, | the sea, and all that there-
16 258 457 168 23
in is : who keepeth his pro-mise for ever ;

37 4 16 258
6 Who helpeth them to right that suf-fer wrong : who
457 168 23
feed-eth the hungry.

347 12568 4 6
7 The Lord looseth men out of pri-son : the Lord giv-eth
123578
sight to the blind.

37 4 12568
8 The Lord helpeth them that are fal-len : the Lord car-
4 15678 23
eth for the righteous.

9 The Lord careth for the strangers ; he defendeth the
347 12568
father-less and wi-dow : as for the way of the ungodly, | he
457 168 23
turn-eth it upside down.

37 4 16
10 The Lord thy God, O Syon, shall be King for ev-er-
258 4 15678 23
more : and throughout all ge- ne-rations.

At Evensong

DAY 30 Ps. 147 *Laudate Dominum* vj. *or* viij. 1

O Praise the Lord, | for it is a good thing to sing praises
37 4 16 258
un-to our God : yea, a joyful and pleasant thing it
457 168 23
is to be thankful.

347 258 16
2 The Lord doth build up Hie-ru-sa-lem : and gather to-
4 15678 23
gether the out-casts of Israel.

37 4 16 258
3 He healeth those that are bro-ken in heart : and giveth
4 15678 23
medicine to heal their sickness.

37 4 16 258 4
4 He telleth the num-ber of the stars : and calleth them
15678 23
all by their names.

37 4 12568
5 Great is our Lord, and great is his pow-er : yea, and
457 168 23
his wis-dom is infinite.

3 47 16 258
6 The Lord set-teth up the meek : and bringeth the un-
4 68 157 23
god-ly down to the ground.

347 12568
7 O sing unto the Lord with thanks-giv-ing : sing praises
·4 15678 23
upon the harp un- to our God ;

8 Who covereth the heaven with clouds, | and prepareth
37 4 16 258
rain for the earth : and maketh the grass to grow upon the
4 15678 23
moun-tains, | and herb for the use of men ;

37 4 12568
9 Who giveth fodder un-to the cat-tle : and feedeth the
4 15678 23
young ravens that call up-on him.

37 4 16 258
10 He hath no pleasure in the strength of an horse : nei-
4 15678 23
ther delighteth he in a- ny man's legs.

347 12568
11 But the Lord's delight is in them that fear him : and
457 168 23
put their trust in his mercy.

347 258 16 4 15678 23
12 Praise the Lord, O Hie-ru-sa-lem : praise thy God, O
Syon.

37 4 16 258
13 For he hath made fast the bars of thy gates : and hath
457 168 23
blessed thy chil-dren with-in thee.

14 He maketh peace ³⁴⁷ in thy ¹²⁵⁶⁸ bor-ders : and filleth thee⁴
¹⁵⁶⁷⁸ ²³
with the flour of wheat.

15 He sendeth forth his ³⁷ com-mand-ment ⁴ up-¹⁶on ²⁵⁸earth : and
⁴ ¹⁵⁶⁷⁸ ²³
his word run-neth ve- ry swiftly.

16 He giveth ³⁴⁷snow ¹⁶like ²⁵⁸wool : and scattereth the hoar-^{.4}
¹⁵⁶⁷⁸ ²³
frost like ashes.

17 He casteth forth his ³⁴⁷ice like ¹²⁵⁶⁸mor-sels : who is a-ble ⁴ ¹⁵⁶⁷⁸to
²³
a-bide his frost ?

18 He sendeth out his ³⁴⁷word, and ²⁵⁸mel-¹⁶teth them : he blow-
^{.4} ¹⁵⁶⁷⁸ ²³
eth with his wind, and the waters flow.

19 He showeth his ³⁴⁷word ¹²⁵⁶⁸un-to Ia-cob : his statutes and
⁴ ¹⁵⁶⁷⁸ ²³
ordinan-ces un- to Israel.

20 He hath not dealt so with ³⁴⁷a-ny ¹²⁵⁶⁸na-tion : neither have
⁴ ¹⁵⁶⁷⁸ ²³
the hea-then know-ledge of his laws.

Ps. 148 *Laudate Dominum* ij. 1 *or* viij. 2

O Praise the ³⁴⁷Lord of ¹²⁵⁶⁸hea-ven : — praise ⁴ ¹⁵⁶⁷⁸him ²³in the height.

2 Praise him, all ye ³⁷an-⁴gels ¹⁶of ²⁵⁸his : — praise ⁴ ¹⁵⁶⁷⁸him, ²³all
his host.

3 Praise him, ³⁴⁷sun ¹⁶and ²⁵⁸moon : praise ⁴ ¹⁵⁶⁷⁸him, ²³all ye stars and
light.

4 Praise him, all ³⁴⁷ye ¹²⁵⁶⁸hea-vens : and ye waters that are a-⁴
¹⁵⁶⁷⁸ ²³
bove the heavens.

37 4 16 258
5 Let them praise the Name of the Lord : for he spake
4
the word, and they were made ; he commanded, and they
15678 23
were cre-ated.

37 4 12568
6 He hath made them fast for ev-er and ev- er : he hath
4 15678 23
given them a law which shall not be broken.

37 4 16 258 457 168 23
7 Praise the Lord up-on earth : ye dra-gons, & all deeps ;

347 12568 4
8 Fire and hail, snow and va-pours : wind and storm, ful-
15678 23
fil-ling his word ;

37 4 16 258 4 6 123578
9 Moun-tains and all hills : fruitful trees and äll cedars ;

34 7 12568 4 68 157 23
10 Beasts and all cat-tle : worms and fea-ther-ed fowls ;

34 7 12568 4 15678
11 Kings of the earth and all peo-ple : princes & all judg-
23
es of the world ;

12 Young men and maidens, old men and children, | praise
37 4 16 258
the Name of the Lord : for his Name only is excellent, | and
4 15678 23
his praise a-bove hea-ven and earth.

347
13 He shall exalt the horn of his people ; all his saints shall
12568 457 168
praise him : even the children of Israel, | even the peo-ple
23
that serveth him.

Ps. 149 *Cantate Domino* vij. 2 *or* 6

37 4 16 258 4
O Sing unto the Lord a new song : let the congrega-tion
6 123578
of säints praise him.

347 12568
2 Let Israel rejoice in him that made him : & let the chil-
457 168 23
dren of Syon be joy-ful in their King.

37 4 16 258
3 Let them praise his Name in the dance : let them sing
4 15678 23
praises unto him with ta- bret and harp.

347 12568 4
4 For the Lord hath pleasure in his peo-ple : and help-eth
6 123578
the mëek-hearted.

37 4 12568 4 15678
5 Let the saints be joy-ful with glo-ry : let them re-joice
23
in their beds.

37 4 16 258
6 Let the praises of God be in their mouth : and a two-
4 15678 23
edg-ed sword in their hands;

347 12568 4 15678 23
7 To be avenged of the hea-then : and to re-buke the
people;

3 47 16 258 4 15678
8 To bind their kings in chains : & their nobles with links
23
of iron.

37 4 12568
9 That they may be avenged of them, as it is writ-ten :
457 168 23
Such ho-nour have all his saints.

Ps. 150 *Laudate Dominum* iv. 5 *or* v. 2

347 258 16
O Praise God in his ho- li-ness : praise him in the firma-
4 15678 23
ment of his power.

3 47 16 258
2 Praise him in his no-ble acts : praise him according to
457 168 23
his ex- cel-lent greatness.

37 4 12568 4
3 Praise him in the sound of the trum-pet : praise him up-
15678 23
on the lute and harp.

37 4 12568 4
4 Praise him in the cym-bals and dan-ces : praise him up-
15678 23
on the strings and pipe.

347 12568
5 Praise him upon the well-tun-ed cym-bals : praise him
4 6 123578
up-on the loüd cymbals.

37 4 16 258 4 15678 23
6 Let every thing that hath breath : — — — praise
the Lord.

Ps. 114 *In exitu Israel*

Irregular or *Peregrine* Tone.

WHen Is- ra- el came out of E-gypt : and the house of

Ia-cob from a-mong the strange peo- ple. 2 Iu- da was his

sanc-tu- a- ry : and Is- ra- el his do-min-ion. 3 The sea saw

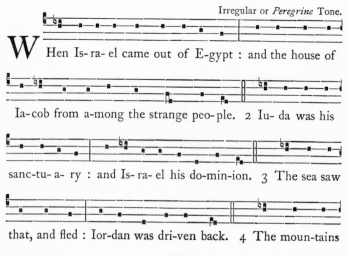

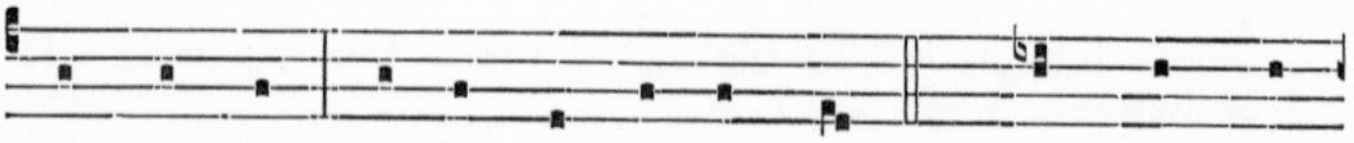

that, and fled : Ior-dan was dri-ven back. 4 The moun-tains

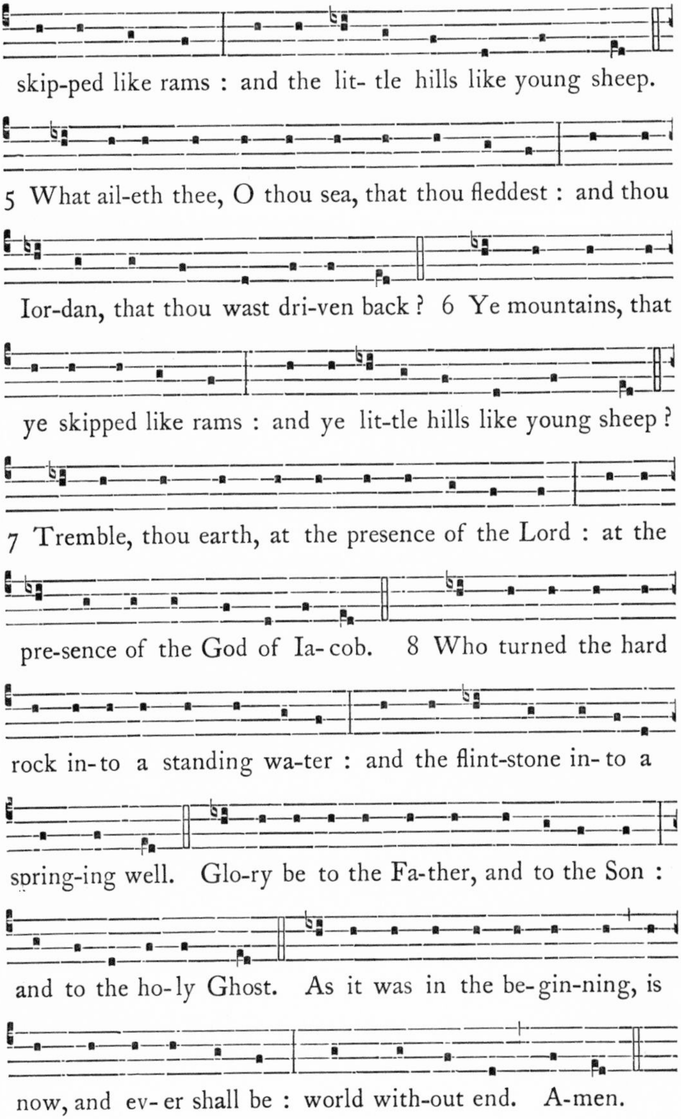
skip-ped like rams : and the lit- tle hills like young sheep.
5 What ail-eth thee, O thou sea, that thou fleddest : and thou
Ior-dan, that thou wast dri-ven back ? 6 Ye mountains, that
ye skipped like rams : and ye lit-tle hills like young sheep ?
7 Tremble, thou earth, at the presence of the Lord : at the
pre-sence of the God of Ia- cob. 8 Who turned the hard
rock in-to a standing wa-ter : and the flint-stone in- to a
spring-ing well. Glo-ry be to the Fa-ther, and to the Son :
and to the ho- ly Ghost. As it was in the be- gin-ning, is
now, and ev- er shall be : world with-out end. A-men.

Ps. 115 *Non nobis, Domine*

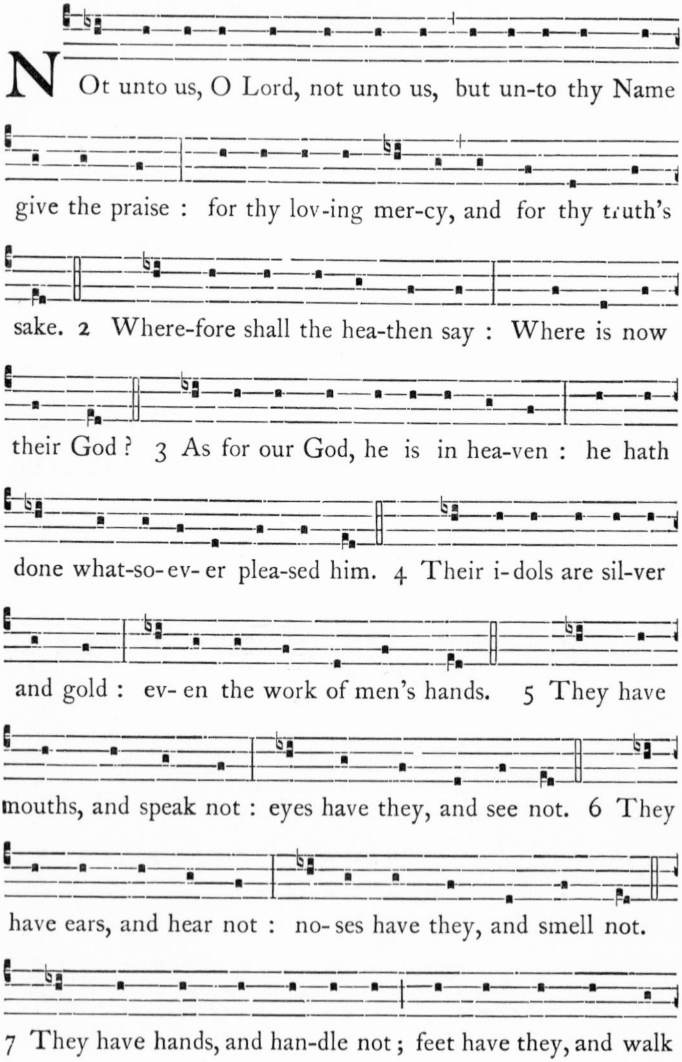

NOt unto us, O Lord, not unto us, but un-to thy Name
give the praise : for thy lov-ing mer-cy, and for thy truth's
sake. 2 Where-fore shall the hea-then say : Where is now
their God ? 3 As for our God, he is in hea-ven : he hath
done what-so-ev-er plea-sed him. 4 Their i-dols are sil-ver
and gold : ev-en the work of men's hands. 5 They have
mouths, and speak not : eyes have they, and see not. 6 They
have ears, and hear not : no-ses have they, and smell not.
7 They have hands, and han-dle not ; feet have they, and walk

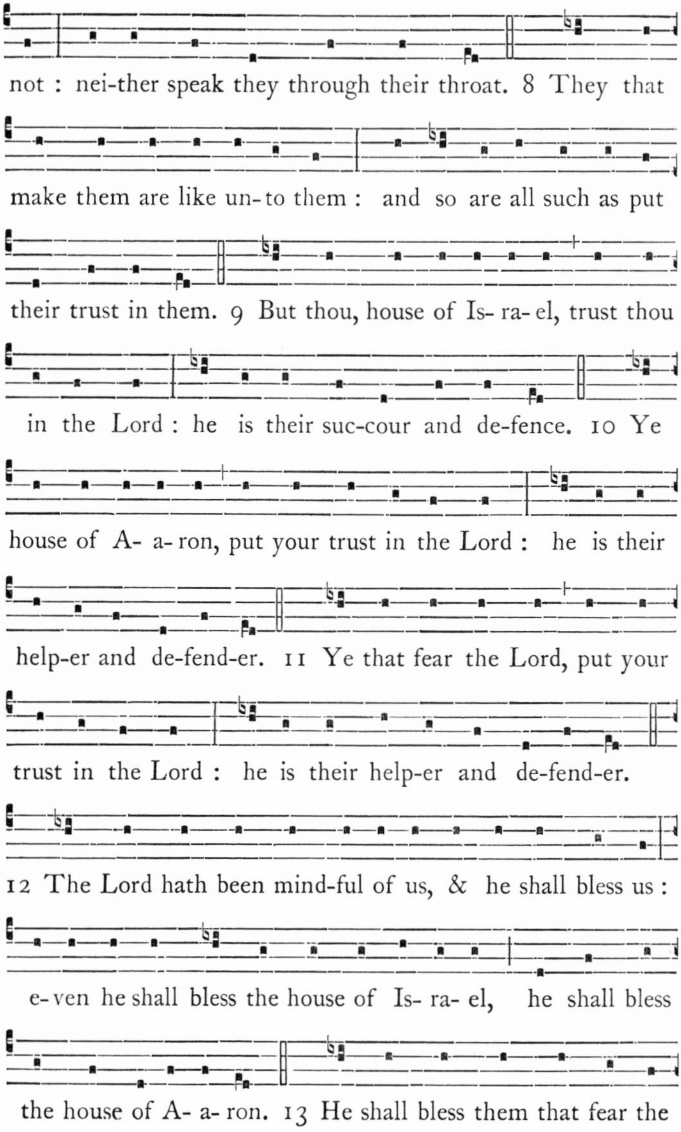
not : nei-ther speak they through their throat. 8 They that
make them are like un-to them : and so are all such as put
their trust in them. 9 But thou, house of Is- ra- el, trust thou
in the Lord : he is their suc-cour and de-fence. 10 Ye
house of A- a- ron, put your trust in the Lord : he is their
help-er and de-fend-er. 11 Ye that fear the Lord, put your
trust in the Lord : he is their help-er and de-fend-er.
12 The Lord hath been mind-ful of us, & he shall bless us :
e- ven he shall bless the house of Is- ra- el, he shall bless
the house of A- a- ron. 13 He shall bless them that fear the

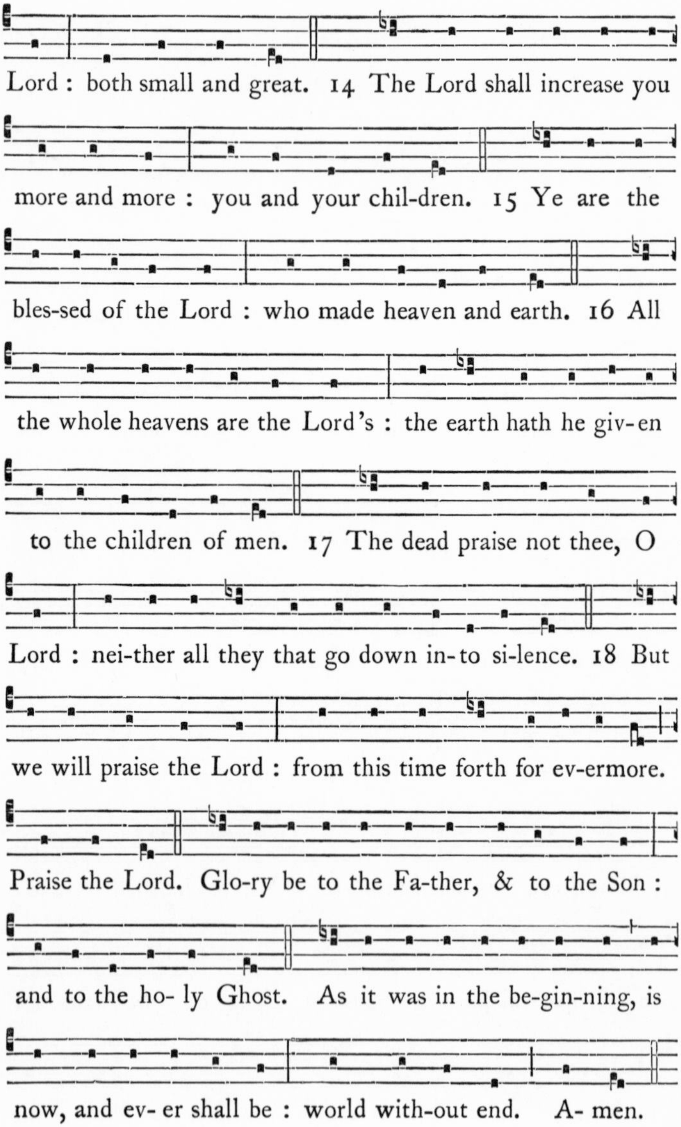
Lord : both small and great. 14 The Lord shall increase you
more and more : you and your chil-dren. 15 Ye are the
bles-sed of the Lord : who made heaven and earth. 16 All
the whole heavens are the Lord's : the earth hath he giv-en
to the children of men. 17 The dead praise not thee, O
Lord : nei-ther all they that go down in-to si-lence. 18 But
we will praise the Lord : from this time forth for ev-ermore.
Praise the Lord. Glo-ry be to the Fa-ther, & to the Son :
and to the ho- ly Ghost. As it was in the be-gin-ning, is
now, and ev- er shall be : world with-out end. A- men.

THE CANTICLES

AT MATTINS

The Invitatory Psalm

Venite, exultemus Domino

37 4 16 258
O Come, let us sing un-to the Lord : let us heartily re-
4 15678 23
joice in the strength of our sal-vation.

347 12568
2 Let us come before his presence with thanks-giv-ing :
4 15678 23
and shew our-selves glad in him with psalms.

37 4 16 258 457 168 23
3 For the Lord is a great God : and a great King a-bove
all gods.

37 4 16 258
4 In his hand are all the cor-ners of the earth : and the
4 6 123578
strength of the hills is hïs also.

347 12568 457 168
5 The sea is his, and he made it : and his hands pre-par-ed
23
the dry land.

37 4 16 258
6 O come, let us wor-ship and fall down : and kneel be-
4 15678 23
fore the Lord our Maker.

3 47 16 258
7 For he is the Lord our God : and we are the people of
4 15678 23
his pasture, | and the sheep of his hand.

37 4 16
8 To-day if ye will hear his voice, hard-en not your
258
hearts : as in the provocation, | and as in the day of tempta-
4 15678 23
tion in the wilderness ;

347 258 16 4 15678 23
9 When your fa-thers temp-ted me : prov-ed me, and saw
my works.

37 4
10 Forty years long was I grieved with this gene-ra-tion,
16 258 4
and said : It is a people that do err in their hearts, | for they
15678 23
have not known my ways.

37 4 16 258
11 Unto whom I sware in my wrath : that they should
4 15678 23
not en-ter in- to my rest.

¶ *On Easter-day, instead of the foregoing Psalm, the following Anthem shall be sung :—*

Pascha nostrum vj.

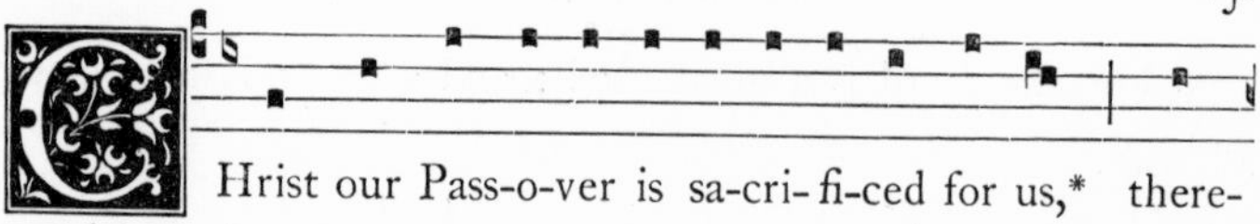

CHrist our Pass-o-ver is sa-cri- fi-ced for us,* there-

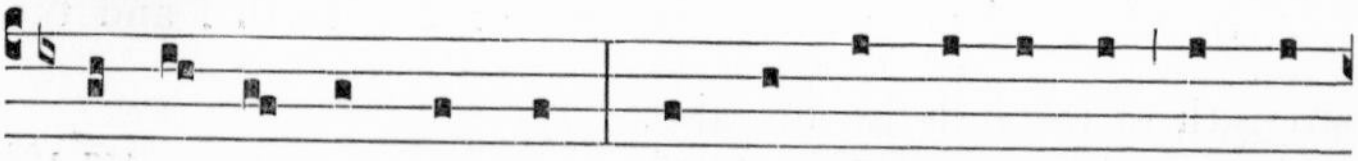

fore let us keep the feast : not with the old leaven, nor with

the leaven of malice and wickedness, but with the unlea-

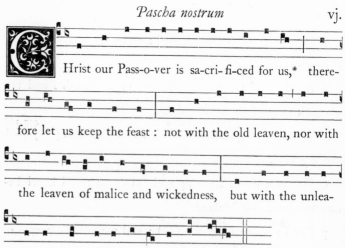

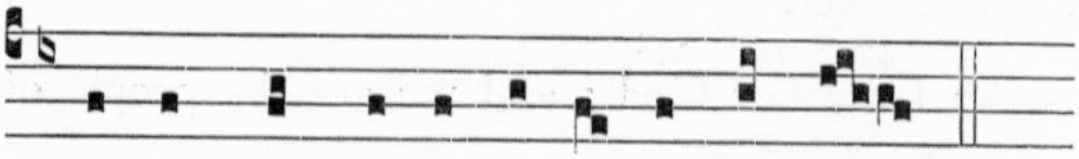

ven-ed bread of sin-ce- ri- ty and truth.

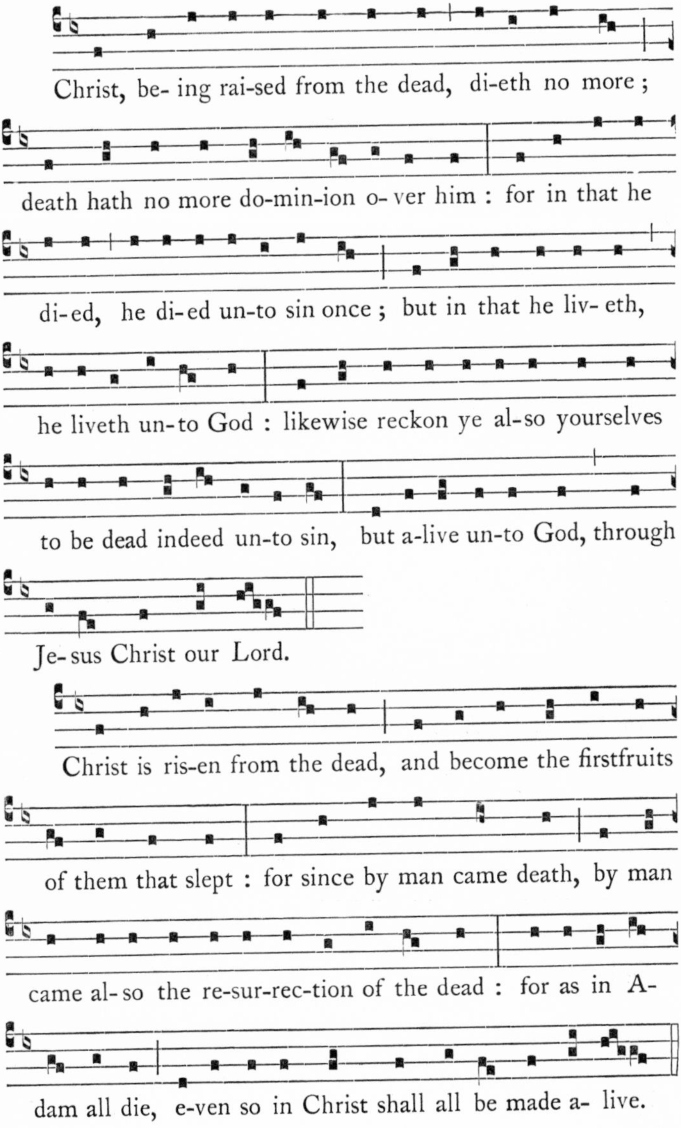
Christ, be- ing rai-sed from the dead, di-eth no more ;
death hath no more do-min-ion o- ver him : for in that he
di-ed, he di-ed un-to sin once ; but in that he liv- eth,
he liveth un-to God : likewise reckon ye al-so yourselves
to be dead indeed un-to sin, but a-live un-to God, through
Je-sus Christ our Lord.
Christ is ris-en from the dead, and become the firstfruits
of them that slept : for since by man came death, by man
came al-so the re-sur-rec-tion of the dead : for as in A-
dam all die, e-ven so in Christ shall all be made a- live.

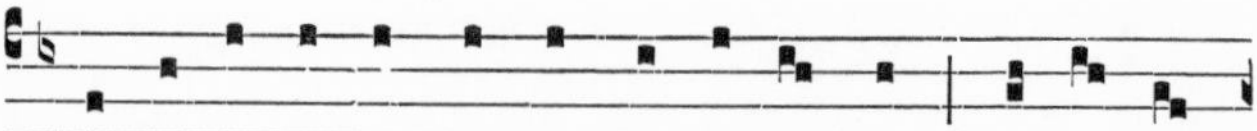

Glo-ry be to the Father, and to the Son, and to the

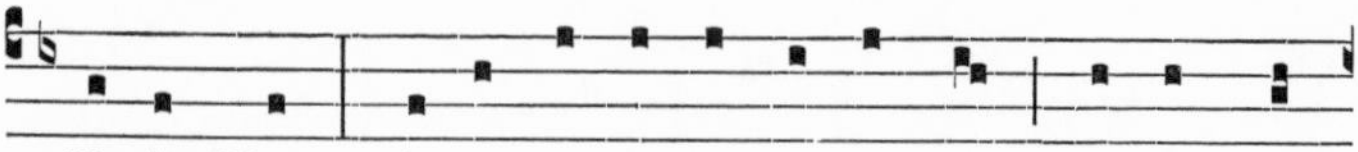

Ho-ly Ghost. As it was in the be-gin-ning, is now, and

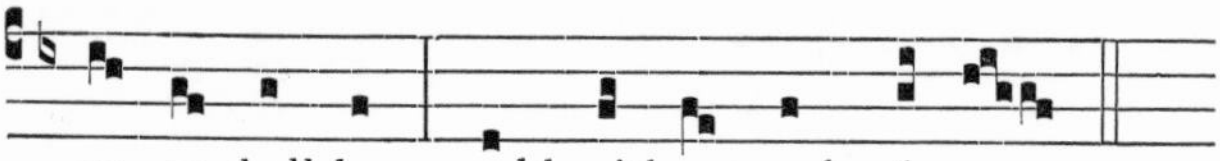

ev- er shall be, world without end. A- men.

The Hymn of SS. Ambrose & Austin

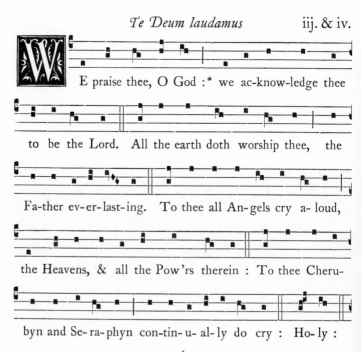

Te Deum laudamus iij. & iv.

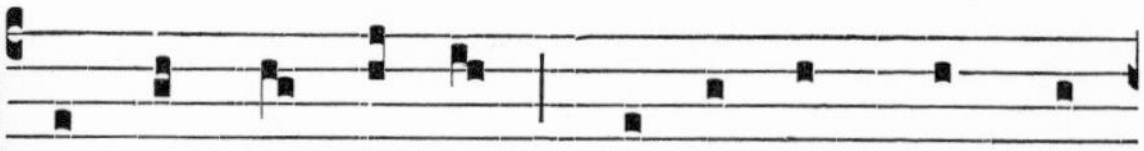

WE praise thee, O God :* we ac-know-ledge thee

to be the Lord. All the earth doth worship thee, the

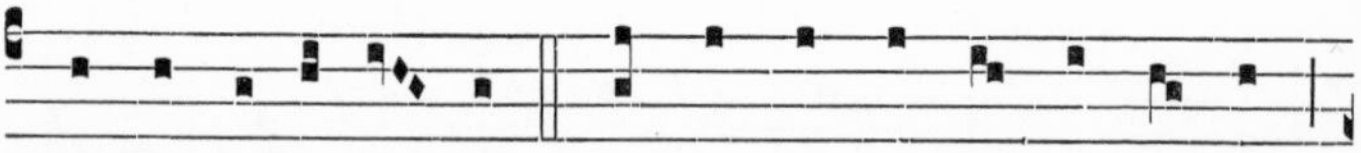

Fa-ther ev-er-last-ing. To thee all An-gels cry a- loud,

the Heavens, & all the Pow'rs therein : To thee Cheru-

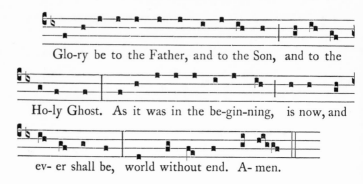

byn and Se- ra- phyn con-tin- u- al- ly do cry : Ho- ly :

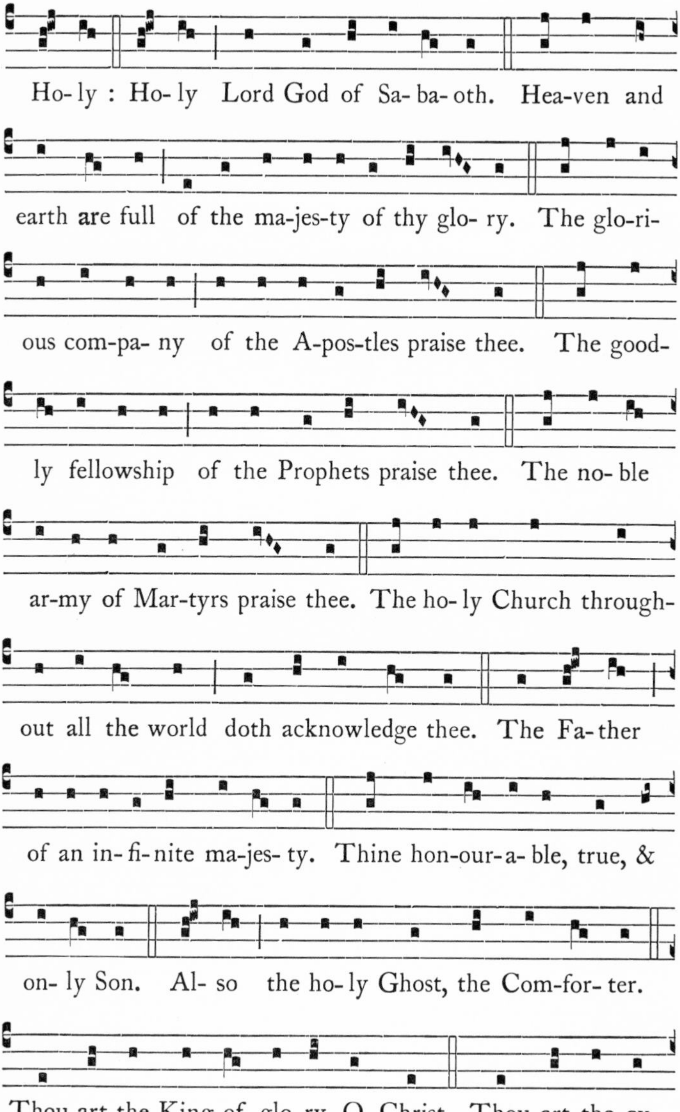
Ho- ly : Ho- ly Lord God of Sa- ba- oth. Hea-ven and
earth are full of the ma-jes-ty of thy glo- ry. The glo-ri-
ous com-pa- ny of the A-pos-tles praise thee. The good-
ly fellowship of the Prophets praise thee. The no- ble
ar-my of Mar-tyrs praise thee. The ho- ly Church throughout all the world doth acknowledge thee. The Fa- ther
of an in- fi- nite ma-jes- ty. Thine hon-our- a- ble, true, &
on- ly Son. Al- so the ho- ly Ghost, the Com-for- ter.
Thou art the King of glo- ry, O Christ. Thou art the ev-

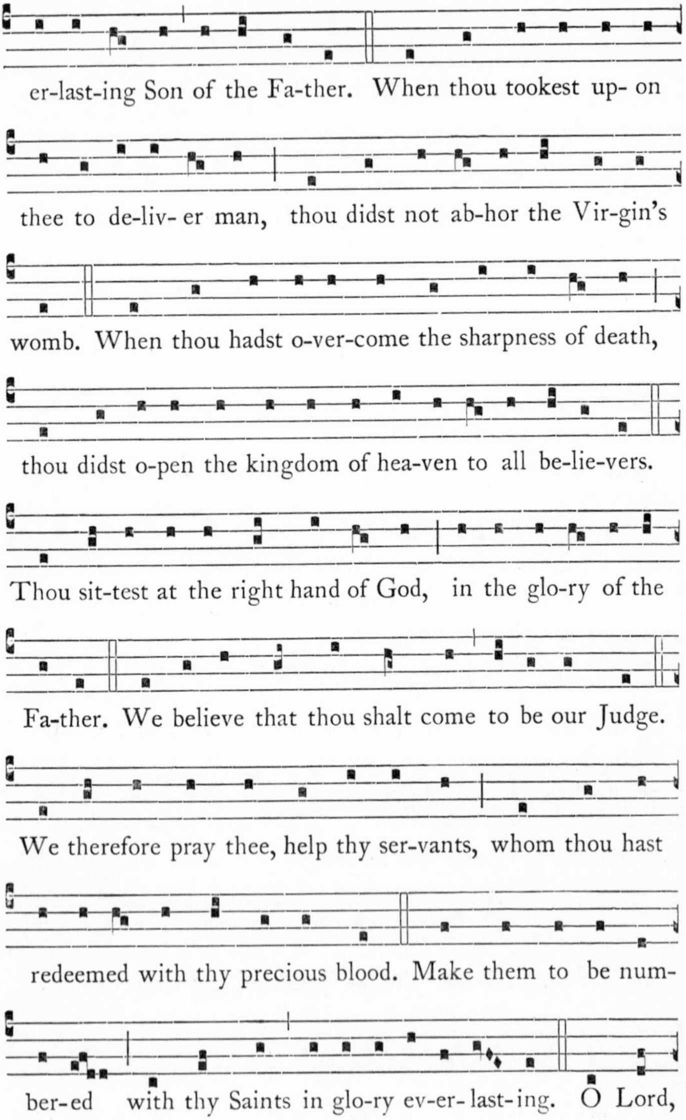
er-last-ing Son of the Fa-ther. When thou tookest up- on
thee to de-liv- er man, thou didst not ab-hor the Vir-gin's
womb. When thou hadst o-ver-come the sharpness of death,
thou didst o-pen the kingdom of hea-ven to all be-lie-vers.
Thou sit-test at the right hand of God, in the glo-ry of the
Fa-ther. We believe that thou shalt come to be our Judge.
We therefore pray thee, help thy ser-vants, whom thou hast
redeemed with thy precious blood. Make them to be num-
ber-ed with thy Saints in glo-ry ev-er- last-ing. O Lord,

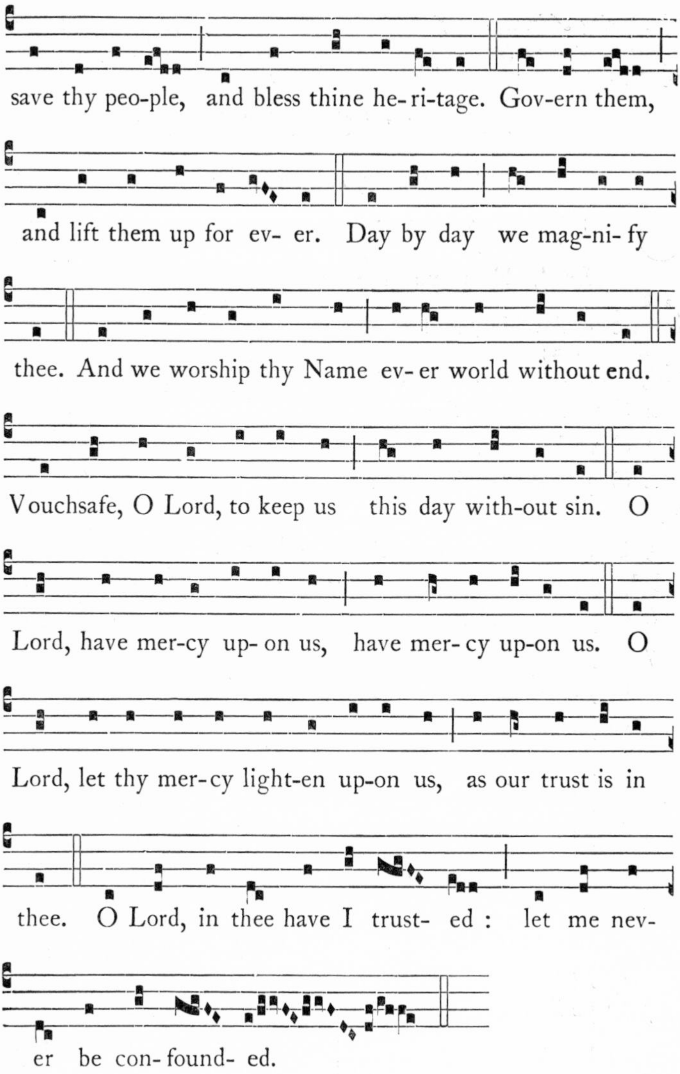
save thy peo-ple, and bless thine he-ri-tage. Gov-ern them,
and lift them up for ev- er. Day by day we mag-ni- fy
thee. And we worship thy Name ev- er world without end.
Vouchsafe, O Lord, to keep us this day with-out sin. O
Lord, have mer-cy up- on us, have mer- cy up-on us. O
Lord, let thy mer-cy light-en up-on us, as our trust is in
thee. O Lord, in thee have I trust- ed : let me never be con- found- ed.

¶ *During Advent, and from Septuagesima to Easter, and on all Vigils and Ember days (except in Whitsun-week), instead of the foregoing Hymn, the following Canticle shall be sung :—*

The Song of the iij Children

Benedicite, omnia opera iij. 6 *or* vij. 8

O All ye works of the Lord, [37]bless [4]ye [16]the [258]Lord : praise him, and mag-[4]ni-fy [15678]him [23]for ever. [&c.

2 O ye angels of the Lord,

3 O ye heavens,

4 O ye waters that be a-bove the firmament,

5 O all ye powers of the Lord,

6 O ye sun and moon,

7 O ye stars of heaven,

8 O ye showers and dew,

9 O ye winds of God,

10 O ye fire and heat,

11 O ye winter & summer,

12 O ye dews and frosts,

13 O ye frost and cold,

14 O ye ice and snow,

15 O ye nights and days,

16 O ye light and darkness,

17 O ye lightnings & clouds,

18 O let the earth [347]bless [16]the [258]Lord : yea, let it praise him &c.

19 O ye mountains and hills,

20 O all ye green things upon the earth,

21 O ye wells,

22 O ye seas and floods,

23 O ye whales, and all that move in the waters,

24 O all ye fowls of the air,

25 O all ye beasts and cattle,

26 O ye children of men,

27 O let Israel [347]bless [16]the [258]Lord :

28 O ye priests of the Lord,

29 O ye servants of the Lord,

30 O ye spirits and souls of the righteous,

31 O ye holy and humble men of heart,

32 O Ananias, Azarias and Misael, [37]bless [4]ye [16]the [258]Lord : praise him, and magni-[4]fy [15678]him [23]for ever.

AT MATTINS

The Song of Zachary

Benedictus Dominus

347 258 16
BLessed be the Lord God of Is-ra-el : for he hath visited
457 168 23
and re-deem-ed his people :

347 12568
2 And hath raised up a mighty sal-va-tion for us : in the
4 15678 23
house of his ser-vant David.

347 12568
3 As he spake by the mouth of his ho-ly Pro-phets : which
4 15678 23
have been since the world began :

347 258 16
4 That we should be saved from our en- e-mies : and from
4 15678 23
the hands of all that hate us :

347 12568
5 To perform the mercy promised to our fore- fa- thers :
4 15678 23
and to remember his ho- ly covenant.

347
6 To perform the oath which he sware to our fore-fa-ther
258 16 4 15678 23
A-bra-ham : that he would give us :

37 4 258 16
7 That we, being delivered out of the hand of our en- e-
·4 15678 23
mies : might serve him with-out fear ;

347 12568 4 15678
8 In holiness and righteous-ness be-fore him : all the days
23
of our life.

347 12568
9 And thou, child, shalt be called the Prophet of the High-
·4 15678 23
est : for thou shalt go before the face of the Lord, to pre-pare
his ways :

347 12568
10 To give knowledge of salvation un-to his peo-ple : for
457 168 23
the re-mis-sion of their sins :

37 4 16 258
11 Through the tender mer-cy of our God : whereby the
4 68 157 23
Day-spring from on high hath vi-sit-ed us :

37
12 To give light to them that sit in darkness, & in the sha-
4 16 258 4 15678 23
dow of death : and to guide our feet in- to the way of peace.

Benedictus Dominus

Irregular Tone.

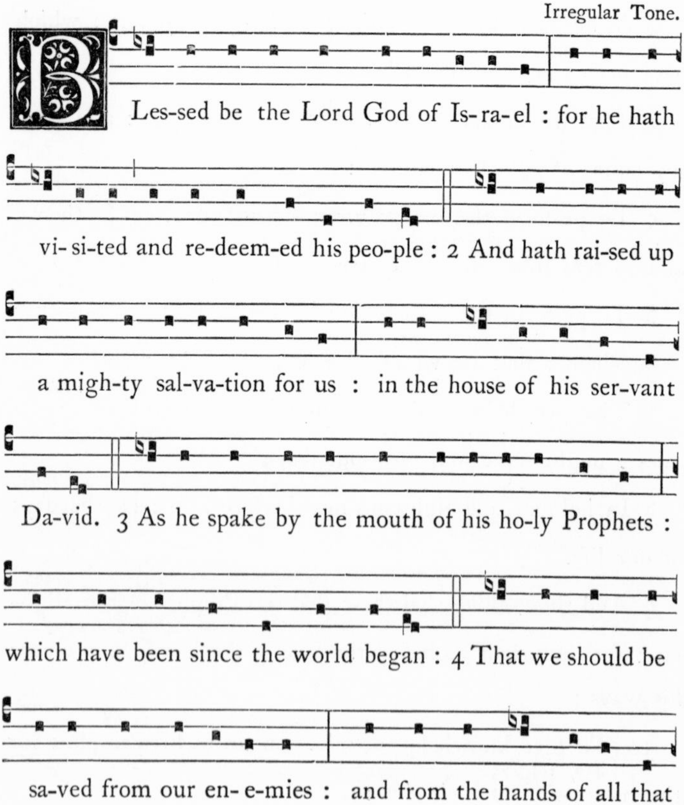
BLes-sed be the Lord God of Is-ra-el : for he hath
vi-si-ted and re-deem-ed his peo-ple : 2 And hath rai-sed up
a migh-ty sal-va-tion for us : in the house of his ser-vant
Da-vid. 3 As he spake by the mouth of his ho-ly Prophets :
which have been since the world began : 4 That we should be
sa-ved from our en-e-mies : and from the hands of all that

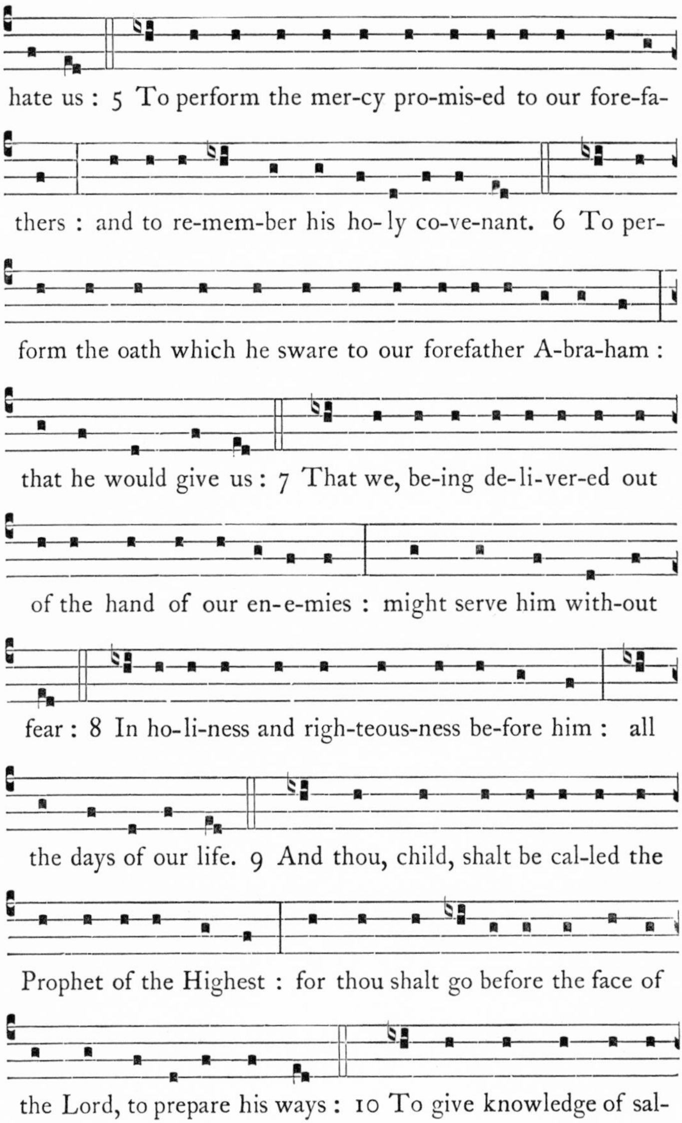
hate us : 5 To perform the mer-cy pro-mis-ed to our fore-fa-
thers : and to re-mem-ber his ho- ly co-ve-nant. 6 To perform the oath which he sware to our forefather A-bra-ham :
that he would give us : 7 That we, be-ing de-li-ver-ed out
of the hand of our en-e-mies : might serve him with-out
fear : 8 In ho-li-ness and righ-teous-ness be-fore him : all
the days of our life. 9 And thou, child, shalt be cal-led the
Prophet of the Highest : for thou shalt go before the face of
the Lord, to prepare his ways : 10 To give knowledge of sal-

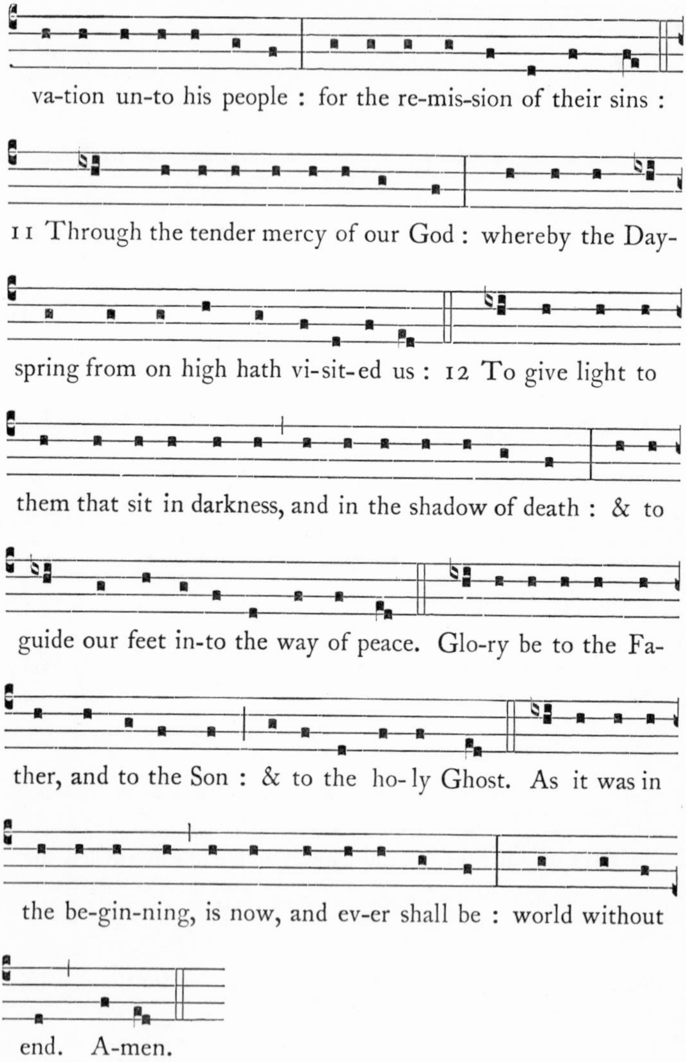
va-tion un-to his people : for the re-mis-sion of their sins :
11 Through the tender mercy of our God : whereby the Day-
spring from on high hath vi-sit-ed us : 12 To give light to
them that sit in darkness, and in the shadow of death : & to
guide our feet in-to the way of peace. Glo-ry be to the Fa-
ther, and to the Son : & to the ho-ly Ghost. As it was in
the be-gin-ning, is now, and ev-er shall be : world without
end. A-men.

¶ *For the Solemn forms of the Mediation, see p. 276.*

The Creed of S. Athanasius

Quicunque vult i. 1

WHosoever will[347] be sa-[12568] ved : before all things it is necessary that he hold[4] the[68] Ca-[157]tho-[23]lick Faith.

2 Which Faith except every one do keep whole and un-[347]de-fi-[12568] led : without doubt he shall pe-rish[4] ev-[15678] er-[23]lastingly.

3 And the Ca-[3]tholick Faith[47] is[16] this[258] : that we worship one God in Trinity, | and Tri-[4]ni-[15678] ty[23] in Unity :

4 Neither con-found-[37]ing[4] the Per-[12568]sons : nor di-vi-[457]ding[168] the[23] Substance.

5 For there is one Person of the Father, | an-o-[37]ther of[4] the[16] Son[258] : and ano-ther[4] of[15678] the[23] holy Ghost.

6 But the Godhead of the Father, of the Son, and of the holy Ghost[37] is[4] all[16] one[258] : the Glory equal, | the Majes-ty[4] co-[15678] e-[23]ternal.

7 Such as the Father is, such[37] is[4] the[16] Son[258] : and such[457] is[168] the[23] holy Ghost.

8 The Father uncreate, the Son[37] un-[4]cre-[16]ate[258] : and the ho-[4]ly[6] Ghöst[123578] uncreate.

9 The Father incomprehensible, | the Son in-com-[347]pre-hen-[258]si-[16]ble : and the holy Ghost in-[4]com-[15678]pre-[23]hensible.

10 The Father eternal, the Son[347] e- ter-[12568]nal : and the ho-ly[4] Ghost[15678] e-[23]ternal.

347 12568 4 15678 23
11 And yet they are not three e-ter-nals : but one e-ternal.

12 As also there are not three incomprehensibles, | nor
347 12568 4 15678
three un-cre- a- ted : but one uncreated, | and one in-com-
23
pre-hensible.

347 12568
13 So likewise the Father is Almighty, the Son Al-migh-
4 15678 23
ty : and the ho-ly Ghost Al-mighty.

347 12568 4 15678
14 And yet they are not three Al-migh-ties : but one
23
Al-migh-ty.

347 16 258 4 15678 23
15 So the Father is God, the Son is God : and the ho- ly
Ghost is God.

37 4 16 258 4 15678 23
16 And yet they are not three Gods : — — but one God.

37 4 16 258 4
17 So likewise the Father is Lord, the Son Lord : and the
15678 23
ho- ly Ghost Lord.

37 4 16 258 4 15678 23
18 And yet not three Lords : — — but one Lord.

347 258 16
19 For like as we are compelled by the Chris-tian ve-ri-ty :
457 168 23
to acknowledge every Person by him-self to be God & Lord;

347 12568
20 So are we forbidden by the Catho-lick re- li- gion : to
4 15678 23
say there be three Gods, or three Lords.

3 47 16 258 4 15678 23
21 The Fa-ther is made of none : neither crea-ted nor be-
gotten.

37 4 16 258
22 The Son is of the Fa-ther a-lone : not made, nor crea-
4 15678 23
ted, but be-gotten.

37 4 16 258
23 The holy Ghost is of the Fa-ther, and of the Son :

4 15678 23
neither made, nor created, nor begot-ten, but pro-ceeding.

37
24 So there is one Father, not three Fathers, | one Son,
4 16 258 .4 15678 23
not three Sons : one holy Ghost, not three holy Ghosts.

347 12568
25 And in this Trinity none is afore, or af-ter o- ther :
457 168 23
none is greater, or less than an-other.

37 4 12568
26 But the whole three Persons are co-e-ter-nal to-ge-
4 15678 23
ther : — and co-equal.

37 4 12568
27 So that in all things, as is a-fore-said : the Unity in
457 168 23
Trinity, and the Trinity in Unity is to be worshipped.
347 12568 457 168
28 He therefore that will be sa- ved : must thus think of
23
the Trinity.

37 4 12568
29 Furthermore, it is necessary to ever-last-ing sal-va-tion :
4 6 123578
that he also believe rightly the Incarnation of our Lörd Jesus

Christ.

37 4 16 258
30 For the right faith is, that we be-lieve and con-fess :
4 15678 23
that our Lord Jesus Christ, the Son of God, is God and Man.

3 47
31 God, of the Substance of the Father, | be-got-ten be-fore
16 258 4 6 123578
the worlds : and Man, of the substance of his Mo-ther, börn

in the world.

37 4 16 258
32 Perfect God and per-fect Man : of a reasonable soul
4 15678 23
and hu-man flesh sub-sisting.

37 4 12568
33 Equal to the Father, as touch-ing his God-head : and
457 168 23
inferior to the Father, as touch-ing his Manhood.

347 16 258 4 15678
34 Who although he be God and Man : yet he is not two,
23
but one Christ :

37 4 16 258
35 One, not by conversion of the God-head in-to flesh :
4 15678 23
but by taking of the Man-hood into God :

37 4 12568
36 One altogether not by con-fu-sion of Sub-stance : but
4 15678 23
by u-ni- ty of Person.

37 4 16 258
37 For as the reasonable soul and flesh is one man : so
4 15678 23
God and Man is one Christ ;

37 4 16 258
38 Who suffered for our salvation, | de-scend-ed in-to hell :
4 15678 23
rose again the third day from the dead.

39 He ascended into heaven, | he sitteth on the right hand
347 12568
of the Father, God Al-migh-ty : from whence he shall come
4 68 157 23
to judge the quick and the dead.

347
40 At whose coming all men shall rise again with their
12568 4 15678 23
bo-dies : and shall give ac-count for their own works.

347
41 And they that have done good shall go into life ev-er-
12568 4 15678 23
last-ing : & they that have done evil in-to ev- er-lasting fire.

37 4 16 258
42 This is the Ca-tho-lick Faith : which except a man be-
457 168 23
lieve faithfully, he can-not be saved.

AT EVENSONG

The Song of the Blessed Virgin Mary

Magnificat

37 4 16 258
MY soul doth mag-ni-fy the Lord : and my spirit hath
4 15678 23
rejoiced in God my Saviour.

347 12568 4 15678 23
* 2 For he hath re-gard-ed : the lowliness of his handmaiden.

347 12568 4 15678
* 3 For be-hold, from hence-forth : all generations shall call
23
me blessed.

37 4 16 258 457 168
4 For he that is mighty hath mag-ni-fi-ed me : and ho- ly
23
is his Name.

347 12568 4
5 And his mercy is on them that fear him : throughout all
15678 23
ge- ne-rations.

37 4 16 258
6 He hath shewed strength with his arm : he hath scat-
457 168 23
tered the proud | in the imagi-na-tion of their hearts.

37 4 16 258
7 He hath put down the migh-ty from their seat : and
4 15678 23
hath exalted the hum-ble and meek.

37 4 16 258
8 He hath filled the hun-gry with good things : and the
4 68 157 23
rich he hath sent emp-ty away.

347 258
9 He, remembering his mercy, hath holpen his ser-vant Is-
16 4
ra-el : as he promised to our forefathers, | Abraham and his
15678 23
seed for ever.

---

* The Intonation of the 4th. Tone is omitted in these verses.

Magnificat

Irregular Tone.

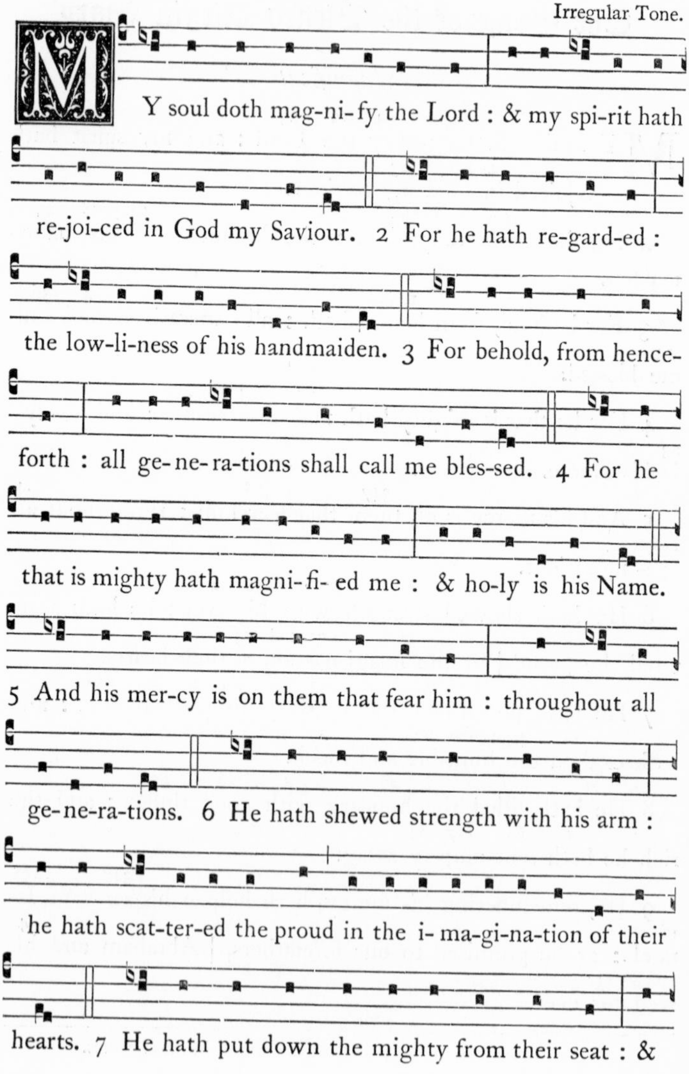
MY soul doth mag-ni-fy the Lord : & my spi-rit hath
re-joi-ced in God my Saviour. 2 For he hath re-gard-ed :
the low-li-ness of his handmaiden. 3 For behold, from hence-
forth : all ge-ne-ra-tions shall call me bles-sed. 4 For he
that is mighty hath magni-fi- ed me : & ho-ly is his Name.
5 And his mer-cy is on them that fear him : throughout all
ge-ne-ra-tions. 6 He hath shewed strength with his arm :
he hath scat-ter-ed the proud in the i- ma-gi-na-tion of their
hearts. 7 He hath put down the mighty from their seat : &

hath ex-alt-ed the hum-ble & meek. 8 He hath fil-led the

hungry with good things : & the rich he hath sent empty a-

way. 9 He, remembering his mer-cy, hath hol-pen his ser-

vant Is- ra- el : as he pro-mis-ed to our forefathers, A-bra-

ham, & his seed for ev- er. Glo-ry be to the Fa-ther, and

to the Son : and to the Ho-ly Ghost. As it was in the be-

ginning, is now, & ev-er shall be : world without end. Amen.

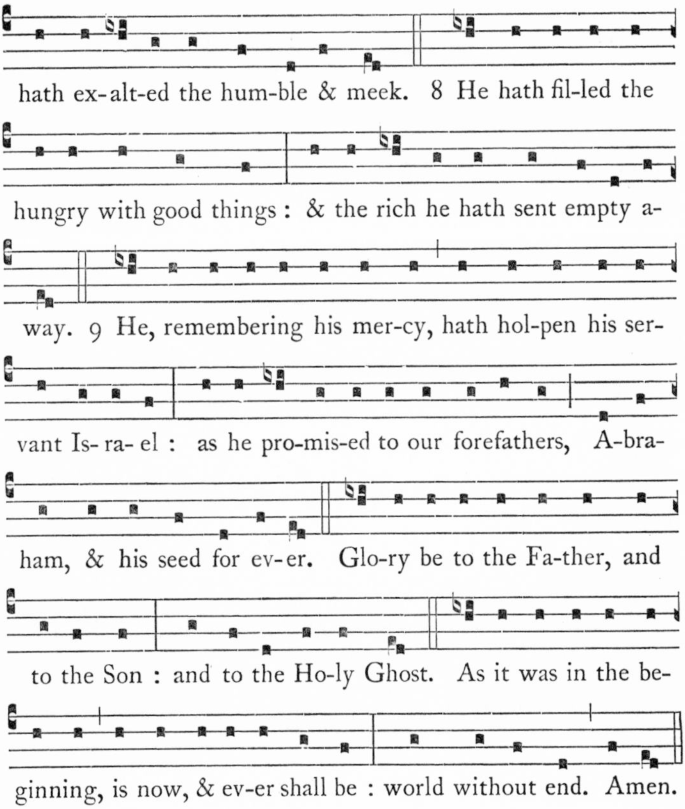

The Song of Symeon

Nunc dimittis

$$\text{3} \qquad \text{47} \quad \text{16} \quad \text{258}$$
Lord, now lettest thou thy ser-vant de-part in peace :
$$\text{457} \quad \text{168} \quad \text{23}$$
ac-cord-ing to thy word.
$$\text{347} \quad \text{16} \quad \text{258} \qquad \text{4} \quad \text{15678} \quad \text{23}$$
2 For mine eyes have seen : — thy sal-vation.

3 Which thou [347]hast [12568]pre-par-ed : be-fore the [4]face [6]of [123578]äll people.

4 To be a light to [37]light-[4]en the [12568]Gen-tiles : and to be the glory of [4]thy [15678]peo-[23]ple Israel.

Solemn Mediations

Benedictus

Tones i & vi

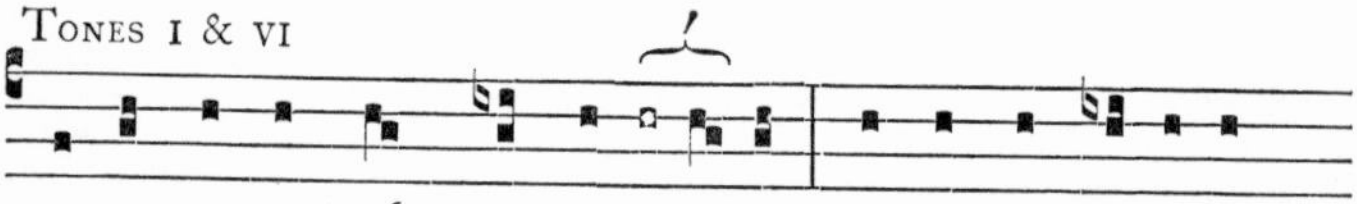

Blessed be the [16]Lord God of Is-ra-el : for he hath ví-si-ted &c.

Tones ii & viii

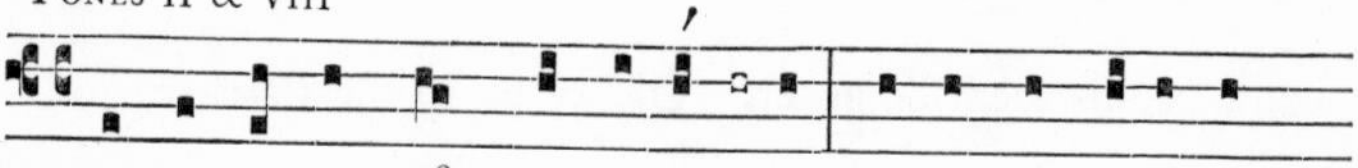

Blessed be the [28]Lord God of Is-ra-el : for he hath ví-si-ted &c.

Tone iv

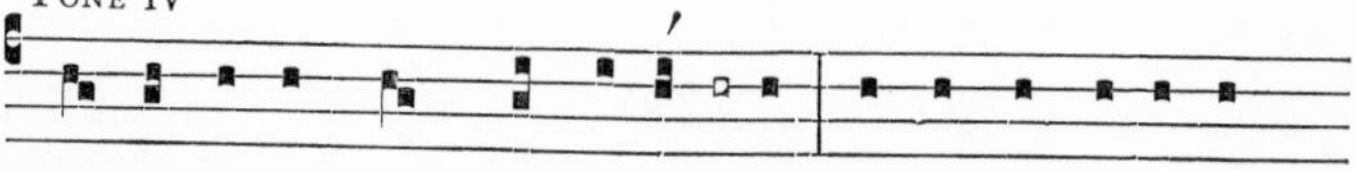

Blessed be the [4]Lord God of Is-ra-el : for he hath vi-si-ted &c.

BLessed be the [12468]Lord God of Ís-ra-el : for he hath vísited and [4]re-[168]deem-[2]ed his people :

2 And hath raised up a mighty [12468]sal-vation fór us : in the [4]hóuse [168]of his [2]ser-vant David.

3 As he spake by the mouth of [12468]his holy Pró-phets : which [4]have [168]been since [2]the world began :

12468

4 That we should be sa-ved from our en-e-mies : and from

4 168 2

the hánds of all that hate us :

12468

5 To perform the mercy promised to our fore-fa-thers :

4 168 2

and to remémber his ho-ly covenant.

12468

6 To perform the oath which he sware to our fore-father

4 168 2

Á-bra-ham : that he would give us :

12468

7 That we, being delivered out of the hand of our en-e-

.4 168 2

mies : might serve him with-out fear :

12468 4 168

8 In holiness and righ-teous-ness be-fore him : all the days

2

of our life.

12468

9 And thou, child, shalt be called the Pro-phet of the High-

.4 168 2

est : for thou shalt gó before the face of the Lord, to pre-pare

his ways :

12468

10 To give knowledge of salvation un-to his peo-ple : for

4 168 2

the re-mis-sion of their sins :

16 248

11 Through the ten-der mer-cy of our God : whereby the

4 68 1 2

Dáy-spring from on high hath vi-si-ted us :

12468

12 To give light to them that sit in darkness, and in the

4 168 2

shadow of death : & to guíde our feet in-to the way of peace.

16 248 4 168 2

Glory be to the Fa-ther, and to the Son : and to the Holy

Ghost.

12468

As it was in the beginning, is now, and ever shall be :

4 168 2

world with-out end. Amen.

SOLEMN MEDIATIONS

Magnificat

TONES I & VI

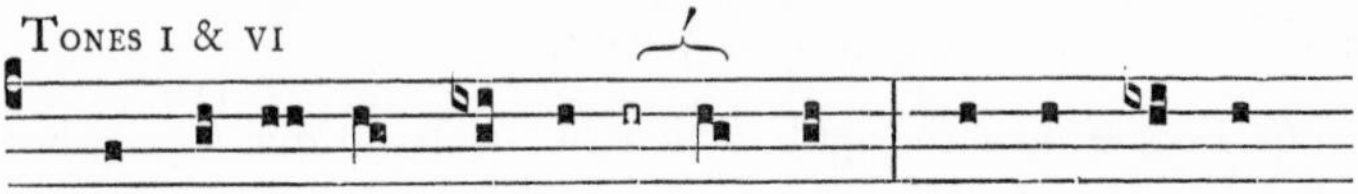

My soul [16]doth mag-ni- fy the Lord : and my spí- rit &c.

TONES II & VIII

Mÿ soul [28]doth mag-ni- fy the Lord : and my spí-rit &c.

TONE IV

My soul [4]doth mag- ni- fy the Lord : and my spi- rit &c.

MY soul [12468]doth magni-fý the Lord : and my spírit hath re-joiced [4]in [168]God [2]my Saviour.

*2 For [12468]he hath re-gárd-ed : the lówliness [4]of [168]his [2]hand-maiden.

*3 For [12468]be- hold, from hénce-forth : all generátions [4]shall [168]call [2]me blessed.

4 For he that is mighty [12468]hath magni-fí-ed me : and [4]ho-[168]ly [2]is his Name.

* The Intonation is omitted in these verses.

12468 ʹ ·4
5 And his mercy is on them that fear him : throughout all
168 2
ge-ne-rations.

12468 ʹ
6 He hath shew-ed strength with his arm : he hath scát-
4 168 2
tered the proud | in the imagi-na-tion of their hearts.

12468 ʹ
7 He hath put down the mighty from their seat : and hath
4 168 2
exálted the hum-ble and meek.

16 248 ʹ
8 He hath filled the hun-gry with good things : and the
4 68 1 2
rích he hath sent emp-ty a-way.

12468
9 He, remembering his mercy, hath holpen his servant
ʹ 4
Is-ra-el : as he prómised to our forefathers, | Abraham and his
168 2
seed for ever.

16 248 ʹ 4 168 2
Glory be to the Fa-ther, and to the Son : and to the Holy
Ghost.

12468 ʹ
As it was in the beginning, is now, and ever shall be :
4 168 2
world with-out end. Amen.

THE VERSICLES & RESPONSES

AT

Mattins & Evensong

¶ *The introductory portion of the Service should be said in a subdued voice and without note.*

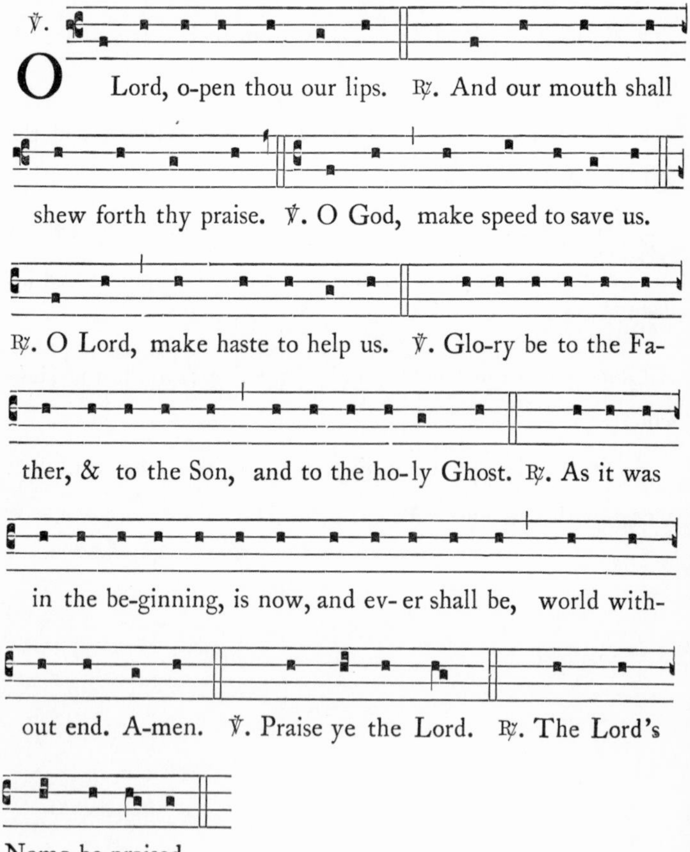

℣. O Lord, o-pen thou our lips. ℟. And our mouth shall
shew forth thy praise. ℣. O God, make speed to save us.
℟. O Lord, make haste to help us. ℣. Glo-ry be to the Fa-
ther, & to the Son, and to the ho-ly Ghost. ℟. As it was
in the be-ginning, is now, and ev- er shall be, world with-
out end. A-men. ℣. Praise ye the Lord. ℟. The Lord's
Name be praised.

* * * * * * *

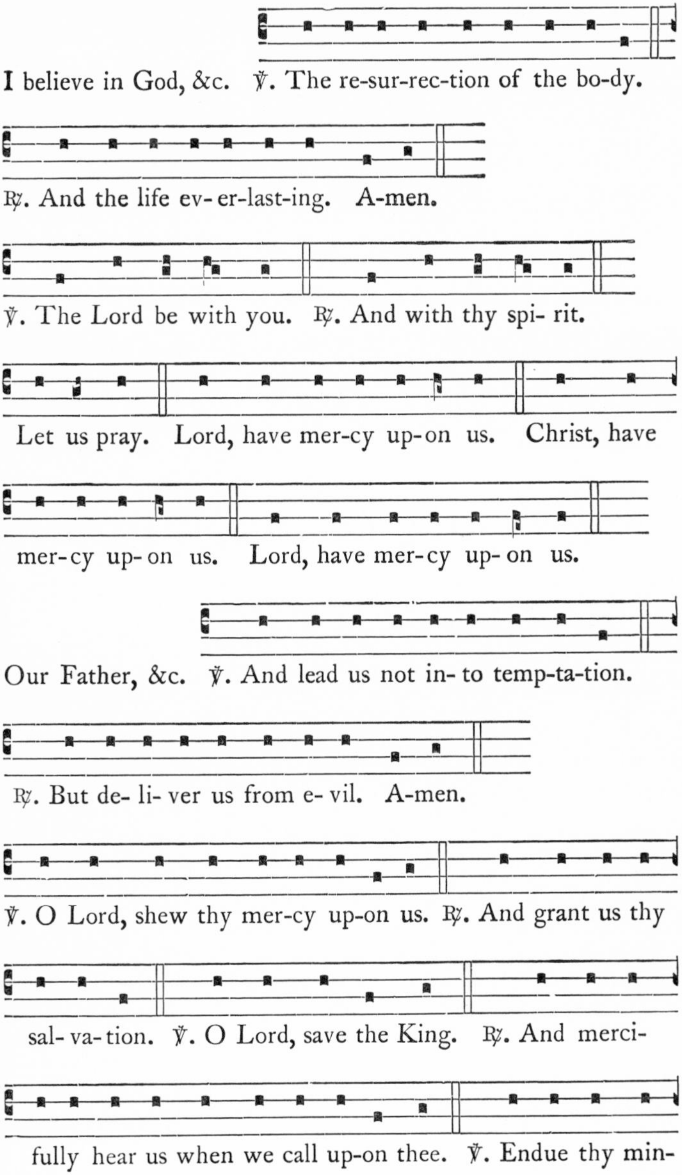
I believe in God, &c. ℣. The re-sur-rec-tion of the bo-dy.
℟. And the life ev- er-last-ing. A-men.
℣. The Lord be with you. ℟. And with thy spi- rit.
Let us pray. Lord, have mer-cy up-on us. Christ, have
mer-cy up-on us. Lord, have mer-cy up-on us.
Our Father, &c. ℣. And lead us not in-to temp-ta-tion.
℟. But de-li-ver us from e-vil. A-men.
℣. O Lord, shew thy mer-cy up-on us. ℟. And grant us thy
sal-va-tion. ℣. O Lord, save the King. ℟. And merci-
fully hear us when we call up-on thee. ℣. Endue thy min-

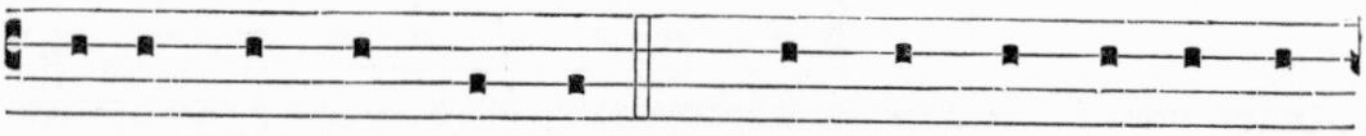

isters with righteousness. ℟. And make thy chosen peo-

ple joyful. ℣. O Lord, save thy people. ℟. And bless thine

in-he-ri-tance. ℣. Give peace in our time, O Lord. ℟. Be-

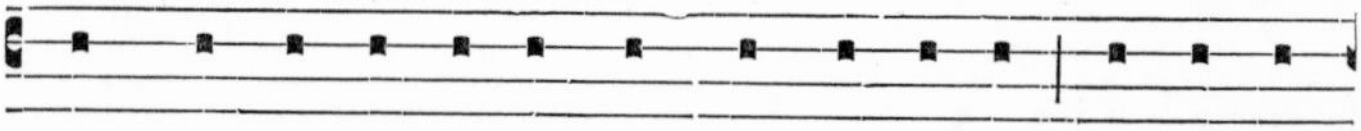

cause there is none other that fighteth for us, but on- ly

thou, O God. ℣. O God, make clean our hearts within us.

℟. And take not thy holy Spi- rit from us.

¶ *The Collect of the Day & the Collect immediately before the Anthem should invariably have their full ending, and be sung throughout on one note until the close, which is inflected as follows :—*

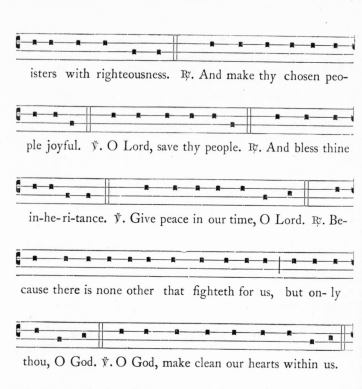

for ev- er and ev- er. A-men.
or world without end.

The same inflexion is used for other Collects, e.g.

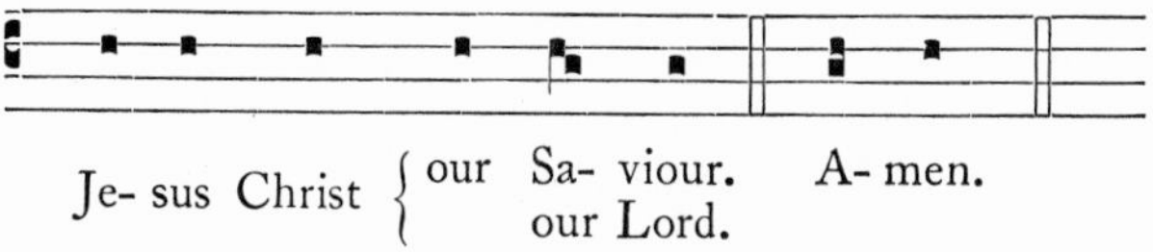
Je- sus Christ
our Sa- viour.
our Lord.
A- men.

¶ *The Prayers following the Anthem should be said on a low note, without any inflexion.*

Deo gracias

Reprinted June 1920
March 1928, January 1933
July 1941, July 1946
October 1948, December 1951
August 1957, and October 1963